McCall's
Best One-Dish Meals

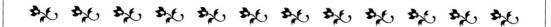

McCall's
Best One-Dish Meals

~

by the Editors of McCall's

LITTLE, BROWN AND COMPANY

BOSTON • NEW YORK • TORONTO • LONDON

First edition

All the recipes in this book were previously published in
McCall's *magazine.*

Recipe photographs by
William Abranowicz, Cynthia Brown, Roger Cabello, John Dugdale,
Tom Eckerle, Dana Gallagher, Beth Galton, Tria Giovan,
Lizzie Himmel, Christopher Lawrence, Rita Maas,
Maria Robledo, and Mark Thomas.

McCall's Books
Director: Margie Chan
Editorial Director: Carol A. Guasti
Managing Editor: Elizabeth Loonan
Project Editor: David Ricketts
Marketing Manager: Jacqueline Varoli
Marketing Project Coordinator: Karen Dragotto
Editorial Intern: Robin Martell

McCall's Magazine
Editor-in-Chief: Kate White
Creative Director: Marilu Lopez
Food Editor: Barbara Chernetz
Senior Food Editor: Mary B. Johnson
Senior Associate Food Editor: Holly Sheppard

Library of Congress Cataloging-in-Publication Data

McCall's best one-dish meals / by the editors of McCall's —
1st ed.
p.   cm.
ISBN 0-316-55351-4
1. Entrées (Cookery)   I. McCall's magazine.
TX740.M34   1994
641.8'2 — dc20   94-1808

10   9   8   7   6   5   4   3   2   1

RRD-OH

Designed by Jeanne Abboud

Published simultaneously in Canada by Little, Brown & Company
(Canada) Limited

Printed in the United States of America

Contents

꽃 꽃 꽃

McCall's
Best One-Dish Meals

Introduction

꙰ ꙰ ꙰

If you're like many people today, you're relying more and more on takeout or convenience food for dinner, lunch, sometimes even breakfast. You love a home-cooked meal, but you just don't have the time to cook, let alone clean up.

A wonderful solution: the one-dish meal. You get a terrifically flavorful meal that generally involves very little fuss — and very little cleanup. At *McCall's* we've found one-dish recipes are among the highest rated in the magazine. That's why we thought you'd enjoy an entire cookbook of them.

Whether prepared in the oven or on top of the stove, whether long-simmering, a quick stir-fry, a make-ahead to refrigerate or freeze, or even a no-cook dish, one-dish meals streamline your time in the kitchen by limiting the number of pots, utensils, and serving dishes you'll need. In those recipes where more than one pot (or other cooking vessel) is needed, we've tried to keep the total number to three.

Many of our recipes contain all three elements of a balanced meal (protein, starch, and vegetable), so you don't have to think of "go-withs" for a meal. Others allow you to add your own starch choice, such as rice, couscous, or noodles. In most cases, adding a simple salad and a loaf of bread will complete your meal.

You'll find a diverse mix of delicious dishes, from hearty meal-in-a-bowl soups to wonderful pasta, chicken, and meat dishes that borrow from a variety of cuisines (Tunisian, Italian, Mexican, Asian, French, and classic American), make-at-home pizzas, and toss-together salads that are a great vehicle for leftovers.

Because many of our one-dish dinners are great for entertaining, we've included guidelines on wines to serve. Delicate food requires delicate wine to balance it; hearty food can stand up to more robust wines. For a listing of food and wine complements, see our Guide to Wines on page 235.

What's the difference between a spice and an herb? Our Guide to Herbs and Spices (page 237) clues you in on the differences, and tells you which seasonings complement which foods. You'll also learn storage methods, how to substitute dried if you don't have fresh on hand, and more. Be sure to use this guide if you run out of a particular spice; you can easily find a good substitute from our list.

Here at *McCall's*, we know how valuable your time is. It is with pride and pleasure that we present this wonderful collection of one-dish meals and offer our own brand of insight to help simplify your kitchen routine.

KATE WHITE
EDITOR-IN-CHIEF

What You Need to Know

❧ ❧ ❧

All the recipes in this book were tested in the *McCall's* kitchens — and that makes them virtually foolproof. As you leaf through the pages, you'll find recipes that are flagged "quick" or "low-fat" or both, and *every* recipe includes a nutrition analysis. Below, you'll find the criteria for these recipe flags, as well as everything you need to know about the basics of good cooking and good eating. And because one-dish meals help streamline your work in the kitchen, we've also included handy advice on utensils for a well-equipped kitchen, and savvy cleanup tips.

NUTRITION ADVICE

The USDA recommends seven dietary guidelines for a healthful diet. (This advice is for Americans two years of age or older.) Follow them to make the smartest food choices for yourself and your family.

- Eat a variety of foods.

- Maintain healthy weight.

- Choose a diet low in fat, saturated fat, and cholesterol.

- Choose a diet with plenty of vegetables, fruits, and grain products.

- Use sugars only in moderation.

- Use salt and sodium only in moderation.

- If you drink alcoholic beverages, do so in moderation.

LOW-FAT RECIPES

As you look through this book, you'll notice that some recipes are flagged "low-fat." In order for a recipe to qualify as "low-fat," no more than 30 percent of the calories in the dish can come from fat. The formula to use: grams of fat in the recipe × 9 calories (there are 9 calories in 1 gram of fat) ÷ total calories in the dish × 100 = percentage of calories attributable to fat. In other words, low-fat is calculated as a ratio of fat to calories in a recipe.

Example: If a recipe has 18 grams of fat per serving and the total calories per serving is 625, the recipe would meet the requirements to qualify as low-fat. However, another recipe having 18 grams of fat and 414 calories per serving would not qualify as low-fat. Here's why:

	Grams of fat ×	9 calories per gram = calories of fat	÷ total calories	× 100 = % of calories attributable to fat
Recipe A	18	162	625	26%
Recipe B	18	162	414	39%

Note, though, that 18 grams of fat in a serving can fit within healthful guidelines if you limit your fat intake in other meals that day.

The chart below tells you the total grams of fat recommended for the calorie levels of children, teenagers, women, and men. Use it as a guideline when you are choosing your foods or recipes. And remember: if you "indulge" in higher-fat foods for a day, keep your fat intake lower for the next day or so to compensate.

	Most women, older adults	Children, teen girls, active women, most men	Teen boys, active men
Calorie level	1,600	2,200	2,800
Total fat (grams)	53	73	93

AND SPEAKING OF LOW-FAT . . .

Whenever our recipes call for low-fat milk, we are referring to 1% milk. We recommend that you substitute low-fat or skim milk in all your recipes that call for milk, and use low-fat milk every day to help lower fat intake.

QUICK RECIPES

When we say quick, we mean it! Each of the dishes that is flagged "quick" takes no more than 30 minutes from prep time to dinnertime — a boon for busy cooks.

POTS AND PANS

To make one-dish cooking really easy, you need to have the appropriate utensils. Ideally, your cookware should be able to go from stove top to oven to refrigerator to freezer to tabletop. For the basic set, consider the following:

- 5- to 6-quart Dutch oven or covered casserole dish

- 1-quart, 2-quart, and 3^1/$_2$-quart saucepans with covers

- 13 × 9-inch glass baking dish

- oval casserole

- 10- and 12-inch skillets

- stockpot

- wok

The material pots are made of will affect how food cooks. **Aluminum** is a terrific heat conductor, but untreated aluminum as a cooking surface will react with acidic foods such as tomato or wine, causing an "off" flavor and occasional discoloration. **Treated** or **anodized aluminum** eliminates these shortcomings. **Stainless steel** is nonreactive but not a good heat conductor, so it needs to be combined with other metals, such as an aluminum core or copper base, to improve conductivity. **Heavy enamelware** or **porcelain** over a steel base is ideal for slow, top-of-the-stove cooking, but this cookware chips easily and is hard to maneuver. **Flameproof** and **ovenproof glass** cookware is perfect for one-dish meals, since it can withstand extremes in temperature and is usually quite attractive.

EASY CLEANUP TIPS

Even the neatest cook can have some serious cleanup work. To make it easier on you, here are a few tricks of the trade:

- Tarnished copper-bottomed pans: Gently rub the copper with a cloth dipped in a mixture of half vinegar and half coarse (kosher) salt. Rinse and dry with a dish towel.

- Burned-on grease on glass baking dishes: Spray the dish with oven cleaner and let stand for about 30 minutes. Wipe off the grease and rinse well.

- Rust stains in the sink: Sprinkle them with baking soda, scrub with a damp cloth or nylon net sponge, and then rinse.

- Discolored rubber spatulas: Soak them for an hour in 1 cup of water mixed with 1 tablespoon of bleach, then rinse.

Chapter One

~

Soups

ᦉ ᦉ ᦉ

Since the cooking pot was first invented, soup has always been the
classic one-dish meal. It can be as easy to fix as our Chilled
Curried Spinach Soup (page 11), or as long-simmering as Mom's
Chicken Soup with Matzo Balls (page 26). The convenience of
most soups is that they can be made a day or two before you want to serve
them. In fact, letting soups "mellow" often improves their flavor.

There's nothing unusually refined about soups. They tolerate mistakes
well, so even the novice cook can create delicious soups with minimal fear
of failure. Soups are a natural for using up leftovers. What's more, they're a
welcome meal just about any time of day — for lunch, dinner, or a snack.
Some people even prefer to start the day with a steaming bowl of soup
instead of oatmeal! Finally, soup travels well, hot or cold, in a thermos.

Check out our variety: The soups here need only a good homemade-style
bread and a salad to make a complete, convenient, and very appealing
meal.

Chilled Curried Spinach Soup

Our deceptively creamy soup actually uses cooked potatoes and low-fat milk to give it a smooth texture and body. Garnished with Tomato Relish and low-fat yogurt, this spinach soup makes a tasty mid-summer meal. Serve with toasted pita bread and a salad of grated carrots with your favorite vinaigrette dressing.

TOMATO RELISH

1/2 cup diced, seeded tomato
1 green onion, trimmed and finely chopped
1 tablespoon chopped fresh cilantro
1 clove garlic, crushed
Pinch of salt

SPINACH SOUP

2 teaspoons olive oil
1/2 cup chopped onion
2 teaspoons curry powder
2 teaspoons grated gingerroot
1/2 teaspoon ground cumin
1 clove garlic, crushed
1 cup low-sodium chicken broth
1 cup pared, cubed potatoes
2 (10-ounce) packages fresh spinach, rinsed and stems trimmed
1 1/2 cups low-fat milk
1 teaspoon salt
1/8 teaspoon ground hot red pepper
1 tablespoon fresh lime juice

1/2 cup plain low-fat yogurt, stirred until smooth

low-fat

make ahead

preparation time:
10 minutes

cooking time:
25 minutes

chilling time:
3 hours

Chilling Soups

Remember that chilling a soup both dulls its flavor and makes it thicker. When preparing a soup to serve cold, adjust the seasonings and the consistency accordingly.

1 • Prepare the Tomato Relish: In a small bowl, combine the diced tomato with the green onion, cilantro, garlic, and salt. Mix the relish well.

2 • Prepare the Spinach Soup: In a large shallow saucepan, heat the olive oil. Add the onion and cook over low heat until the onion is soft, about 5 minutes. Stir in the curry powder, grated ginger, cumin, and garlic until blended. Add the chicken broth and potatoes. Over medium heat, bring the mixture to boiling. Reduce the heat and simmer, covered, until the potatoes are soft, about 10 minutes. Stir in the spinach. Cook, covered, for 8 minutes or until the spinach is tender, stirring occasionally.

3 • Place the spinach mixture in a food processor or blender. Process until the mixture is puréed. With the motor running, pour in 1 cup of the milk. Process until all the ingredients are blended. Pour the mixture into a large bowl. Stir in the salt and hot red pepper until blended. Cover the bowl and refrigerate the soup until it is cold, about 3 hours.

4 • Just before serving, stir the remaining ½ cup of milk into the soup. Add the lime juice and blend well.

5 • To serve: Ladle the soup into 4 large soup bowls. Swirl a dollop of the yogurt in the center of each serving. Sprinkle some Tomato Relish over each serving.

Makes 4 servings. Per serving: 209 calories, 12 g protein, 34 g carbohydrate, 5 g fat, 5 mg cholesterol, 914 mg sodium.

Chilled Curried Spinach Soup and Potato-Leek Soup

Potato-Leek Soup

This filling soup takes just 25 minutes to cook. Although it is traditionally eaten cold, it's equally delicious when served hot. A swirl of Green Pea Purée adds a dramatic touch. Crusty whole-wheat bread would make a perfect accompaniment.

low-fat

quick

make ahead

chilling time:
3 hours

1 tablespoon olive oil
1 to 4 leeks (12 ounces total), trimmed, halved lengthwise, rinsed
*   well, and coarsely chopped*
2 cups pared, cubed potatoes
1 clove garlic, crushed
1 cup low-sodium chicken broth
2 cups low-fat milk
1 teaspoon salt
⅛ teaspoon ground hot red pepper
⅛ teaspoon nutmeg (optional)

GREEN PEA PURÉE

1 cup fresh or frozen small green peas
½ cup low-sodium chicken broth
¼ cup low-fat milk
2 tablespoons chopped fresh mint leaves
Pinch of ground hot red pepper
Pinch of salt
1 teaspoon fresh lime juice

1 • In a large shallow saucepan, heat the olive oil. Add the leeks and cook over low heat, stirring, about 5 minutes or until the leeks are softened. Add the potatoes, garlic, and chicken broth. Bring the mixture to boiling. Reduce the heat and simmer, covered, until the vegetables are very tender, about 10 minutes. Remove the saucepan from the heat and let the mixture cool slightly.

2 • Place the potato-leek mixture in a blender and process until the mixture is puréed. With the blender running, pour in the milk and process until smooth. Pour the mixture into a large bowl. Stir in the salt and hot red pepper, and the nutmeg if desired, until blended. Cover the bowl and refrigerate the soup until it is cold, about 3 hours.

3 • Prepare the Green Pea Purée: In a small saucepan, combine the peas and chicken broth. Over medium heat, bring the mixture to boiling. Reduce the heat and simmer, covered, until the peas are soft, about 10 minutes. Place the pea mixture in a blender. Add the milk and chopped mint. Process until the mixture is puréed. Pour the pea purée into a small bowl. Stir in the hot red pepper, salt, and lime juice until blended. Cover the bowl and refrigerate the purée until it is cold.

4 • To serve: Ladle the soup into 4 large soup bowls. Swirl some of the Green Pea Purée in the center of each serving.

Makes 4 servings. Per serving: 294 calories, 12 g protein, 50 g carbohydrate, 6 g fat, 5 mg cholesterol, 920 mg sodium.

Taste Tips for Slender Soups

The problem with most low-calorie soups is that when you take out the fat, you also lose the flavor and that rich, creamy texture. But there are easy ways to cut back on the calories and fat without destroying the soup. To thicken soups without fat, use cooked potatoes, turnips, sweet potatoes, or parsnips, puréed until smooth. To add a flavor boost, stir in chopped fresh herbs, such as basil or thyme, just before serving the soup. Finally, make slender soups look lusciously creamy by garnishing them with a swirl of low-fat plain yogurt, or puréed carrot, beet, or sweet red pepper. See our recipes for Potato-Leek and Carrot-Ginger Soups for good examples of "swirl appeal."

Creamy Potato-Pepper Soup

The pears add a subtle sweetness to this peppery soup. Serve with a watercress and endive salad or shredded romaine, tossed with your favorite dressing, and chunks of crusty bread. To keep the fat content of this soup at a moderate level, try garnishing with low-fat sour cream.

4 tablespoons unsalted butter
2 large onions, chopped
4 cloves garlic, minced
2 baking potatoes, pared and diced
4 (7½-ounce) jars roasted red peppers, drained, patted dry, and chopped
5 cups chicken broth
2 (16-ounce) cans pear halves, packed in juice, drained and chopped
⅛ teaspoon ground black pepper
⅛ teaspoon cayenne pepper
Sour cream (optional)
Chopped fresh parsley (optional)

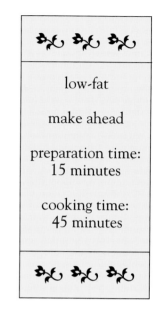

low-fat

make ahead

preparation time:
15 minutes

cooking time:
45 minutes

Creamy Potato-Pepper Soup

1 • In a large saucepan or Dutch oven, over medium heat, melt the butter. Add the onion and garlic; sauté for 10 minutes or until very tender. Add the potato and red pepper; sauté for 10 minutes. Add the chicken broth; heat to boiling. Reduce the heat; simmer for 15 to 20 minutes or until the vegetables are tender.

2 • Remove the pan from the heat. Strain the vegetables through a sieve placed over a bowl; reserve the liquid. In batches, purée the vegetables and pears in a food processor. Pour the purée back into the same saucepan. Add the cooking liquid, black pepper, and cayenne; mix well. Heat through. Garnish with a swirl of sour cream and sprinkle with parsley.

Makes 10 servings. Per serving: 185 calories, 5 g protein, 31 g carbohydrate, 6 g fat, 12 mg cholesterol, 398 mg sodium.

Carrot-Ginger Soup

make ahead

preparation time:
20 minutes

cooking time:
40 minutes

chilling time:
3 hours

The piquant spice of fresh ginger enhances the sweetness of carrots in this chilled soup, and the sun-dried tomato purée adds another dimension of flavor. Herb muffins and a cucumber salad would round out the soup to make a delicious lunch or light supper. If you'd like to serve this soup at a picnic, bring the soup in a chilled thermos and the purée in a separate container.

> 2 tablespoons vegetable oil
> 1 (1-inch-long) piece gingerroot, pared and thinly sliced
> 1$\frac{1}{2}$ pounds carrots, pared and diced
> 2 leeks, thinly sliced and washed
> 2 large cloves garlic, crushed
> 2 (14-ounce) cans low-sodium chicken broth
> 1 teaspoon ground coriander
> $\frac{1}{2}$ teaspoon salt
> $\frac{1}{2}$ cup cold water

SUN-DRIED TOMATO PURÉE

6 sun-dried tomato halves (not in oil)
$1/2$ cup cold water
2 tablespoons vegetable oil
$1/4$ teaspoon chili powder
Pinch of ground hot red pepper

2 tablespoons buttermilk
Fresh chives, for garnish

1 • In a large saucepan, heat the vegetable oil over medium-high heat. Add the ginger, carrots, leeks, and garlic. Sauté about 5 minutes or until the leeks have wilted. Add half of 1 can of chicken broth. Partially cover the saucepan; cook for 10 minutes or until the broth is reduced and the carrot mixture begins to dry out. Add the remaining half-can of chicken broth. Cover the saucepan partially again; cook for 10 minutes more or until the vegetables soften. Stir in the coriander and salt. Cook the carrot mixture for 5 minutes.

2 • Place the carrot mixture in a food processor. Process until the mixture is puréed. With the motor running, pour in the remaining can of chicken broth through the feed tube. Process until all the ingredients are blended. Pour the mixture into a large bowl. Stir in the $1/2$ cup of cold water. Cover the bowl and refrigerate the soup until it is cold, about 3 hours.

3 • Prepare the Sun-Dried Tomato Purée: In a 2-cup glass measure, combine the sun-dried tomatoes with the $1/2$ cup of cold water. Cover the measure and microwave on HIGH for $1 1/2$ minutes; let stand for 10 minutes. (Or, in a small saucepan over high heat, bring the water to boiling. Add the sun-dried tomatoes. Remove the saucepan from the heat, cover it, and let stand for 10 minutes.) Place the tomatoes with the liquid in a blender or food processor. Process until the mixture is puréed. With the motor running, pour in the vegetable oil through the feed tube. Process until all the ingredients are blended. Pour the tomato purée into a small bowl. Stir in the chili powder and hot red pepper.

4 • To serve: Ladle the chilled soup into 6 soup bowls. Spoon some of the Sun-Dried Tomato Purée on top of each serving. Drizzle some of the buttermilk and sprinkle fresh chives over each serving.

Makes 6 servings. Per serving: 180 calories, 4 g protein, 20 g carbohydrate, 10 g fat, 0 mg cholesterol, 523 mg sodium.

Pass the Crackers

Crackers are a natural choice for a soup side dish, but don't just reach for the obvious varieties. Have fun instead: Experiment with Scandinavian flatbreads, no-salt tortilla chips, wheat thins, melba toast, cheese straws, bagel chips, or anything else that tickles your fancy.

Squash Soup

quick

The secret to the rich flavor of this vegetable soup is to sauté the onion just enough to bring out its natural sweetness and not to overcook the other vegetables. For a light luncheon, serve the soup with a simple green salad and your favorite dressing.

2 tablespoons olive oil
1 large onion, chopped
3 cups water
2 yellow squash (about 12 ounces), chopped
2 large ripe tomatoes, coarsely chopped
1 sweet red pepper, cored, seeded, and chopped
1 sweet yellow pepper, cored, seeded, and chopped
1 zucchini (6 ounces), chopped
3 large cloves garlic, minced
1½ teaspoons salt
½ teaspoon fennel seeds
¼ teaspoon ground black pepper
½ cup grated Parmesan or shredded Gruyère (optional)

Tomato-Mozzarella Sandwich (page 35) and Squash Soup

1 • In a Dutch oven or large saucepan, heat the oil over medium heat. Add the onion; sauté for 5 minutes or until softened. Add the water, yellow squash, tomatoes, sweet red and yellow peppers, zucchini, garlic, salt, fennel seeds, and black pepper. Heat to boiling. Reduce the heat; simmer for 15 minutes or until the vegetables are tender.

2 • Place 2 ½ cups of the soup in a food processor; purée. Return the purée to the pan with the remaining soup. Heat through. Sprinkle with the cheese, if you wish, and serve.

> Makes 6 servings. Per serving: 101 calories, 3 g protein, 14 g carbohydrate, 5 g fat, 0 mg cholesterol, 545 mg sodium.

Pumpkin-Peanut Soup

A delicious cool-weather soup that captures the best flavors of the autumn. Make a day or two ahead, and then gently reheat. Serve with a zucchini quick bread or another bread of your choice.

make ahead

preparation time:
15 minutes

baking time:
1 hour

cooking time:
30 minutes

1 sugar pumpkin or butternut squash (3 pounds) (see Note)
1 teaspoon salt
¼ teaspoon ground black pepper
4 tablespoons butter
1 cup chopped onion
½ cup finely diced sweet red pepper
1 large jalapeño pepper, cored, seeded, and minced
4 cups chicken broth
¼ cup creamy peanut butter
½ cup heavy cream or milk
2 tablespoons fresh lime juice
Thinly sliced green onion

1 • Preheat the oven to 350°F. Line a jelly-roll pan with aluminum foil. Halve the pumpkin lengthwise; remove the seeds. Sprinkle the inside of the pumpkin with ½ teaspoon of the salt and ⅛ teaspoon of the black pepper. Place the pumpkin halves, cut side down, on the prepared pan.

2 • Bake the pumpkin halves in the preheated 350°F oven for 1 hour or until the flesh is soft. Set aside until the pumpkin is cool enough to handle. With a spoon, scoop out the flesh into a bowl.

3 • In a Dutch oven, melt the butter over medium heat. Add the onion; sauté for 15 minutes or until golden brown. Add the pumpkin, red pepper, jalapeño, and chicken broth. Heat to boiling. Cover; reduce the heat to low. Simmer for 10 minutes, stirring occasionally, to break up the pumpkin. Remove all but 2 cups of the soup solids to a food processor. Purée, in batches. Pour the purée into the reserved soup in the pot. Add the peanut butter and heavy cream. Over low heat, cook, stirring until the peanut butter melts. Add the lime juice and remaining salt and pepper. Sprinkle each serving with green onion.

NOTE: You can substitute 4 cups of canned solid-pack pumpkin purée (not pie filling) for the cooked fresh pumpkin.

Makes 8 servings. Per serving: 222 calories, 7 g protein, 15 g carbohydrate, 16 g fat, 36 mg cholesterol, 897 mg sodium.

Pumpkin-Peanut Soup

Dutch Vegetable Soup

~

Bacon, potatoes, and Gouda cheese are frequently used in Dutch cooking, although today there is a greater emphasis on using more vegetables. This hearty soup can be prepared a day or two ahead and makes enough for a hungry crowd. Bonus: This recipe provides its own savory bread accompaniment.

1/2 pound bacon, cut into 1-inch pieces
2 large carrots, pared and cut crosswise into thin slices
2 medium leeks, cut crosswise into thin slices and rinsed
1 medium onion, diced
2 large potatoes, pared and coarsely chopped
1 medium head cauliflower, separated into florets
5 3/4 cups low-sodium chicken broth (about 4 cans)
1 loaf Italian bread, cut into 3/4-inch-thick slices (about 16 slices)
2 cups shredded Gouda cheese (about 8 ounces)
1/4 cup chopped fresh parsley

1 • In an 8-quart Dutch oven over medium heat, sauté the bacon until it is crisp, about 10 minutes. With a slotted spoon, remove the bacon to paper towels to drain.

2 • Remove and discard all but 1/4 cup of the bacon drippings from the pot. To the hot drippings, add the carrots, leeks, and onion; sauté for 5 minutes. Add the potatoes and cauliflower; sauté for 10 minutes. Add the chicken broth and bring the mixture to boiling. Reduce the heat and simmer, uncovered, for 30 minutes.

3 • Meanwhile, place the bread slices in a single layer on a baking sheet. About 8 minutes before serving the soup, broil the slices 5 inches from the heat, turning the slices once, until they are toasted on both sides. Sprinkle the Gouda cheese, divided equally, over the bread slices. Set aside half of the bacon. Sprinkle the remaining bacon over the cheese-topped bread slices. Broil the bread slices just until the cheese melts.

4 • To serve: Ladle the soup into 8 large soup bowls. Sprinkle some of the parsley and the remaining bacon over each serving. Serve the bread slices with the soup.

Makes 8 servings. Per serving: 581 calories, 29 g protein, 64 g carbohydrate, 24 g fat, 57 mg cholesterol, 1,310 mg sodium.

❧ ❧ ❧

make ahead

preparation time:
15 minutes

cooking time:
1 hour

Freezing Soups

Soups can often be frozen for up to 6 months, but keep in mind that cream, yogurt, sour cream, and other dairy additions will separate when the soup is thawed and reheated. To avoid this, prepare without the dairy ingredient and freeze. After thawing, gently reheat the soup and stir in the dairy ingredient. Also, pasta and many vegetables can lose their texture when frozen and thawed. As above, add the particular ingredient while gently reheating the soup.

❧ ❧ ❧

Country Vegetable Soup with Pistou

make ahead

soaking time
for beans:
1 hour

preparation time:
20 minutes

cooking time:
1¼ hours

Pistou is a savory mixture of garlic, basil, Parmesan cheese, and tomatoes; it is used as a flavor accent in many French Provençal dishes. This recipe makes enough for a large crowd. Make it the day before, as the flavor improves with age.

³/₄ cup dry great Northern or navy beans
Water
2 large red potatoes, pared and cut into ¹/₂-inch dice
2 large leeks, halved lengthwise, cut crosswise into ¹/₂-inch slices, and rinsed
4 small carrots, pared, halved lengthwise, and sliced crosswise
¹/₂ small butternut squash (¹/₂ pound), pared, seeds removed, and cut into ¹/₂-inch dice
¹/₂ pound green beans, trimmed and cut into ³/₄-inch pieces
1 large onion, chopped
1¹/₂ quarts chicken broth
¹/₂ pound Swiss chard, cut into ¹/₂-inch pieces
1 large zucchini, cut into ¹/₂-inch cubes
1 small yellow squash, cut into ¹/₂-inch cubes
¹/₂ cup uncooked elbow macaroni
1 teaspoon salt
¹/₂ cup frozen peas

PISTOU

1 large clove garlic
¹/₂ cup packed fresh basil leaves
¹/₂ cup freshly grated Parmesan cheese
¹/₂ cup olive oil
3 ripe plum tomatoes, seeded and finely chopped
¹/₄ teaspoon freshly ground pepper
¹/₄ teaspoon salt

1 • In a stockpot or Dutch oven, combine the great Northern or navy beans with enough water to cover; let the beans soak overnight. Or, to quick-soak, in the stockpot, cover the beans with water. Bring the water to boiling, and boil for 2 to 3 minutes. Remove the pot from the heat and let the beans soak for 1 hour.

2 • Drain the soaked beans. In the stockpot, combine the beans and 1 quart of water. Bring the water to boiling. Cover the pot, reduce the heat, and simmer about 45 minutes or until the beans are tender but not mushy. Add the red potatoes, leeks, carrots, butternut squash, green beans, onion, and chicken broth. Bring the mixture to boiling again. Cover the pot, reduce the heat, and simmer for 15 minutes.

3 • Add the Swiss chard, zucchini, yellow squash, macaroni, and salt. Cover the pot and bring the mixture to boiling. Reduce the heat and simmer for 5 minutes. Add the peas and simmer until all of the vegetables are tender.

4 • Meanwhile, prepare the Pistou: In a food processor, mince the garlic. Add the basil and process until it is finely chopped. Add the Parmesan cheese. With the motor running, add the olive oil through the feed tube. Process until all the ingredients are blended. Add the tomatoes, pepper, and salt; mix well. Pour the Pistou into a small serving bowl.

5 • With a slotted spoon, transfer 1½ cups of vegetable solids from the soup to the cleaned food processor. Process until the vegetable mixture is puréed. Stir the purée back into the soup.

6 • To serve: Ladle the soup into a large soup bowl. If the Pistou has separated while standing, stir it to blend the ingredients again. Serve the soup hot, drizzled with some of the Pistou.

> *Makes 16 servings. Per serving: 197 calories, 8 g protein, 24 g carbohydrate, 9 g fat, 2 mg cholesterol, 540 mg sodium.*

Double-Duty Squash

Many varieties of squash, both summer and winter, are superb additions to soup. But winter squash have another use, too. An uncooked pumpkin or Hubbard squash, filled with a vegetable soup, such as our Country Vegetable Soup with Pistou, makes an unusual serving tureen for a festive meal. If you want to further the theme, use acorn squash halves as individual bowls.

Pasta and Bean Soup

low-fat

make ahead

preparation time:
10 minutes

cooking time:
30 minutes

Fill a pretty basket with flatbreads to serve alongside this hearty soup. Pair it with a watercress and endive salad, and you have a meal in less than 45 minutes. Try a steaming mug of this soup to satisfy a snack attack, too.

> 1 tablespoon olive oil
> 1 (2-ounce) slab bacon, diced (about ¹/₂ cup)
> 2 carrots, chopped
> 1 medium onion, chopped
> 3 cloves garlic, crushed
> 3 (14-ounce) cans chicken broth
> 2 (14¹/₂-ounce) cans diced tomatoes in juice
> ³/₄ teaspoon dried marjoram leaves, crushed
> ¹/₂ teaspoon dried sage leaves, crushed
> ¹/₂ teaspoon salt
> 4 ounces uncooked orecchiette pasta (about 1 heaping cup)
> 1 (19-ounce) can garbanzo beans (chickpeas)
> 1 (10-ounce) package frozen chopped kale or collard greens, thawed
> ¹/₂ teaspoon freshly ground pepper
> Grated Parmesan cheese

1 • In a stockpot or Dutch oven, heat the olive oil. Add the bacon and sauté over medium heat for 3 to 4 minutes or until the bacon is lightly browned. Add the carrots, onion, and garlic. Cover the pot and cook for 5 minutes or until the vegetables are soft.

2 • Stir in the chicken broth, tomatoes with their juice, marjoram, sage, and salt. Bring the mixture to boiling; stir in the pasta. Cover the pot and cook, stirring frequently, as the package label directs, until the pasta is al dente (page 93). Add the garbanzo beans with their liquid and the kale. Heat the soup through. Stir in the pepper.

3 • To serve: Ladle the soup into 6 large soup bowls. Sprinkle some Parmesan cheese over each serving.

> *Makes 6 servings. Per serving: 384 calories, 20 g protein, 53 g carbohydrate, 11 g fat, 8 mg cholesterol, 1,206 mg sodium.*

Pasta and Bean Soup

Mom's Chicken Soup
with Matzo Balls

The classic comfort food and home remedy for whatever ails you. To make the soup preparation easier, the broth and shredded chicken can be made a day or two ahead and refrigerated. The matzo ball mixture is blended together 4 hours before serving.

MATZO BALLS

> 2 large eggs, well beaten
> 3 tablespoons seltzer water, club soda, or sparkling mineral water
> 2 tablespoons vegetable oil or chicken fat
> ¹/₄ teaspoon freshly ground pepper
> ¹/₄ teaspoon salt
> ¹/₂ cup matzo meal

CHICKEN SOUP

> 1 (3¹/₂- to 4-pound) chicken, quartered
> 2¹/₂ to 3 quarts cold water
> 5 large carrots, thinly sliced
> 3 celery stalks with leaves, sliced
> 3 small parsnips, sliced
> 1 large onion, quartered
> 4 sprigs parsley
> 2 teaspoons salt
> ¹/₄ teaspoon freshly ground pepper
> 1 tablespoon minced parsley

1 • Prepare the Matzo Balls: In a medium bowl, combine the eggs, seltzer, vegetable oil or chicken fat, pepper, and salt. Gradually stir in the matzo meal until the ingredients are blended. Cover the bowl and refrigerate the dough for 4 hours.

2 • Meanwhile, prepare the Chicken Soup: In a large stockpot or Dutch oven, combine the chicken and water. Heat the water to boiling, skimming off the foam with a metal spoon. Set aside 1¹/₂ cups of the carrots. Add the remaining carrots, the celery, parsnips, onion, parsley sprigs, 1¹/₂ teaspoons of the salt, and the pepper to the chicken mixture. Reduce the heat and simmer, partially covered, until the chicken is cooked through, about 1 hour.

3 • With a slotted spoon, remove the chicken to a plate. When the chicken is cool enough to handle, remove the meat from the bones; discard the bones and skin. Shred the chicken meat into bite-sized pieces; keep warm.

4 • To cook the Matzo Balls: Bring a large saucepan of salted water to boiling. Using cool, wet hands, shape the matzo dough into 8 (1½-inch-diameter) balls. Carefully drop the Matzo Balls into the boiling water. Reduce the heat, cover the saucepan, and simmer for 25 minutes.

5 • Meanwhile, strain the soup through a cheesecloth-lined sieve into another large clean pot, pressing the solids with the back of a spoon to extract as much liquid as possible. Add the remaining ½ teaspoon of salt and the reserved carrots. Simmer the soup, covered, for about 15 minutes or until the carrots are tender.

6 • To serve: Ladle the hot soup into 8 large soup bowls. Add the shredded chicken and matzo balls, divided equally, to each serving and sprinkle the minced parsley over the tops.

> *Makes 8 servings. Per serving: 225 calories, 28 g protein, 8 g carbohydrate, 8 g fat, 136 mg cholesterol, 717 mg sodium.*

Mom's Chicken Soup with Matzo Balls

Yellow Split Pea Soup

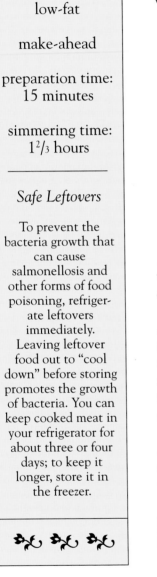

low-fat

make-ahead

preparation time:
15 minutes

simmering time:
1²/₃ hours

Safe Leftovers

To prevent the
bacteria growth that
can cause
salmonellosis and
other forms of food
poisoning, refriger-
ate leftovers
immediately.
Leaving leftover
food out to "cool
down" before storing
promotes the growth
of bacteria. You can
keep cooked meat in
your refrigerator for
about three or four
days; to keep it
longer, store it in
the freezer.

A marvelous use for leftover cooked pork, this winter soup is rich and filling, and very easy to make. Serve the soup with a salad of blanched broccoli mixed with roasted red peppers and dressed with vinaigrette, and lots of warm crusty bread.

> 1 pound dried yellow split peas, washed
> 1 (1-pound) piece cooked pork or about 3 cups julienned pork
> 8 cups water
> 1 bay leaf
> 2 tablespoons butter or margarine
> 2 celery stalks, chopped
> 1 large onion, chopped
> 2 teaspoons salt
> ¹/₂ teaspoon ground cumin
> ¹/₂ teaspoon dried marjoram leaves, crushed
> ¹/₂ teaspoon freshly ground pepper

1 • In a 6-quart Dutch oven, combine the yellow split peas, pork, water, and bay leaf. Bring the mixture to boiling. Reduce the heat, cover the pot, and simmer the mixture for 1 hour, stirring occasionally.

2 • Meanwhile, in a large skillet, melt the butter or margarine over medium-high heat. Add the celery and onion. Sauté for about 5 minutes or until the vegetables are tender-crisp. Stir in the salt, cumin, marjoram, and pepper. Add the vegetable mixture to the split pea mixture. Cover the pot and simmer the soup for 40 minutes, stirring occasionally.

3 • If the pork is in one piece, remove it from the soup with a slotted spoon. When the pork is cool enough to handle, remove the meat from the bone; discard the bone. Return the shredded meat to the soup.

> *Makes 8 servings. Per serving: 371 calories, 33 g protein, 37 g carbohydrate, 11 g fat, 72 mg cholesterol, 633 mg sodium.*

Portuguese Soup

Kale is a much-used ingredient in Portuguese cuisine. If fresh kale is unavailable, substitute four 10-ounce packages of frozen kale or fresh spinach. Serve this soup with thick slices of Portuguese bread (a sweet white bread) or peasant bread.

> 1 tablespoon extra-virgin olive oil
> 1 cup chopped onion
> 1 medium carrot, peeled and cut into $^1/_2$-inch dice
> 1 tablespoon minced garlic
> $^1/_4$ teaspoon crushed red-pepper flakes
> $^3/_4$ pound kale, stems removed and leaves cut into $^1/_2$-inch-thick strips
> Bone from a cooked ham (optional)
> $1^1/_2$ cups cooked ham, cut into $^3/_4$-inch dice
> 2 large potatoes, peeled, quartered, and cut into $^1/_2$-inch-thick slices
> 4 (14-ounce) cans low-sodium chicken broth plus enough water to equal 8 cups liquid

1 • In a Dutch oven, heat the olive oil over medium heat. Add the onion and carrot. Cover the pot and cook about 3 minutes or until the onion is translucent, stirring occasionally. Add the garlic and red-pepper flakes; sauté for 30 seconds.

2 • Add the kale, ham bone if using, diced ham, potatoes, and chicken broth–water mixture. Increase the heat to high and bring the mixture to boiling. Reduce the heat and simmer, partially covered, about 25 minutes or until the vegetables are tender. Remove and discard the ham bone. Skim off any visible fat with a metal spoon before serving.

Makes 6 servings. Per serving: 220 calories, 16 g protein, 27 g carbohydrate, 6 g fat, 20 mg cholesterol, 590 mg sodium.

low-fat

make ahead

preparation time:
15 minutes

cooking time:
30 minutes

Wide Bowls

Thick soups with chunks of meat or vegetables, or both, such as our Portuguese Soup, look particularly appetizing when served in a wide, shallow bowl. These bowls show off the soup ingredients to their best advantage and emphasize the hearty consistency.

Seafood Chowder

~

This speedy chowder recipe, which uses no butter, oil, or cream, is ready in less than 20 minutes! Ideal for a Saturday night "shore leave" dinner with pilot crackers, or oyster crackers, and a beet salad.

1 • Pour the juice reserved from the chopped clams into a 2-cup glass measure. Add enough water to make 1½ cups. Pour the clam juice mixture into a medium saucepan and bring the mixture to boiling; skim off any foam from the top of the liquid with a metal spoon. Add the carrot, corn kernels, leek, potato, garlic, basil, and dillweed. Heat the mixture to simmering and cook for 10 minutes, stirring occasionally.

2 • In a cup, combine the cornstarch with 1 tablespoon of water; stir until well blended. Pour the milk into a small bowl; stir the cornstarch mixture into the milk. Add the cornstarch-milk mixture to the saucepan. Bring the combined mixtures to a simmer, stirring; simmer for 2 minutes.

3 • Add the flounder, snapper, shrimp, and clams to the saucepan. Cook the chowder for 2 to 3 minutes or until the shellfish are just cooked and the fish are opaque. Garnish the chowder with the parsley and serve hot.

NOTE: You can substitute 1 (6½-ounce) can of clams, drained and rinsed, and 1 (8-ounce) bottle of clam juice for the fresh clams.

Makes 4 servings. Per serving: 181 calories, 23 g protein, 13 g carbohydrate, 3 g fat, 80 mg cholesterol, 228 mg sodium.

Seafood Chowder

Chapter Two

~

Sandwiches and Pizzas

꙰ ꙰ ꙰

Once you get beyond peanut butter and jelly, what you put between the bread can be practically limitless. Should your sandwich be portable or open-faced; hot or at room temperature; multilayered or delicate? Some sandwiches, such as Tuna Niçoise Sandwich (page 49), can be made ahead, while others, an Avocado BLT (page 39) for instance, are best assembled at the last minute. Sandwiches are no longer relegated to the lunch box either — serve them for snacks, brunch, or a light supper.

As for pizzas, the *idea* is nothing new — they began with the Greeks. But we doubt they came up with a creation such as our Gorgonzola-Chicken extravaganza (page 54). Most pizzas are best eaten fresh and hot from the oven. *But . . .* with ready-made bread dough, pita breads, and even pie crusts, pizzas can be created in practically no time at all. Homemade pizzas are a fun (and flavorful!) way to beat the midweek blahs, or the perfect fare for a relaxed, easy-on-you Saturday-night party.

Tomato-Mozzarella Sandwiches

Focaccia, the "base" of this sandwich (shown on page 18), is nothing more than a dimpled pizza without all the toppings. Use the Focaccia for all kinds of other sandwiches.

FOCACCIA

2 pounds pizza dough, thawed if frozen
2 tablespoons extra-virgin olive oil
2 large cloves garlic, minced
$1/2$ teaspoon dried rosemary, crushed
$1/4$ teaspoon crushed red-pepper flakes
$1/4$ teaspoon ground black pepper

$1/4$ cup prepared pesto
$1/2$ pound thinly sliced fresh mozzarella cheese
2 ripe tomatoes (1 pound), thinly sliced

1 • Prepare the Focaccia: Grease a 13 × 9 × 2-inch baking pan. Press the pizza dough over the bottom of the prepared pan. Cover the dough with plastic wrap and a clean kitchen towel. Let the dough rise in a warm place for 40 minutes or until it is almost doubled in bulk.

2 • Meanwhile, in a small saucepan, combine the oil and garlic. Heat over low heat for 2 minutes (do not brown). Add the rosemary, red-pepper flakes, and black pepper; set aside.

3 • Preheat the oven to 400°F. With floured fingers, poke about 16 evenly spaced indentations into the dough. Brush the dough gently with the oil mixture.

4 • Bake the dough in the 400°F oven for 25 to 30 minutes or until it is browned. With a spatula, remove the Focaccia to a wire rack to cool.

5 • With a serrated knife, cut the Focaccia into 6 equal pieces; split each piece in half horizontally. Lightly brush one cut side with the pesto. Divide the cheese and tomato slices evenly over the 6 pieces of Focaccia spread with pesto, then cover with the remaining pieces.

Makes 6 servings. Per serving: 542 calories, 18 g protein, 63 g carbohydrate, 25 g fat, 30 mg cholesterol, 683 mg sodium.

rising time:
40 minutes

preparation time:
20 minutes

baking time:
25 minutes

*Low-Fat
Taste Tricks*

If you're trying to keep your fat intake down, skip the mayonnaise on sandwiches. Instead, combine low-fat yogurt, fresh or bottled horseradish, and snipped fresh chives for a lively, low-fat sandwich spread.

Grilled-Vegetable and Feta Hero

This is a flavorful, lighter version of the classic submarine sandwich. The vegetables can be cooked in a special, ridged grill skillet, or broiled indoors, or grilled on the outdoor barbecue. For a no-fuss dinner, make the sandwich ahead of time, wrap well, and refrigerate.

> 1/4 cup Tapenade (olive paste; recipe follows)
> 5 tablespoons olive oil
> 1 Spanish onion, cut into 1/2-inch-thick slices
> 2 medium zucchini, cut lengthwise into 1/4-inch-thick slices
> 1 tablespoon balsamic vinegar
> 1/4 teaspoon freshly ground black pepper
> 2 loaves semolina Italian bread (10 ounces each)
> 1/2 roasted sweet red pepper, trimmed, seeded, and cut into strips
> 1/2 roasted sweet yellow pepper, trimmed, seeded, and cut into strips
> 6 ounces feta cheese, thinly sliced

1 • Prepare the Tapenade according to the recipe instructions.

2 • Drizzle 1 tablespoon of the olive oil over a cast-iron ridged grill skillet or a regular cast-iron skillet; heat the oil over medium-high heat. Add the Spanish onion slices, in batches if necessary. Cook for 7 to 8 minutes on each side or until the onion slices are browned; set aside. Repeat with another tablespoon of oil and the zucchini, grilling for 6 to 8 minutes on each side or until the zucchini is browned; set aside. Or, if desired, brush the onion and zucchini with the oil and broil or cook on an outdoor grill, turning once, until the vegetables are browned. Set aside the grilled vegetables.

3 • In a small jar with a tight-fitting lid, combine the remaining 3 tablespoons of olive oil with the balsamic vinegar and ground pepper. Cover the jar and shake to blend the ingredients.

4 • Cut the loaves of Italian bread in half horizontally; if desired, remove some of the soft bread in the centers. Drizzle the cut sides of the loaves with the oil-vinegar mixture. Spread the bottom half of each loaf with 2 tablespoons of the Tapenade; top with the grilled onion and zucchini, the roasted sweet peppers, and the feta cheese, divided evenly. Replace the top half of each loaf.

---

quick

make ahead

To Roast a Pepper

Roast whole sweet peppers in the broiler 5 to 6 inches from the heat, turning them frequently with tongs, until the peppers are blackened on all sides, about 15 to 20 minutes. Place the roasted peppers in a paper bag and seal the bag. When the peppers are cool enough to handle, remove them from the bag. Cut the peppers in half, and remove the core and seeds. With a paring knife, remove the skins and discard. Use as directed, or refrigerate them for up to 2 days in a tightly covered container.

---

5 • To serve: Cut each loaf in thirds crosswise to make a total of 6 sandwiches.

> Makes 6 servings. Per serving: 435 calories, 14 g protein, 54 g carbohydrate, 19 g fat, 25 mg cholesterol, 931 mg sodium.

Grilled-Vegetable and Feta Hero

Tapenade (Olive Paste)

quick

make ahead

Tapenade is an exuberantly flavored paste — a little goes a long way. It will keep in the refrigerator for a week or two. Bottled tapenade is available at specialty food stores or better supermarkets.

1 cup niçoise olives, pitted
3 anchovy fillets
1 tablespoon drained capers
1 teaspoon olive oil, preferably extra-virgin
$^1/_2$ teaspoon fresh thyme leaves

In a food processor, combine the niçoise olives, anchovies, capers, olive oil, and thyme. Using an on-and-off pulse, process until the mixture is finely chopped.

Makes $^2/_3$ cup. Per tablespoon: 22 calories, 1 g protein, 1 g carbohydrate, 2 g fat, 1 mg cholesterol, 154 mg sodium.

Sandwich Breads

A baguette sliced lengthwise is a fitting bed for thinly shaved flavorful meats such an oven-roasted turkey breast and prosciutto, layered with mild cheese such as provolone, fresh mozzarella, or Muenster, and finished with roasted red peppers. Or spread the bread with chutney and mound on grilled vegetables such as eggplant, red pepper, zucchini, onions, and a little garlic. For a more snackable sandwich, slice the bread crosswise into small rounds before topping.

With dark breads (dark rye, 7-grain, pumpernickel), pile on the strong tastes: smoked hams, salami, grilled sausages; pungent cheese such as an Italian Taleggio, Brie, or blue; and garnish with assertive greens — escarole, arugula, or chicory. Go wild with these creations — the bread will stand up to it.

The bagel classic is a slather of cream cheese topped with smoked salmon, but other spreadables (tuna salad, curried egg salad, and even peanut butter and jelly) go fine atop a bagel.

Pita breads make salads and other loose sandwich fillers portable. Stuff the pockets with a marinated Greek vegetable salad; an avocado, salsa, and black bean extravaganza; or even a pasta salad.

Avocado BLT

~

A yummy new version of an old favorite, this BLT has been updated with slices of avocado and Jalapeño-Lime Mayonnaise. For the best flavor, assemble the sandwich just before serving.

¹/₂ cup Jalapeño-Lime Mayonnaise (recipe follows)
1 (8-inch-diameter) round-loaf Italian bread (about 1 pound)
6 leaves Boston lettuce, washed and patted dry
12 slices tomato
12 slices bacon, cooked crisp (about ³/₄ pound)
2 avocados, pared, pitted, and cut in six slices lengthwise
¹/₄ teaspoon freshly ground pepper
¹/₈ teaspoon salt

quick

1 • Prepare the Jalapeño-Lime Mayonnaise according to the recipe instructions.

2 • Starting from the center, cut 12 slices from the loaf of Italian bread; reserve the remaining bread for another use.

3 • Spread one side of each bread slice with the Jalapeño-Lime Mayonnaise, divided equally. Top 6 slices with 1 lettuce leaf, 2 tomato slices, 2 slices of bacon, and 2 avocado slices. Sprinkle with the pepper and salt. Place the remaining bread slices on top, spread side down. Serve immediately.

> *Makes 6 servings. Per serving: 453 calories, 12 g protein, 51 g carbohydrate, 23 g fat, 11 mg cholesterol, 907 mg sodium.*

Avocado BLT

Jalapeño-Lime Mayonnaise

quick

make ahead

Spoon a little of this spicy-good spread over cold poached fish or use it as a dressing for tuna salad.

> 1 cup reduced-fat, cholesterol-free mayonnaise
> 3 jalapeño peppers, trimmed, seeded, and minced
> 2 green onions, minced
> 2 tablespoons minced fresh cilantro
> 1 teaspoon grated lime zest (colored part of peel)
> 1/4 teaspoon chili powder
> 1 teaspoon fresh lime juice

In a small bowl, combine the mayonnaise, jalapeños, green onions, cilantro, lime zest, chili powder, and lime juice. Stir until all the ingredients are well blended.

> *Makes 1 cup. Per tablespoon: 44 calories, 0 g protein, 4 g carbohydrate, 3 g fat, 0 mg cholesterol, 162 mg sodium.*

Easy Snacks for Entertaining

Sandwiches are the perfect meal for impromptu guests. By keeping some of the following goodies on hand, you can let your guests munch while you throw together one of our fabulous sandwiches. These hassle-free finger foods will get you out of the kitchen fast.

- Mango-Melon Salsa: Toss diced mango, watermelon, and honeydew with grated lemon zest and fresh lemon juice. Serve with blue tortilla chips.

- Red-and-Yellow Salsa: Combine chopped red and yellow cherry tomatoes with hot pepper, fresh cilantro, and lime juice. Serve with tortilla chips.

- Marinated Olives: Cover niçoise, giant Sicilian, and calamata olives with a good-quality olive oil. Add garlic, cracked pepper, orange zest, and fresh rosemary to taste.

- Vegetable Kebabs: Skewer chunks of raw vegetables, such as carrot, zucchini, tomato, and sweet yellow, red, and green pepper. Serve the kebabs with a dip made from 1 cup plain low-fat yogurt, $1/2$ tablespoon lemon juice, $1^{1}/_{2}$ teaspoons each ground cumin and chopped fresh parsley, and ground black pepper to taste.

- Bruschetta: Brush toasted or grilled Italian bread slices with olive oil and rub with garlic. Top with slices of fresh tomato and fresh basil or mint.

Barbecued Pork Sandwich

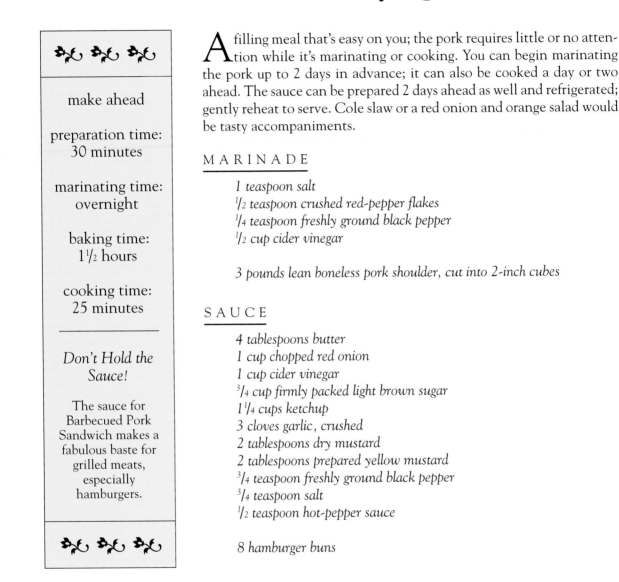

A filling meal that's easy on you; the pork requires little or no attention while it's marinating or cooking. You can begin marinating the pork up to 2 days in advance; it can also be cooked a day or two ahead. The sauce can be prepared 2 days ahead as well and refrigerated; gently reheat to serve. Cole slaw or a red onion and orange salad would be tasty accompaniments.

MARINADE

1 teaspoon salt
$^1/_2$ teaspoon crushed red-pepper flakes
$^1/_4$ teaspoon freshly ground black pepper
$^1/_2$ cup cider vinegar

3 pounds lean boneless pork shoulder, cut into 2-inch cubes

SAUCE

4 tablespoons butter
1 cup chopped red onion
1 cup cider vinegar
$^3/_4$ cup firmly packed light brown sugar
$1^1/_4$ cups ketchup
3 cloves garlic, crushed
2 tablespoons dry mustard
2 tablespoons prepared yellow mustard
$^3/_4$ teaspoon freshly ground black pepper
$^3/_4$ teaspoon salt
$^1/_2$ teaspoon hot-pepper sauce

8 hamburger buns

---

make ahead

preparation time:
30 minutes

marinating time:
overnight

baking time:
$1^1/_2$ hours

cooking time:
25 minutes

Don't Hold the Sauce!

The sauce for Barbecued Pork Sandwich makes a fabulous baste for grilled meats, especially hamburgers.

---

1 • Prepare the Marinade: In a large bowl, combine the salt, red-pepper flakes, black pepper, and cider vinegar. Stir until the ingredients are well blended. Add the pork; toss to coat the pork with the Marinade. Cover the bowl and refrigerate the mixture overnight or up to 2 days.

2 • Preheat the oven to 375°F. Place the pork with the Marinade in a large Dutch oven; over medium heat, bring the mixture to boiling. Cover the pot, place it in the preheated oven, and bake for 1½ hours, stirring once, until the pork is very tender. Transfer the pot to the stove top. Over medium-high heat, cook the mixture, stirring, until the liquid evaporates. Using two forks, shred the pork; set aside.

3 • Prepare the Sauce: In a medium saucepan, over medium heat, melt the butter. Add the red onion and sauté for 5 minutes. Add the cider vinegar, brown sugar, ketchup, garlic, dry mustard, yellow mustard, black pepper, salt, and hot-pepper sauce. Stir until the ingredients are well blended. Bring the Sauce to boiling; reduce the heat and simmer for 15 minutes, stirring occasionally.

4 • Add 1½ cups of the Sauce to the shredded pork; stir to coat the pork well. Heat the pork mixture over medium-low heat.

5 • To serve: Open each hamburger bun. Spoon some of the pork mixture onto the bottom half of each bun; top with the remaining bun half. Pass the remaining Sauce separately.

Makes 8 servings. Per serving: 659 calories, 39 g protein, 40 g carbohydrate, 38 g fat, 147 mg cholesterol, 1,059 mg sodium.

Keep Your Kitchen Safe

- To prevent your cutting board from slipping while you are chopping, slicing, or dicing on it, place a damp cloth on the counter underneath the board.

- Never use a damp rag to lift hot pots; the heat can travel through the moisture in the rag and burn your hands.

- Don't wear baggy or loose clothing when cooking. Loose material can catch on skillet or saucepan handles and utensils, potentially causing severe accidents.

- Don't use dull knives. Because they require more pressure, dull knives increase the risk of the knife slipping while you cut.

- Never lift the lid off a machine, such as a blender or food processor, while the motor is running—something may fly out at you. Use the feed tube to add ingredients while you blend. And never poke a utensil into a machine while the motor is running.

Pork, Pepper, and Onion Sandwich

quick

Fast and fantastic, this sandwich is full of flavor, and it's ready in 15 minutes. Serve with deli potato salad.

2 teaspoons chopped fresh thyme or ¼ teaspoon dried thyme leaves, crushed
½ teaspoon salt
¼ teaspoon freshly ground black pepper
4 (¼- to ⅓-inch-thick) boneless pork loin chops (about 12 ounces total weight)
1 tablespoon olive oil
1 sweet green or yellow pepper, cut into ½-inch-wide strips
1 medium Spanish onion, halved lengthwise and cut lengthwise again into ¼-inch-wide slices
2 plum tomatoes, cut into ¼-inch-wide wedges
1 clove garlic, crushed
2 tablespoons red-wine vinegar
4 thick slices peasant-style bread, toasted

1 • In a cup, combine the thyme, salt, and ground pepper. Stir until the ingredients are blended. Sprinkle ¼ teaspoon of the mixture over the pork chops; reserve the remaining mixture.

2 • In a nonstick skillet, heat 1 teaspoon of the olive oil over medium-high heat. Add the pork chops and cook for 1½ to 2 minutes on each side; transfer the pork chops to a platter. Add the remaining 2 teaspoons of olive oil, the sweet pepper, and the Spanish onion to the skillet; sauté until the vegetables are coated with the oil. Cover the skillet and cook over medium heat for 5 minutes, stirring once. Add the plum tomatoes, garlic, and remaining thyme mixture; sauté for 2 minutes.

3 • Return the pork chops and any juices on the platter to the skillet. Gently reheat the chops, stirring, until all the ingredients are blended. Sprinkle with the red-wine vinegar. Cook, stirring, until the juices boil.

4 • To serve: Place each bread slice on a plate. Top with 1 pork chop, some of the vegetable mixture, and some of the pan juices.

Makes 4 servings. Per serving: 310 calories, 25 g protein, 26 g carbohydrate, 12 g fat, 63 mg cholesterol, 492 mg sodium.

Pork, Pepper, and Onion Sandwich

Grilled Bratwurst with Mustard-Apple-Onion Relish

~

An appetizing alternative to hot dogs, bratwurst makes a satisfying meal either grilled or broiled. The snappy relish can be made ahead and reheated. Fill up the plate with store-bought Scandinavian whole-grain flatbread.

MUSTARD-APPLE-ONION RELISH

2 tablespoons olive oil
2 Vidalia or other sweet onions, halved lengthwise and sliced crosswise
1 large Golden Delicious apple, pared, cored, and cut into ¼-inch dice
¼ cup coarse Dijon mustard
¼ cup reduced-fat sour cream

6 bratwurst
6 kaiser rolls, split
¾ cup shredded reduced-fat Cheddar cheese (about 3 ounces)

relish can be made ahead

preparation time:
15 minutes

cooking time:
25 minutes

1 • Prepare the Mustard-Apple-Onion Relish: In a large skillet, heat the olive oil over medium-high heat. Add the sweet onions and sauté about 10 minutes or until the onions are tender. Add the diced apple, Dijon mustard, and sour cream. Stir until the ingredients are well blended. Gently heat the relish through for 1 to 2 minutes. Remove the skillet from the heat; keep the relish warm.

2 • Split each bratwurst in half lengthwise without cutting all the way through. Grill or broil the bratwurst 4 inches from the heat source for 4 to 5 minutes on each side. Toast the kaiser rolls. Sprinkle the Cheddar cheese over the bottom halves of the rolls; grill or broil about 1 to 2 minutes or until the cheese is melted. Top each roll bottom half with some of the relish, a bratwurst, and the top of the roll. Serve immediately.

> *Makes 6 servings. Per serving: 548 calories, 22 g protein, 39 g carbohydrate, 34 g fat, 65 mg cholesterol, 887 mg sodium.*

Grilled Bratwurst with Mustard-Apple-Onion Relish

Pepper, Onion, and Steak Sandwich

~

Leftover steak or roast? Here's a great way to put it to irresistible use. (If you don't have leftovers, substitute deli roast beef.) The Garlic Butter brings out the best in beef, but it's also great tossed with hot cooked vegetables. Serve the sandwich with a ripe-tomato salad.

GARLIC BUTTER

6 tablespoons unsalted butter, softened
3 tablespoons olive oil
1/2 cup grated Parmesan cheese
2 teaspoons minced garlic
1/4 teaspoon freshly ground black pepper

2 (12-inch-long) loaves semolina or Italian bread, split lengthwise

FILLING

2 tablespoons olive oil
1 large red onion, halved lengthwise and sliced crosswise
1 large sweet red pepper, julienned
1/2 large sweet green pepper, julienned
1/2 large sweet yellow pepper, julienned
10 to 12 ounces leftover grilled steak, thinly sliced
1/4 teaspoon salt

quick

1 • Prepare the Garlic Butter: In a small bowl, combine the butter, the 3 tablespoons of olive oil, the Parmesan cheese, garlic, and black pepper. Stir until the ingredients are well blended. Spread the Garlic Butter over the cut sides of the loaves of bread. Place the bread halves, buttered side up, on a baking sheet. Broil until the bread is golden; set aside.

2 • Prepare the Filling: In a large skillet, heat the 2 tablespoons of olive oil over high heat. Add the red onion and the sweet peppers. Sauté about 4 to 5 minutes or until the vegetables are tender-crisp. Add the steak and salt; heat the mixture through.

3 • To serve: Top each bread bottom half with half of the steak mixture, then the bread top. Cut each loaf in thirds to make a total of 6 sandwiches. Serve immediately.

Makes 6 servings. Per serving: 568 calories, 26 g protein, 44 g carbohydrate, 32 g fat, 80 mg cholesterol, 745 mg sodium.

Pepper, Onion, and Steak Sandwich

Tuna Niçoise Sandwich

A luscious variation on the classic salad, this spiced-up version is served on Italian bread. The salad mixture can be prepared a day ahead and refrigerated.

2 (6½-ounce) cans tuna packed in olive oil

VINAIGRETTE DRESSING

Olive oil
2 tablespoons fresh oregano leaves or ½ teaspoon dried oregano
   leaves, crushed
¼ teaspoon salt
¼ teaspoon freshly ground black pepper
3 tablespoons red-wine vinegar
1 teaspoon Dijon mustard
1 clove garlic

PEPPER FILLING

1 sweet red pepper
1 sweet yellow pepper
1 pickled jalapeño pepper, seeded and minced
¼ cup diced red onion
2 tablespoons chopped pitted niçoise or calamata olives
2 tablespoons capers

1 (12-ounce) loaf Italian bread, split in half lengthwise
1 bunch watercress, coarse stems removed

1 • Drain the oil from the cans of tuna into a 1-cup glass measure; reserve the tuna.

2 • Prepare the Vinaigrette Dressing: To the oil in the glass measure, add enough olive oil to equal ⅓ cup. Pour the combined oil into a blender and add the oregano, salt, black pepper, red-wine vinegar, Dijon mustard, and garlic. Process until the mixture is smooth and well blended.

3 • Prepare the Pepper Filling: Roast, peel, core, seed, and julienne the sweet red and yellow peppers (page 36). Place the sweet peppers in a medium bowl and add the jalapeño pepper, red onion, olives, and capers.

make ahead

preparation time:
20 minutes

total broiling
time:
20 minutes

Storing Canned Tuna

Like all canned foods, tuna should be stored in a cool, dark place. For optimum nutrient value and the best texture, tuna packed in water should be eaten within three years of purchase; tuna packed in oil can last up to five years.

4 • Remove some of the soft bread from inside the Italian loaf halves. Brush the insides of the bread halves with some of the Vinaigrette Dressing; add the remaining dressing to the pepper mixture. Add the tuna to the pepper mixture and stir gently to combine all the ingredients, leaving the tuna in large chunks.

5 • Broil or grill the bread halves, oiled side toward heat, 2 to 3 minutes, or until they are toasted. Pile the tuna mixture onto the bottom bread halves. Top with some of the watercress and the top bread halves. Slice the loaves crosswise in half to make a total of 4 sandwiches.

> *Makes 4 servings. Per serving: 558 calories, 34 g protein, 50 g carbohydrate, 25 g fat, 16 mg cholesterol, 1,044 mg sodium.*

Tuna Niçoise Sandwich and Barley and Black-Eyed Pea Salad (page 84)

Tuna Salad – Stuffed Pita

A quick-to-fix sandwich that family or guests can easily assemble themselves at an informal dinner or lunch. Serve with carrot sticks and iced tea.

low-fat

quick

DRESSING

2 tablespoons reduced-calorie mayonnaise
1 tablespoon fresh lemon juice
$1/4$ teaspoon dried thyme leaves, crushed

TUNA SALAD

1 (16-ounce) can cannellini beans, drained
1 cup frozen peas, thawed
1 (7-ounce) can water-packed white tuna
4 green onions, chopped

8 (4-inch-diameter) pita pocket breads
8 lettuce leaves, washed and crisped
1 large tomato, cut crosswise into 8 slices

1 • Prepare the Dressing: In a large bowl, combine the mayonnaise, lemon juice, and thyme. Stir until the ingredients are well blended.

2 • Prepare the Tuna Salad: To the Dressing in the bowl, add the cannellini beans, peas, tuna, and green onions. With a fork, mix the ingredients well.

3 • Split open the pita breads along the edge, forming a pocket. Into each pita pocket, insert 1 lettuce leaf, 1 tomato slice, and some of the Tuna Salad, divided equally. Serve immediately.

Makes 8 servings. Per serving: 301 calories, 20 g protein, 50 g carbohydrate, 3 g fat, 15 mg cholesterol, 460 mg sodium.

Deep-Dish Turkey Pizza

make ahead

preparation time:
20 minutes

cooking time:
10 minutes

baking time:
30 minutes

The pizza Chicago made famous with a twist: turkey! More than just a great supper, this pizza is also perfect for after-school meetings and tailgate parties, since it can be served at room temperature. You can use deli-roasted turkey breast in this recipe.

> 2 tablespoons olive oil
> 2 medium celery stalks, sliced
> 1 medium red onion, cut into wedges
> 1 large sweet red pepper, diced
> 1 teaspoon dried rosemary leaves, crushed
> 1/8 teaspoon freshly ground black pepper
> 4 cups coarsely chopped cooked turkey (about 1 1/2 pounds)
> 2 cups shredded Swiss cheese (about 8 ounces)
> 1/2 cup halved, pitted canned black olives
> 1 (1.6-ounce) package mushroom-soup mix
> 1 (1-pound) package hot-roll mix

1 • In a large skillet, heat the olive oil over medium heat. Add the celery, red onion, sweet red pepper, rosemary, and ground pepper. Sauté about 10 minutes or until the vegetables are tender.

2 • In a large bowl, combine the vegetable mixture with the turkey, 1 3/4 cups of the Swiss cheese, the olives, and the mushroom-soup mix. Stir until the ingredients are well mixed.

3 • Preheat the oven to 425°F. Grease a 10-inch springform pan.

4 • Prepare the hot-roll mix as the package label directs for a pizza crust. Remove and set aside 1/2 cup of the dough. Roll or stretch the remaining dough into a 14-inch round. Place the dough round in the prepared pan, pressing the dough over the bottom and up the sides of the pan. Bake the crust for 5 minutes; remove from the oven. Spoon the turkey mixture onto the crust. Sprinkle the remaining 1/4 cup of Swiss cheese over the turkey mixture. Cut the remaining 1/2 cup of dough into 3 equal pieces; roll each piece into a 10-inch rope. Arrange the dough ropes, spoke fashion, on top of the cheese, pinching the ends of the ropes to the top of the crust sides. Bake the pizza about 25 minutes or until the crust is golden.

> Makes 8 servings. Per serving: 465 calories, 35 g protein, 36 g carbohydrate, 20 g fat, 80 mg cholesterol, 876 mg sodium.

Deep-Dish Turkey Pizza and Italian Strata (page 226)

Keeping Cool in the Kitchen

When warm weather hits, sandwiches are a terrific choice for meals, as they require little cooking (if any) that might heat up the kitchen. Here are some other ideas for keeping kitchen temperatures at a minimum.

- When you have to cook on steamy days, keep your kitchen well ventilated. Place an electric fan at least 3 feet from an open window and point the fan away from the window on a diagonal. The fan will catch even the smallest breeze from outside and bring it in to cool the room.

- Whenever possible, use the microwave oven. This ultraquick method of cooking is particularly good for boneless chicken breasts (the moist heat keeps it juicy) and fish fillets (the minimal cooking time helps preserve their delicate texture).

- Do heavy-duty baking (cakes or fruit pies, for example) in the morning, when outside temperatures are at their lowest.

- A quick refresher while you're preparing dinner: Place a damp bandanna in the freezer for 15 minutes, then tie it loosely around your neck.

- Stay cool — and quench your thirst — by keeping a bunch of grapes in the freezer to munch on while you're preparing dinner.

Gorgonzola-Chicken Pizza

preparation time:
15 minutes

cooking time:
35 minutes

baking time:
15 minutes

Gorgonzola is a crumbly, sharp, and tangy-tasting blue cheese of Italian origin that pairs well with mild chicken breast to make a sophisticated pizza. Other blue cheeses like Roquefort or Stilton can be used if Gorgonzola is not available. Using frozen bread dough for the pizza crust in this recipe speeds things along.

2 teaspoons olive oil
2 teaspoons cornmeal

TOPPING

2 tablespoons butter or margarine
2 tablespoons olive oil
1 boneless chicken breast, skinned and cut into strips (about $^3/_4$ pound)
1 tablespoon chopped fresh sage leaves
$^1/_2$ teaspoon freshly ground pepper
$^1/_2$ teaspoon salt
2 large Vidalia or Spanish onions, thinly sliced
2 large cloves garlic, thinly sliced

$^1/_3$ (3-pound) package frozen bread dough, thawed (1 loaf)
$^1/_4$ pound Gorgonzola cheese, crumbled
2 tablespoons grated Parmesan cheese

Gorgonzola-Chicken Pizza

1 • Grease a 14-inch pizza pan with the 2 teaspoons of olive oil; sprinkle the cornmeal over the oiled pan.

2 • Prepare the Topping: In a large skillet over medium heat, melt the butter in the olive oil. Add the chicken, sage, pepper, and salt. Sauté the mixture for 3 minutes. With a slotted spoon, remove the chicken mixture to a bowl. In the drippings in the pan, sauté the Vidalia or Spanish onions and the garlic about 15 to 20 minutes over medium-low heat, or until they are golden and caramelized.

3 • Preheat the oven to 450°F. Pat the bread dough into the prepared pan to form a thin crust, folding under the edge $1/4$ inch. Bake for 5 minutes. Remove the pan from the oven. Spread the onion mixture over the crust, then sprinkle the chicken mixture and the Gorgonzola and Parmesan cheeses evenly over the top. Bake about 10 minutes more or until the crust is golden brown and the cheese is melted and bubbly. Cool the pizza for 5 minutes before slicing.

Makes 4 servings. Per serving: 673 calories, 30 g protein, 72 g carbohydrate, 28 g fat, 76 mg cholesterol, 1,574 mg sodium.

Pita Pizzas

B ring out these crispy-crusted, individual pizzas at your next summer get-together. Pita breads serve as the ready-made pizza crusts in this quick-to-fix meal you prepare on the outdoor grill or under the broiler.

quick

RED-ONION TOPPING

$1/4$ cup olive oil
1 small red onion, sliced
$1/4$ teaspoon dried oregano leaves, crushed
$1/4$ teaspoon crushed red-pepper flakes

TOMATO-CHEESE TOPPING

2 tablespoons chopped sun-dried tomatoes in oil
2 tablespoons shredded mozzarella cheese
2 tablespoons ricotta cheese
2 tablespoons grated Parmesan cheese
8 mini pita breads, split in half

ADDITIONAL TOPPINGS

Crumbled goat cheese
Julienned fresh sage or basil leaves
Coarse (kosher) salt
Roasted sweet red and yellow peppers, julienned

1 • Prepare the Red-Onion Topping: In a small skillet, heat the olive oil over medium heat. Add the red onion, oregano, and red-pepper flakes, and sauté about 6 minutes or until the onion is tender; set aside.

2 • Prepare the Tomato-Cheese Topping: In a small bowl, combine the sun-dried tomatoes with the mozzarella, ricotta, and Parmesan cheeses. Stir until all the ingredients are well mixed; set aside.

3 • Grill or broil each pita bread half on the unbrowned side about 1 minute or until lightly toasted. Place the toasted pita bread halves on a platter, toasted side up. Spread each with some of the Red-Onion Topping, then sprinkle with some of the Tomato-Cheese Topping and any other additional toppings. Place the pizzas on the grill rack and grill, covered, about 1 to 2 minutes or until the pizzas are browned and crisp. Or, place the pizzas on a broiler-pan rack and broil until browned and crisp.

Makes 8 servings. Per serving: 179 calories, 5 g protein, 20 g carbohydrate, 9 g fat, 6 mg cholesterol, 216 mg sodium.

Pita Pizzas

Pizza Rustica

~

A two-crusted, hearty pizza that makes good use of leftover cooked pork, especially a large roast. Serve with a green salad dressed with balsamic vinaigrette.

1 tablespoon olive oil
1 medium onion, chopped
¹/₂ pound mushrooms, sliced
1 cup prepared tomato sauce
1 pound part-skim ricotta cheese
2 large eggs
¹/₄ cup grated Parmesan cheese
2 tablespoons chopped parsley
¹/₂ teaspoon freshly ground pepper
¹/₂ teaspoon salt
1 (15-ounce) package refrigerated, all-ready pie crust (2 crusts)
¹/₂ pound cooked pork, cubed (1¹/₂ cups)
¹/₂ pound part-skim mozzarella cheese, thinly sliced

1 • Preheat the oven to 425°F. In a large skillet, heat the olive oil over medium-high heat. Add the onion and mushrooms and sauté until the onion is wilted and the mushrooms release their liquid. Bring to boiling; boil until the liquid evaporates. Stir in the tomato sauce; set aside.

2 • In a large bowl, combine the ricotta cheese, eggs, Parmesan cheese, parsley, pepper, and salt. Stir until the ingredients are well blended.

3 • Line a 9-inch pie plate with 1 of the pie crusts. Sprinkle half of the pork over the crust; top with half of the ricotta mixture and half of the mushroom mixture. Cover with half of the sliced mozzarella. Repeat the layering with the remaining pork, ricotta, and mushroom mixtures and the mozzarella cheese. Top with the remaining pie crust; crimp the crust edges together to seal.

4 • Bake the pizza for about 35 to 40 minutes or until the crust is golden. Let the pizza stand for 30 minutes before serving.

---

preparation time:
20 minutes

cooking time:
10 minutes

baking time:
35 minutes

standing time:
30 minutes

The Right Way to Measure Cheese

If a recipe calls for grated or shredded cheese, grate or shred the cheese before measuring. Then lightly pack the cheese into a dry measuring cup.

Makes 8 servings. Per serving: 530 calories, 27 g protein, 33 g carbohydrate, 32 g fat, 117 mg cholesterol, 925 mg sodium.

Ham and Greens Pizza

preparation time:
20 minutes

dough rising time:
15 minutes

total baking time:
20 minutes

You can use cooked deli ham for this recipe, and feel free to experiment with other combinations of greens. Serve with cherry tomatoes tossed in a low-fat salad dressing.

PIZZA DOUGH

1 package fast-rising yeast
1 teaspoon honey
$^1/_2$ cup warm water (105°F to 115°F)
$1^1/_2$ cups unsifted all-purpose flour
1 teaspoon salt
1 tablespoon olive oil

TOPPING

2 tablespoons olive oil plus 1 teaspoon to grease pan
$^1/_4$ cup water
$^1/_2$ pound Swiss chard, stems removed
$^1/_2$ pound spinach, stems removed
1 cup cooked ham, cut into $^3/_4$-inch dice
$^1/_4$ cup finely chopped onion
Pinch of crushed red-pepper flakes
2 teaspoons minced garlic
$^3/_4$ cup whole-milk ricotta cheese
$^1/_4$ cup grated Parmesan cheese
1 tablespoon chopped fresh parsley
1 teaspoon chopped fresh thyme or $^1/_2$ teaspoon dried thyme
$^1/_4$ teaspoon freshly ground black pepper

1 • Prepare the Pizza Dough: In a small bowl, stir together the yeast, honey, and warm water; let the mixture stand for 2 minutes. In a food processor, combine the flour and salt; pulse to mix. With the motor running, pour the yeast mixture and 1 tablespoon of olive oil through the feed tube; process until the dough begins to leave the sides of the work bowl and forms a ball. Process for 1 minute more or until the dough is smooth and elastic. Remove the dough from the processor and shape it into a ball. Place the ball in an oiled bowl and turn the dough so the oiled side is up. Cover the bowl or place it in a plastic food-storage bag (remove any air from the bag, and seal); let stand in a warm, draft-free place about 15 to 20 minutes or until the dough is doubled in bulk.

2 • Preheat the oven to 425°F. Grease a 12-inch pizza pan with the 1 teaspoon of olive oil. Pat the Pizza Dough into a 12-inch round and press into the pan. Brush with 1 tablespoon of the remaining oil and prick holes in the dough with a fork. Bake about 10 minutes or until the crust is lightly browned.

3 • Prepare the Topping: While the crust is baking, heat the 1/4 cup of water to boiling in a large skillet. Add the Swiss chard and spinach in batches, stirring until the greens begin to wilt. Cover the skillet and cook about 3 minutes or until the greens are completely wilted. Drain the greens well; coarsely chop.

4 • In the same skillet, dried, heat the remaining 1 tablespoon of olive oil over medium-high heat. Add the ham, onion, and red-pepper flakes. Sauté about 2 minutes or until the onion is translucent. Add the garlic and sauté for 30 seconds. Add greens and sauté for 5 minutes.

5 • In a small bowl, combine the ricotta and Parmesan cheeses with the parsley, thyme, and black pepper. Stir until the mixture is well blended. Remove the crust from the oven; sprinkle with the ham mixture. Spoon dollops of the cheese mixture over the ham mixture. Bake the pizza for 10 minutes.

> *Makes 4 servings. Per serving: 464 calories, 25 g protein, 45 g carbohydrate, 21 g fat, 47 mg cholesterol, 1,321 mg sodium.*

Easy Pizza Crusts

- Ready-to-top, premade bread pizza crusts, packaged in cellophane, are available in most supermarkets in large and small sizes. Layer on one of our toppings or use your own impromptu combination, and bake according to the package directions.

- Refrigerated pizza crusts that come in flavors, such as herb and tomato, are just waiting for your favorite toppings and a little baking. Refrigerated bread dough also works extremely well.

- English muffins have been popular since Day One for making individual, quick pizzas. Lightly toast the muffin first for extra crispness. Then top and toast again just to heat everything through. You can do the same thing with pita pockets split in half. One advantage of these minipizzas — they'll fit into a toaster oven.

- Scandinavian flatbreads or even matzoth make very crunchy, no-fuss bases for a party pizza hors d'oeuvre.

Pizza Dough

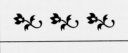

Here's our basic pizza dough, quickly mixed with the aid of a food processor. On pages 64–66, we offer you three easy toppings. See our instructions below for refrigerating and freezing the dough.

1 package dry yeast
1 teaspoon sugar
$^3/_4$ cup warm water (105°F to 115°F)
$2^1/_4$ cups unsifted all-purpose flour (see Note)
1 $^1/_2$ teaspoons salt
1 tablespoon olive oil
Nonstick cooking spray

1 • In a small glass measure, stir together the yeast, sugar, and warm water; let the mixture stand about 5 minutes or until foamy.

2 • In a food processor, combine the flour, salt, and olive oil. With the motor running, pour the yeast mixture through the feed tube. Process until the dough forms a ball and pulls cleanly away from the sides of the work bowl. Process for 1 minute to knead the dough. (The dough will be sticky; if it's too wet, mix in additional flour, 1 tablespoon at a time. If the dough is too dry, mix in additional water, 1 teaspoon at a time.) Remove the dough from the processor. Pat the dough into a ball.

3 • Lightly coat the inside of a 3-gallon plastic food-storage bag with nonstick cooking spray; add the dough. Squeeze out any air from the bag and close the top with a twist tie. Let the dough rise in a warm, draft-free place about 1 hour or until the dough is doubled in bulk.

4 • Remove the dough from the plastic bag. Punch the dough down and divide it in half. To refrigerate up to 4 days, place the dough in another plastic bag, leaving a little room for expansion. Tightly seal the bag and refrigerate. Let the dough come to room temperature before using as directed in a recipe. Or, freeze the dough in a freezer-safe plastic bag up to 1 month. To use, thaw the dough in the refrigerator for 12 hours or overnight. Let the dough come to room temperature before using.

NOTE: For whole-wheat dough, replace $^1/_2$ cup of the all-purpose flour with an equal amount of whole-wheat flour.

Makes enough dough for two 10-inch-diameter pizzas.

---

make ahead

preparation time:
15 minutes

rising time:
1 hour

Flavored Crusts

Adding ingredients to a pizza crust can introduce a whole range of subtle flavor combinations as well as visual variations. To the flour, add from a teaspoon to a tablespoon of a dried herb or spice such as oregano, rosemary, basil, cracked black pepper, chili powder, coriander, and so on. Chopped green onions, black olives, and roasted red peppers are other crust additions you might consider.

TO MAKE A PIZZA CRUST

1. Add the proofed yeast through the feed tube to the flour mixture in the food processor while the motor is running.

2. Let the dough rise in a sealed plastic bag in a warm place until doubled in bulk, about 1 hour.

3. Roll the dough out or stretch it with your hands on a lightly floured work surface into a 10-inch round; the round should be thicker around the edges.

4. Place the dough in a prepared pizza pan.

Wild-Mushroom Pizza

~

pizza dough can
be made ahead

preparation time:
20 minutes

cooking time:
10 minutes

baking time:
8 minutes

Cutting Pizza

To slice your pizza, we recommend transferring it to a cutting surface to avoid scratching the pan. Use a pizza cutting wheel for speedy slicing.

Shiitake mushrooms mixed with regular button mushrooms create a rich, "woodsy" taste for this pizza. Be sure to wipe the mushrooms very clean with damp paper towels. Serve with a salad of yellow, green, and red roasted peppers (page 36) drizzled with olive oil and balsamic vinegar.

> *Olive oil*
> *1 teaspoon cornmeal*
> *½ recipe whole-wheat Pizza Dough (page 60)*
> *2 teaspoons dried rosemary leaves, crushed*
> *¼ cup grated Parmesan cheese (about 1 ounce)*
> *½ pound shiitake mushrooms, sliced*
> *¼ pound regular mushrooms, sliced*
> *2 cloves garlic, crushed*
> *1 teaspoon soy sauce*
> *1 cup shredded Gruyère cheese (about 4 ounces)*
> *4 green onions, sliced*
> *Freshly ground pepper*

1 • Preheat the oven to 500°F. Grease a 12-inch black pizza pan with a little olive oil. Sprinkle the cornmeal over the oiled pan.

2 • On a lightly floured work surface, flatten the dough; with a rolling pin or your hands, roll or stretch the dough into a 10-inch-diameter round, with the dough thicker around the edges. Place the dough in the prepared pan.

3 • In a cup, combine 2 teaspoons of olive oil and the rosemary. Brush the mixture over the dough; sprinkle with half of the Parmesan cheese.

4 • In a large skillet, heat 2 tablespoons of olive oil over medium heat. Add the shiitake and regular mushrooms; sauté about 8 minutes or until the mushrooms release their liquid and the liquid evaporates. Add the garlic and soy sauce; cook, stirring, for 1 minute more.

5 • Spread the mushroom mixture over the dough to within ½ inch of the edge. Sprinkle the Gruyère and remaining Parmesan cheese over the mushrooms, then the green onions and ground pepper over all.

6 • Bake about 8 to 12 minutes or until the crust is dark golden brown and the cheeses are bubbly.

> *Makes 4 servings (8 slices). Per serving: 338 calories, 18 g protein, 35 g carbohydrate, 15 g fat, 36 mg cholesterol, 707 mg sodium.*

Shown clockwise from top: Wild-Mushroom Pizza, Pizza Puttanesca (page 65), and Pesto Pizza with Ricotta and Peppers (page 64)

Pesto Pizza with Ricotta and Peppers

~

pizza dough can be made ahead

preparation time: 15 minutes

baking time: 8 minutes

Pizza Pans

You can use all sorts of pans for baking pizzas: 12-inch rounds in dark or black steel, shiny aluminum pans, flat pans with a lip or a rippled edge, jelly-roll pans, ordinary baking sheets, round layer-cake pans, cast-iron skillets, even springform pans.

Pesto, the classic basil mixture, provides the tempting sauce for this pizza (shown on page 63), and can be found in the refrigerator section in your supermarket. Creamy ricotta cheese, plum tomatoes, and sweet red and yellow pepper strips make a colorful presentation.

Olive oil
1 teaspoon cornmeal
1/2 recipe Pizza Dough (page 60)
2 teaspoons dried basil leaves, crushed
2 large ripe plum tomatoes, thinly sliced lengthwise
1/4 cup grated Parmesan cheese (about 1 ounce)
1/2 cup ricotta cheese
1/4 cup prepared pesto
1/2 sweet red pepper, cut into strips
1/2 sweet yellow pepper, cut into strips
1 tablespoon toasted pine nuts
Freshly cracked pepper

1 • Preheat the oven to 500°F. Grease a 12-inch black pizza pan with a little olive oil. Sprinkle the cornmeal over the oiled pan.

2 • On a lightly floured work surface, flatten the dough; with a rolling pin or your hands, roll or stretch the dough into a 10-inch-diameter round, with the dough thicker around the edges. Place the dough in the prepared pan.

3 • In a cup, combine 2 teaspoons of olive oil with the basil; brush the mixture over the dough. Cover the dough with plum tomato slices to within 1/2 inch of the edge. Sprinkle half of the Parmesan cheese over the tomatoes. Spoon dollops of the ricotta cheese over the tomatoes; repeat with the pesto. Arrange the sweet red and yellow pepper strips over the top and sprinkle with the pine nuts, cracked pepper, and remaining Parmesan cheese.

4 • Bake about 8 to 12 minutes or until the crust is dark golden brown and the cheeses are bubbly.

Makes 4 servings (8 slices). Per serving: 385 calories, 14 g protein, 36 g carbohydrate, 22 g fat, 26 mg cholesterol, 587 mg sodium.

Pizza Puttanesca

~

This spicy, black-olive topping reportedly was first created by ladies of the evening as a quick dish to serve customers. The three cheeses, mozzarella, provolone, and Parmesan, give this pizza (shown on page 63) robust flavor.

Olive oil
1 teaspoon cornmeal
1/2 recipe Pizza Dough (page 60)
2 teaspoons dried oregano leaves, crushed
1/2 cup Sun-Dried Tomato Sauce (page 67)
1/2 teaspoon crushed red-pepper flakes
1 cup shredded mozzarella cheese (about 4 ounces)
1/2 cup shredded provolone cheese (about 2 ounces)
1/4 cup grated Parmesan cheese (about 1 ounce)
1 small red onion, thinly sliced crosswise
1/2 cup Greek olives, pitted, halved

ЖЖЖ

pizza dough can
be made ahead

preparation time:
15 minutes

baking time:
8 minutes

ЖЖЖ

1 • Preheat the oven to 500°F. Grease a 12-inch black pizza pan with a little olive oil. Sprinkle the cornmeal over the oiled pan.

2 • On a lightly floured work surface, flatten the dough; with a rolling pin or your hands, roll or stretch the dough into a 10-inch-diameter round, with the dough thicker around the edges. Place the dough in the prepared pan.

3 • In a cup, combine 2 teaspoons of olive oil with the oregano; brush the mixture over the dough. In another cup, stir together the tomato sauce and red-pepper flakes. Spread the tomato-sauce mixture over the dough to within 1/2 inch of the edge. In a bowl, combine the mozzarella, provolone, and Parmesan cheeses; stir to mix well. Sprinkle half of the cheese mixture over the tomato sauce; top with the red-onion rings and Greek olives. Sprinkle the remaining cheese mixture over all.

4 • Bake about 8 to 12 minutes or until the crust is dark golden brown and the cheeses are bubbly.

Makes 4 servings (8 slices). Per serving: 395 calories, 18 g protein, 40 g carbohydrate, 19 g fat, 37 mg cholesterol, 995 mg sodium.

Turkey Sausage and Goat-Cheese Pizza

~

Turkey sausage and goat cheese impart rich flavor in this whole-wheat-crusted pizza.

pizza dough can
be made ahead

preparation time:
15 minutes

cooking time:
15 minutes

baking time:
8 minutes

Olive oil
1 teaspoon cornmeal
½ recipe whole-wheat Pizza Dough (page 60)
2 tablespoons chopped fresh thyme leaves or 2 teaspoons dried thyme
   leaves, crushed
¼ cup grated Parmesan cheese (about 1 ounce)
½ pound Italian-style turkey sausage
½ cup Sun-Dried Tomato Sauce (page 67)
6 ounces goat cheese, crumbled
Freshly ground pepper

1 • Preheat the oven to 500°F. Grease a 12-inch black pizza pan with a little olive oil. Sprinkle the cornmeal over the oiled pan.

2 • On a lightly floured work surface, flatten the dough; with a rolling pin or your hands, roll or stretch the dough into a 10-inch-diameter round, with the dough thicker around the edges. Place the dough in the prepared pan.

3 • In a cup, combine 2 teaspoons of olive oil with 1 tablespoon of fresh thyme or 1 teaspoon of dried thyme; brush the mixture over the dough. Sprinkle with half of the Parmesan cheese.

4 • In a large skillet, heat 1 tablespoon of olive oil over medium heat. Remove the sausage from its casing; add the sausage to the skillet. Sauté the sausage, breaking up pieces with a spoon, until it is browned. Remove the skillet from the heat and drain off the fat. Stir in the tomato sauce until it is well mixed.

5 • Spread the sausage mixture over the dough to within ½ inch of the edge. Sprinkle the goat cheese, the remaining Parmesan cheese and thyme, and the pepper over all.

6 • Bake about 8 to 12 minutes or until the crust is dark golden brown and topping is bubbly.

> Makes 4 servings (8 slices). Per serving: 414 calories, 21 g protein,
> 43 g carbohydrate, 18 g fat, 54 mg cholesterol, 908 mg sodium.

Sun-Dried Tomatoes

- Like other dried fruit, such as raisins and apricots, sun-dried tomatoes are full of intense flavor and are very chewy.

- Sun-dried tomatoes packed in oil come in a jar and are ready to use. To remove excess oil and fat, rinse the tomatoes and pat them dry with paper towels.

- Dry-pack sun-dried tomatoes usually come in plastic packets. Since they are crisp and somewhat brittle, they must be softened before using. Place the tomatoes in a bowl and cover them with boiling water. Let the tomatoes stand until softened, about 5 to 10 minutes. Drain the tomatoes, reserving the soaking liquid for soup, sauces, casseroles, and other dishes. Blot the tomatoes dry with paper towels and use as directed in the recipe.

Sun-Dried Tomato Sauce

This sauce is not only good spread over pizza but also makes an exciting sauce when tossed with rotelle or ziti pasta. Prepare the sauce a few days ahead if you like and refrigerate.

1/2 cup sun-dried tomatoes (not packed in oil)
2 tablespoons olive oil
1 medium onion, chopped
1 (14-ounce) can Italian plum tomatoes in purée
2 cloves garlic, crushed
1 tablespoon dried basil leaves, crushed

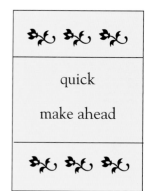

quick

make ahead

1 • In a medium bowl, cover the sun-dried tomatoes with boiling water. Let the mixture stand for 5 minutes.

2 • In a large skillet, heat the olive oil over medium heat. Add the onion and sauté about 5 minutes or until the onion is tender. Drain the sun-dried tomatoes; add them to the onion in the skillet. Add the plum tomatoes, garlic, and basil. Bring the mixture to boiling, breaking up the plum tomatoes with a spoon. Reduce the heat and simmer about 15 minutes or until the mixture is thickened. Place the tomato mixture in a food processor and process until it is a smooth purée.

> *Makes 1½ cups sauce. Per ¼ cup: 105 calories, 3 g protein, 15 g carbohydrate, 5 g fat, 0 mg cholesterol, 276 mg sodium.*

Chapter Three

~

Salads

Everywhere you look, supermarkets, urban green markets, and roadside farm stands are overflowing with a huge assortment of fruit and vegetables. And that gives you a rainbow of wonderful ingredients with which to create salads, from enoki mushrooms and napa cabbage to frisée and papaya. Though salads are often first courses or side dishes, with the right ingredients they can be a meal unto themselves. Include protein, such as small amounts of meat or fish. You can also create main-dish salads with health-smart choices such as the aromatic rices — basmati and Texmati — as well as legumes and variously shaped pasta.

When you cook vegetables for meals, save any leftovers and chill them. Chilled vegetables add flavor, texture, and a nutritional boost to salads, and because they're already cooked, they're ready to add in seconds. Broccoli, cauliflower, summer squash, carrots, and peas all make great additions to salads.

To make your salads even more nutritionally sound, sample some of the new low-fat salad dressings. For real savings, create your own — turn the traditional formula of three parts oil to one part acid (vinegar, lemon juice, and so on) around 180 degrees. Instead, combine three parts acid to one part oil. Add plenty of fresh herbs and garlic and you'll never miss the oil.

To get a jump on salad-making time, wash salad greens a day or two ahead and store in a plastic bag in the refrigerator to keep them crisp. Then you simply assemble at the last minute.

Once you've made a few salads using our recipes, you'll be ready to experiment with your own creations, taking advantage of whatever looks the best in the market.

Pronto Pasta Salad

This salad can be made several hours ahead and refrigerated. Serve with *grissini* — very thin Italian breadsticks.

DRESSING

²/₃ cup low-fat cottage cheese
²/₃ cup nonfat plain yogurt
³/₄ teaspoon dried dillweed
¹/₂ teaspoon sugar
1 tablespoon fresh lemon juice
1 teaspoon Dijon mustard

SALAD

1 cup uncooked tricolor rotini twists
1 cup snow peas
4 ounces part-skim mozzarella cheese, cut into thin strips
4 ounces low-fat ham, cut into thin strips
4 celery stalks, thinly sliced
3 large green onions, thinly sliced

1 • Prepare the Dressing: In a blender or food processor, combine the cottage cheese, yogurt, dillweed, sugar, lemon juice, and Dijon mustard. Process until the mixture is a smooth purée. Pour the Dressing into a jar with a tight-fitting lid and refrigerate until serving time.

2 • Prepare the Salad: Cook the rotini as the package label directs. During the last minute of cooking time, add the snow peas and cook for 1 minute. Drain the pasta and snow peas and immediately rinse them with cold water.

3 • In a large bowl, combine the cooked rotini and snow peas with the mozzarella cheese, ham, celery, and green onions. Shake the jar of Dressing to combine the ingredients, then immediately pour the Dressing over the Salad. Toss gently to coat the Salad with the Dressing. Cover the bowl and refrigerate the Salad for at least 1 hour before serving.

Makes 6 servings and 2 cups Dressing. Per serving: 130 calories, 13 g protein, 14 g carbohydrate, 2 g fat, 13 mg cholesterol, 526 mg sodium.

Warm Chicken Salad

An elegant yet easy main-dish salad that can serve as a midweek supper or noteworthy light dinner for company. The raspberries add a touch of color and tangy flavor.

make ahead

preparation time:
20 minutes

roasting time:
30 minutes

cooling time:
20 minutes

DRESSING

2 shallots, minced
1 teaspoon fresh thyme leaves, chopped
$^{1}/_{4}$ teaspoon freshly ground pepper
$^{1}/_{4}$ teaspoon salt
$^{1}/_{3}$ cup raspberry vinegar
2 teaspoons Dijon mustard
$^{1}/_{2}$ cup olive oil
$^{1}/_{4}$ cup vegetable oil

CHICKEN SALAD

4 bone-in chicken-breast halves
2 teaspoons fresh thyme leaves, chopped
$^{1}/_{2}$ teaspoon freshly ground pepper
$^{1}/_{2}$ teaspoon salt
2 teaspoons olive oil
12 cups mixed salad greens
$^{1}/_{2}$ cup toasted walnut pieces
4 ounces Gorgonzola cheese, crumbled
$^{1}/_{2}$ pint fresh raspberries
Freshly ground pepper

1 • Prepare the Dressing: In a medium bowl, combine the shallots, 1 teaspoon of fresh thyme, $^{1}/_{4}$ teaspoon of pepper, $^{1}/_{4}$ teaspoon of salt, raspberry vinegar, and Dijon mustard. Whisk until the mixture is blended. Add the $^{1}/_{2}$ cup of olive oil and the vegetable oil in a steady stream, whisking constantly, until the Dressing is blended and smooth. Set aside the Dressing.

2 • Prepare the Chicken Salad: Preheat the oven to 425°F. Cover the broiler pan with aluminum foil. Place the chicken breasts on the foil-covered pan. In a cup, combine the 2 teaspoons of fresh thyme, $^{1}/_{2}$ teaspoon of pepper, $^{1}/_{2}$ teaspoon of salt, and 2 teaspoons of olive oil; stir to mix the ingredients well. Brush the thyme mixture over the chicken breasts. Roast about 30 minutes or until the chicken is cooked through. Drizzle the chicken with 2 tablespoons of the Dressing and let the chicken cool. When the chicken is cool enough to handle, pull the meat off the bones; thinly slice the meat.

3 • Tear the salad greens into bite-sized pieces and place them in a large salad bowl or divide them equally among 6 salad plates. Arrange the chicken meat, toasted walnuts, Gorgonzola cheese, and raspberries over the salad greens. Sprinkle the salad with freshly ground pepper to taste and the remaining Dressing.

Makes 6 servings. Per serving: 524 calories, 37 g protein, 9 g carbohydrate, 38 g fat, 94 mg cholesterol, 708 mg sodium.

A Change of Oil

When preparing your own salad dressings, don't limit yourself to ordinary vegetable oil. The highest quality and most interesting in flavor of olive oils is extra-virgin, which has the lowest acidity. Extra-virgin olive oil comes in a wide range of colors, from amber to dark green. The flavor can vary widely, depending upon which variety of olives are crushed and where the olives are grown. Use small amounts of this oil in salad dressings or toss a little with cooked vegetables.

Not only is there a vast array of olive oils available from all over the world, but there are also other oils you may have overlooked: Oriental sesame oil has a rich dark color and an almost-roasted flavor; safflower, peanut, canola, corn, and vegetable oils add a lighter flavor; nut oils, such as walnut, almond, and hazelnut, can lend a woodsy flavor; and herb and other flavored oils such as garlic, pepper, and citrus can make a simple dressing sensational.

The more delicate and flavorful the oil, the more you will need to pay attention to its storage. Nut and seed oils tend to be very perishable and should be stored in airtight containers in a cool dark place or, during hot weather, in the refrigerator. Use these oils within 6 months of purchase. Store olive oil, well sealed, in a cool, dark place. If your pantry gets hotter than 72°F to 80°F, store olive oil in the refrigerator. If refrigerated, the oil will become thick or even solid; place the bottle under hot running water until the oil liquefies again. Properly stored, olive oil can keep up to one year.

Turkey Teriyaki Salad

Deli turkey, enoki mushrooms, sweet red peppers, and a teriyaki-sauce dressing combine to make a colorful, exotic salad. Served with flatbreads, crackers, or bread, this dazzling salad is a meal in itself — and it literally takes just minutes to prepare.

1 (³/₄-pound) napa, or Chinese, cabbage, washed, crisped, and torn into bite-sized pieces
2 cups large pieces romaine lettuce, washed and crisped
³/₄ pound sliced cooked turkey breast, cut into ¹/₂-inch-long strips
1 (3¹/₂-ounce) package enoki mushrooms, rinsed, patted dry, and separated
2 sweet red peppers, julienned
¹/₂ pint cherry tomatoes, halved
2 celery stalks, sliced diagonally
¹/₂ cup alfalfa or other sprouts

DRESSING

¹/₂ cup bottled reduced-calorie vinaigrette dressing
2 tablespoons teriyaki sauce
1 medium clove garlic, crushed

1 • In a large salad bowl, combine the napa cabbage and romaine lettuce. Arrange the turkey, enoki mushrooms, sweet red peppers, cherry tomatoes, celery, and sprouts over the greens.

2 • Prepare the Dressing: In a small bowl, combine the vinaigrette dressing, teriyaki sauce, and garlic. Whisk with a fork until the Dressing is blended. Pour the Dressing over the salad and toss to coat the ingredients.

Makes 6 servings. Per serving: 181 calories, 20 g protein, 11 g carbohydrate, 7 g fat, 53 mg cholesterol, 390 mg sodium.

make-ahead

quick

What's an Enoki Mushroom?

Mild-flavored and creamy white, enoki mushrooms have long stems (like pieces of straw) and tiny caps. Enoki mushrooms make a wonderful addition to salads both for their texture and for their appearance.

Napa Cabbage

Also known as Chinese cabbage, napa cabbage is mild-flavored, with long, deeply crinkled, pale green to whitish leaves. Remove the hard core from the cabbage before using the leaves.

Turkey Teriyaki Salad

Lentil Salad with Smoked Turkey

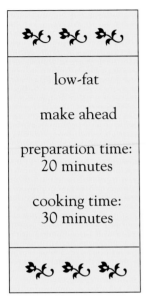

low-fat

make ahead

preparation time:
20 minutes

cooking time:
30 minutes

The lentils for this salad can be prepared earlier in the day and refrigerated. Let the lentils come to room temperature before completing the salad.

8 cups water
1 pound lentils
3 carrots, pared and diced (about 12 ounces)

DIJON VINAIGRETTE

2 large cloves garlic
1 cup fresh parsley leaves
1/3 cup vegetable oil
1/4 cup fresh lemon juice
1/4 cup red-wine vinegar
2 tablespoons Dijon mustard
1 teaspoon salt
1 teaspoon grated lemon zest (colored part of peel)
1/2 teaspoon or more freshly ground pepper, to taste

1/2 pound smoked turkey, diced
6 large green onions, chopped
4 cups mixed salad greens

1 • In a large saucepan, bring the water to boiling. Add the lentils, reduce the heat, and simmer for 30 minutes. Add the carrots for the last 2 minutes of the cooking time.

2 • Meanwhile, prepare the Dijon Vinaigrette: In a blender or food processor, mince the garlic. Add the parsley leaves and process until they are finely chopped. Add the vegetable oil, lemon juice, red-wine vinegar, Dijon mustard, salt, lemon zest, and pepper. Process until all the ingredients are blended.

3 • Drain the lentil mixture and place it in a large bowl. Add the smoked turkey and green onions. Pour the vinaigrette over the lentil-turkey mixture and toss to coat all the ingredients with the dressing.

4 • Arrange the mixed salad greens on each of 10 salad plates. Place the lentil salad over the greens on each plate.

Makes 10 servings. Per serving: 261 calories, 18 g protein, 31 g carbohydrate, 8 g fat, 10 mg cholesterol, 433 mg sodium.

Lentil Salad with Smoked Turkey

Cleaning and Storing Greens

- When purchasing greens, avoid those that are wilted or show signs of bruising.

- Wash greens in a large bowl of warm water or in a clean sink. Swish the greens around to loosen any grit and let them sit in the water for a few minutes. Using your hands, gently lift the greens out of the water, letting greens drain. If the greens are especially sandy, such as arugula or spinach, repeat the washing a few times, changing the water, until the water is clear. Dry greens in a salad spinner or blot them dry with paper towels.

- Wrap washed and dried greens in paper towels, place in plastic bags, and refrigerate.

- Tender-leaf greens, such as arugula or Bibb lettuce, can be stored up to 2 days; loose-leaf lettuce, such as Boston lettuce, can be stored up to 4 days; and the sturdier greens, such as iceberg and romaine lettuce, will keep up to 1 week.

Rice, Lentil, and Vegetable Salad

Lentils combine with Texmati rice and a variety of vegetables to make a colorful salad that provides high-quality vegetable protein — with no meat!

DRESSING

¹/₂ cup olive oil
¹/₃ cup fresh lemon juice
¹/₄ cup Dijon mustard
3 large cloves garlic
1 teaspoon salt
³/₄ teaspoon freshly ground black pepper

SALAD

6 cups water
1 teaspoon salt
1 cup Texmati rice
1 cup dried lentils
1 large carrot, pared and chopped
1 large celery stalk, chopped
6 large radishes, chopped
¹/₂ seedless cucumber, chopped
4 green onions, sliced
1 sweet red pepper, trimmed and diced
1 sweet yellow pepper, trimmed and diced
1 bunch arugula, large stems discarded and leaves cut into ¹/₂-inch pieces
2 ounces crumbled feta cheese

1 • Prepare the Dressing: In a blender or food processor, combine the olive oil, lemon juice, Dijon mustard, garlic, 1 teaspoon of salt, and the ground pepper. Process until the Dressing is smooth and creamy. Set aside the Dressing.

2 • Prepare the Salad: In a medium saucepan, combine 1³/₄ cups of the water and ¹/₂ teaspoon of the salt; bring the mixture to boiling. Stir in the Texmati rice; reduce the heat to medium-low, cover the saucepan, and simmer until the rice is tender and the liquid is absorbed, about 12 minutes. Let the rice stand for 3 minutes. Place the rice in a large bowl and set aside.

---

make ahead

preparation time:
20 minutes

cooking time:
40 minutes

Texmati Rice

Like basmati rice, Texmati rice is one of the aromatic rices. Texmati is available in both white and brown versions in most supermarkets.

---

3 • In a medium saucepan, heat the remaining 4¼ cups of water and ½ teaspoon of salt to boiling. Add the lentils, reduce the heat, and simmer until the lentils are tender but not soft, about 25 minutes. Drain the lentils well and add them to the rice. Add the carrot, celery, radishes, cucumber, green onions, sweet red and yellow peppers, arugula, feta cheese, and the Dressing. Gently toss the Salad to coat the ingredients with the Dressing. Serve at room temperature.

Makes 12 servings. Per serving: 233 calories, 8 g protein, 28 g carbohydrate, 11 g fat, 4 mg cholesterol, 499 mg sodium.

Dressed to Perfection

The word *salad* comes from the Latin *herba salata*, meaning "greens sprinkled with salt." Fortunately, these days we enjoy a much greater variety of dressings. Here's how to choose the best dressing for your favorite greens.

- Iceberg lettuce: Its crunchy, sturdy leaves hold up to rich, creamy dressings like Thousand Island and French. To enhance the mild flavor, top the salad with radishes, celery, and shredded carrots.

- Romaine lettuce: Toss this nutty, cool-tasting lettuce with an orange-juice vinaigrette or a lime-cilantro dressing.

- Boston, Bibb, and red- and green-leaf lettuce: The delicate, subtly sweet taste of these types of lettuce lends itself to dressings made with mild vinegars (such as white-wine or champagne variety) and soft, creamy toppings like blue cheese and avocado.

- Radicchio, endive, and chicory: To offset their sharp and slightly bitter flavor, top these greens with mildly sweet dressings, such as a sherry-wine vinaigrette.

- Arugula and watercress: The peppery flavor of these greens is best paired with a lemon-juice or balsamic vinaigrette. Nice complements include fresh herbs (such as chives, basil, and parsley), niçoise olives, and shaved Parmesan cheese.

Protein Packs

A "protein" is a long chain of amino acids. Proteins from most animal sources — meat, fish, eggs, poultry, and dairy products — usually are "complete," meaning they have a complete chain of the amino acids needed for a healthy diet. Proteins from plant sources usually are incomplete and need to be paired with other complementary proteins to provide all the necessary amino acids — for instance, rice with beans or peanut butter with milk.

Confetti Greek Pasta Salad

A sparkling salad to feed a crowd, this savory combination of orzo, Greek olives, and black-pepper feta cheese is a terrific choice for a picnic or buffet party.

VINAIGRETTE DRESSING

$^1/_4$ cup fresh lemon juice
6 tablespoons olive oil
1 teaspoon grated lemon zest (colored part of peel)
1 small clove garlic, crushed
$^1/_2$ teaspoon dried oregano leaves, crushed

SALAD

2 cups uncooked orzo pasta
2 cups shredded romaine lettuce
1 sweet red pepper, diced
1 sweet yellow pepper, diced
$^1/_2$ European cucumber, peeled, seeded, and diced
$^1/_2$ cup diced red onion
2 carrots, diced
$^1/_3$ cup Greek olives, chopped
1 (4-ounce) package black-pepper feta cheese or plain feta cheese

1 • Prepare the Vinaigrette Dressing: In a small bowl, combine the lemon juice, olive oil, lemon zest, garlic, and dried oregano. Whisk until all the ingredients are blended. Set aside the dressing.

2 • Prepare the Salad: Cook the orzo pasta as the package label directs and drain. Rinse the orzo under running cold water and drain again. Set aside.

3 • In a large bowl, combine the romaine lettuce, sweet red and yellow peppers, European cucumber, red onion, carrots, and Greek olives. Stir to mix the ingredients well. Add the orzo to the lettuce mixture. Add the Vinaigrette Dressing and black-pepper or plain feta cheese. Toss to coat the ingredients with the dressing.

Makes 8 servings. Per serving: 317 calories, 8 g protein, 39 g carbohydrate, 15 g fat, 13 mg cholesterol, 228 mg sodium.

---

make ahead

quick

Orzo

This looks like rice but is really a rice-shaped pasta. Orzo can be used as a side dish, tossed with a little butter or olive oil and parsley if you wish. Substitute orzo for rice in your favorite rice salad or use it in pasta salads.

Confetti Greek Pasta Salad

Curly Endive, Tomato, and Bacon Pasta Salad

~

A festive salad just right for a midsummer brunch. You can substitute romaine lettuce for the radicchio in this recipe.

2 cups torn radicchio leaves
4 cups torn curly endive leaves
$^1/_2$ cup whole parsley leaves
2 tablespoons fresh tarragon leaves (optional)
3 ounces goat cheese, crumbled (scant $^1/_2$ cup)
8 ounces farfalle pasta (bow ties)
2 large cloves garlic
$^1/_8$ teaspoon salt
$^1/_4$ pound slab bacon, cut into $^1/_2$-inch dice
1 pint cherry tomatoes, halved
$^1/_2$ teaspoon freshly ground pepper
2 tablespoons extra-virgin olive oil
2 tablespoons red-wine vinegar

make ahead

quick

1 • In a large serving bowl, combine the radicchio, curly endive, parsley leaves, tarragon if using, and goat cheese. Toss gently to mix the ingredients.

2 • Cook the farfalle pasta as the package label directs. Drain the pasta, rinse it under cold running water, and drain the pasta again well. Place the pasta in the bowl with the endive mixture.

3 • Meanwhile, on a cutting board, mince the garlic with the salt until the mixture becomes a paste; set aside the garlic paste. In a medium skillet, sauté the bacon about 5 to 8 minutes or until it is browned. With a slotted spoon, remove the bacon to the bowl with the endive-pasta mixture. Remove all but 1 tablespoon of bacon fat from the skillet; heat the fat over medium-high heat. Add the cherry tomatoes and sauté for 1 minute. Add the garlic paste and sauté for 30 seconds more. Add the pepper, olive oil, and red-wine vinegar; stir until the ingredients are well blended. Pour the hot dressing over the endive-pasta mixture in the bowl. Toss to coat the ingredients with the dressing.

> *Makes 4 servings. Per serving: 471 calories, 21 g protein, 48 g carbohydrate, 22 g fat, 26 mg cholesterol, 524 mg sodium.*

Curly Endive, Tomato, and Bacon Pasta Salad

Warm Pasta and Escarole Salad

～

An inviting warm pasta salad that uses a very small amount of pancetta (see page 96) for flavoring. The entire salad can be finished in just the amount of time it takes to cook the pasta.

RED-PEPPER VINAIGRETTE

1 (7-ounce) jar roasted red peppers, drained
1/4 cup red-wine vinegar
2 tablespoons olive oil
1 teaspoon salt
1/2 teaspoon crushed red-pepper flakes

SALAD

1 1/2 cups uncooked small pasta shells or ditalini (about 6 ounces)
1 1/2 ounces pancetta or slab bacon, diced
1 large yellow onion, chopped
1 head escarole, rinsed and torn into 2-inch pieces
1 (16-ounce) can cannellini beans, drained and rinsed

1 • Prepare the Red-Pepper Vinaigrette: In a blender or food processor, combine the roasted red peppers, red-wine vinegar, olive oil, salt, and red-pepper flakes. Process until the dressing is smooth.

2 • Prepare the Salad: Cook the pasta shells or ditalini as the package label directs. Drain the pasta in a colander.

3 • Meanwhile, in a large saucepan over medium heat, sauté the pancetta or bacon until it is browned. With a slotted spoon, remove the pancetta to paper towels to drain. In the drippings in the pan, sauté the onion about 5 minutes or until it is tender. Add the escarole and cook, stirring, until it is tender.

4 • Add the pasta, cannellini beans, and Red-Pepper Vinaigrette to the saucepan. Toss to coat the salad with the dressing. Place the salad in a serving dish and sprinkle with the pancetta. Serve the salad warm.

Makes 8 servings. Per serving: 232 calories, 9 g protein, 32 g carbohydrate, 8 g fat, 7 mg cholesterol, 355 mg sodium.

---

quick

The World of Vinegars

Vinegar adds sharpness and tang to salad dressings. By using a high proportion of vinegar to oil, you can reduce the fat and calories in dressings. Even local supermarkets now stock a wide variety of vinegars, including red- and white-wine, sherry, balsamic, rice, berry, herb, and the usual cider and distilled white. Many small producers create regional favorites, such as cranberry and jalapeño, so check out local farm stands and specialty shops.

Barley and Black-Eyed Pea Salad

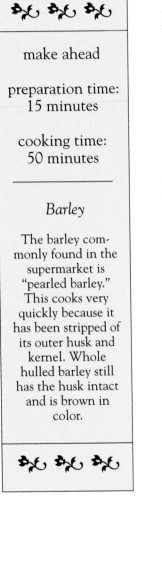

Ideal for hearty appetites, this savory salad (shown on page 50) can be prepared a day ahead and is a great choice for a picnic or take-along lunch.

2 tablespoons olive oil
1 cup uncooked barley
4 cups cold water
³/4 teaspoon salt
2 cups cooked black-eyed peas (or canned, drained; or frozen, thawed)

VINAIGRETTE DRESSING

2 large cloves garlic
¹/2 teaspoon salt
1 teaspoon coarsely ground black pepper
2 tablespoons fresh lemon juice
2 tablespoons red-wine vinegar
¹/4 cup extra-virgin olive oil

2 cups finely julienned savoy cabbage
2 cups finely julienned spinach
³/4 cup crumbled feta cheese
1 medium red onion, chopped
1 (7-ounce) jar roasted red peppers, drained and diced
¹/4 cup chopped fresh parsley
20 oil-cured olives, pitted and diced
1 tablespoon chopped fresh oregano leaves

1 • In a large saucepan, heat the 2 tablespoons of olive oil over medium-high heat. Add the barley and sauté about 2 to 3 minutes or until the barley is lightly toasted. Add the water and the ³/4 teaspoon of salt. Bring the mixture to boiling; reduce the heat, cover the saucepan, and simmer for 25 minutes. Stir in the black-eyed peas. Cook, covered, for 20 minutes more, stirring occasionally.

2 • Meanwhile, prepare the Vinaigrette Dressing: On a cutting board, mince the garlic with the ¹/2 teaspoon of salt until a paste forms. Scrape the garlic paste into a small jar with a tight-fitting lid; add the black pepper, lemon juice, red-wine vinegar, and extra-virgin olive oil. Put the lid on the jar and shake to blend the ingredients. Set aside the dressing.

Sidebar

make ahead

preparation time:
15 minutes

cooking time:
50 minutes

Barley

The barley commonly found in the supermarket is "pearled barley." This cooks very quickly because it has been stripped of its outer husk and kernel. Whole hulled barley still has the husk intact and is brown in color.

3 • Transfer the barley mixture to a large bowl and let the mixture cool. Add the savoy cabbage, spinach, feta cheese, red onion, roasted red peppers, parsley, olives, oregano leaves, and the Vinaigrette Dressing. Toss gently to coat the ingredients with the dressing.

Makes 12 servings. Per serving: 185 calories, 5 g protein, 22 g carbohydrate, 10 g fat, 6 mg cholesterol, 381 mg sodium.

Frisée, Bacon, and Goat-Cheese Salad

A feast for the eyes as well as the palate: rounds of mild goat cheese sautéed to golden brown sit atop a bed of tangy greens tossed with a warm sweet-and-sour vinaigrette. Serve with a thin, crispy baguette. Frisée is a type of curly endive.

quick

2 heads frisée or 1 head curly endive
1 large head radicchio
¹/₂ large head romaine lettuce
1 (11-ounce) log goat cheese
¹/₂ cup all-purpose flour
1 large egg
2 tablespoons water
¹/₃ cup fine dried bread crumbs
2 tablespoons chopped fresh chives
¹/₂ pound slab bacon, cut into ¹/₂-inch dice
3 tablespoons balsamic vinegar
1 tablespoon coarse-grain Dijon mustard
Vegetable oil for deep-frying

1 • Wash, dry, and tear the frisée or curly endive, radicchio, and romaine lettuce into bite-sized pieces. Set aside the greens.

2 • Preheat the oven to 300°F. Cut the log of goat cheese crosswise into 12 disks, patting the cheese rounds together if they crumble. Place the flour in a shallow bowl. In a second bowl, with a fork, beat the egg and water together until they are well blended. In a third shallow bowl, stir together the bread crumbs and chives. Working in batches, first coat each goat-cheese disk with the flour, shaking off the excess, then dip the disk in the egg mixture and drain, and finally coat the disk with the bread-crumb mixture. Place the coated cheese disks on a sheet of waxed paper.

3 • Line a baking sheet with paper towels. In a large skillet over medium-high heat, cook the bacon until it is crisp. With a slotted spoon, remove the bacon to the prepared baking sheet; keep the bacon warm in the 300°F oven. Into the bacon drippings in the skillet, whisk the balsamic vinegar and Dijon mustard until the mixture is blended. Over low heat, keep the vinegar mixture warm.

4 • In a medium skillet over medium-high heat, bring 1 inch of the vegetable oil to 350°F. Working in batches, fry the goat-cheese disks until they are golden brown, about 1 to 2 minutes. Transfer the goat-cheese disks to the baking sheet with the bacon; keep the disks warm.

5 • In a large salad bowl, toss the greens with the warm vinegar mixture. Arrange the greens, divided equally, on 6 dinner plates. Sprinkle the greens with the bacon. Place 2 goat-cheese disks on each salad. Serve the salads immediately.

> *Makes 6 servings. Per serving: 443 calories, 25 g protein, 16 g carbohydrate, 31 g fat, 72 mg cholesterol, 705 mg sodium.*

Frisée, Bacon, and Goat-Cheese Salad

Thai Beef Salad with Lime and Papaya

Create a dinner tonight that showcases the refreshingly hot and tart flavors of Thai cuisine.

³/4 pound well-trimmed boneless sirloin, about 1-inch thick
1 clove garlic, crushed
1 teaspoon soy sauce
1 teaspoon peanut oil or other vegetable oil

LIME DRESSING

¹/2 cup fresh lime juice
¹/3 cup peanut oil or other vegetable oil
¹/4 cup Asian fish sauce (available at Asian grocery stores)
1 jalapeño pepper, seeded and minced
1 clove garlic, crushed
2 teaspoons grated lime zest (colored part of peel)
1 teaspoon sugar

SALAD

1 head romaine lettuce, torn into 2-inch pieces
1 lime, pared, white pith removed, and sections cut from membrane
1 ripe papaya, halved, seeded, pared, and cut into ¹/2-inch wedges
1 cup chopped fresh cilantro
1 cup chopped fresh mint
¹/2 cucumber, pared and thinly sliced
¹/2 red onion, thinly sliced
¹/2 sweet red pepper, thinly sliced
¹/3 cup chopped salted or unsalted dry-roasted peanuts

preparation time:
20 minutes

marinating time:
20 minutes

cooking time:
8 minutes

The Heartburn of Hot and Spicy

Chili peppers and other fiery spices can give some of us heartburn. Combat this by pairing hot dishes with a cooling dairy product (such as sour cream or yogurt) to dilute the concentration of seasonings and alleviate possible discomfort.

1 • Marinate the beef: On a plate, rub the steak with the clove of garlic and the soy sauce. Let the beef stand for 20 minutes at room temperature. Heat the 1 teaspoon of peanut or other vegetable oil in a large nonstick skillet over medium-high heat. Add the steak; cook about 3 to 4 minutes on each side for rare to medium-rare. Remove the steak to a cutting board and let stand until the beef cools to room temperature.

2 • Meanwhile, prepare the Lime Dressing: In a medium bowl, combine the lime juice, the $1/3$ cup of peanut or other vegetable oil, Asian fish sauce, jalapeño pepper, clove of garlic, lime zest, and sugar. Whisk until the dressing is blended.

3 • Prepare the Salad: In a large bowl, combine the romaine lettuce, lime sections, papaya wedges, cilantro, mint, cucumber, red onion, and sweet red pepper. Cut the steak crosswise into very thin slices. In a small bowl, toss the steak slices with 1 tablespoon of the Lime Dressing. Add the remaining Lime Dressing to the Salad and toss to coat all the ingredients with the dressing. Arrange the steak slices on top of the Salad and sprinkle the chopped peanuts over all. Serve the salad immediately.

Makes 4 servings. Per serving: 449 calories, 27 g protein, 23 g carbohydrate, 30 g fat, 54 mg cholesterol, 1,176 mg sodium.

Lamb and Lentil Salad with Olives

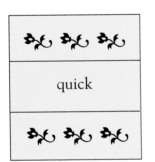

quick

Rich with the flavors of the Middle East, this memorable salad can be made with leftover pork instead of the lamb. Try serving with a cucumber and yogurt salad.

2 quarts water
1 teaspoon ground coriander
$1/2$ bay leaf
$1/8$ teaspoon crushed red-pepper flakes
1 cup dried lentils
1 teaspoon salt

DRESSING

3 tablespoons extra-virgin olive oil
2 tablespoons fresh lemon juice
2 tablespoons chopped pitted black Greek olives

2 tablespoons chopped fresh parsley
1 tablespoon chopped capers
1 teaspoon minced garlic
1 teaspoon ground cumin
$1/4$ teaspoon freshly ground pepper
$1/4$ teaspoon salt

$3/4$ pound cooked lamb, cut into $1/2$-inch dice (about $2^1/2$ cups)
1 carrot, pared and finely diced
1 small celery stalk, finely diced
4 cups torn arugula leaves
1 cup cherry tomatoes, halved

1 • In a large saucepan, bring the water, coriander, bay leaf, and red-pepper flakes to boiling. Stir in the lentils and the 1 teaspoon of salt. Reduce the heat, cover the saucepan, and simmer about 20 to 30 minutes or until the lentils are tender. Drain the lentils.

2 • Meanwhile, prepare the Dressing: In a large bowl, combine the extra-virgin olive oil, lemon juice, Greek olives, fresh parsley, capers, garlic, cumin, pepper, and the $1/4$ teaspoon of salt. Whisk until the Dressing is blended.

3 • To the Dressing in the bowl, add the lamb, drained lentils, carrot, and celery. Toss to coat the ingredients with the Dressing. Add the arugula and toss just until the arugula is wilted. Garnish the salad with the cherry tomatoes.

Makes 4 servings. Per serving: 408 calories, 32 g protein, 36 g carbohydrate, 16 g fat, 51 mg cholesterol, 727 mg sodium.

Chapter Four

~

Pasta

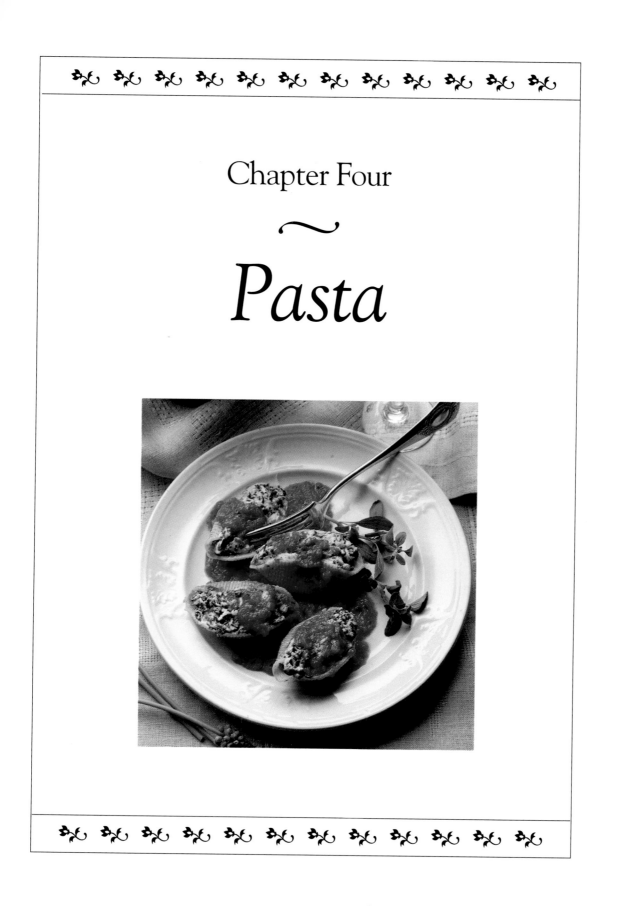

☙ ☙ ☙

Is there anyone who *doesn't* love pasta? It comes in a huge variety of shapes, sizes, colors, and flavors, and you just can't beat it for ease of preparation. In the time it takes to boil the water and cook the pasta (usually not more than 15 minutes), you can easily prepare a dish such as our Pasta with Ricotta and Swiss Chard (page 108) and Fusilli with Peppers (page 93).

What's more, we've given you one-dish options ranging from the classic, long-simmered Bolognese sauce to toss-togethers that spotlight more uncommon ingredients, such as Three-Mushroom Fettuccine (page 97) and Fresh Tuna Vermicelli (page 116). We also offer several recipes for the always popular lasagna, from an Italian Vegetable Lasagna with Escarole (page 128) to a slightly more daring Creole Mushroom Lasagna (page 133).

Ever wonder why there are so many different pasta shapes? Check out page 114 to discover which pastas work best with particular sauces — for example: fusilli with creamy sauces or penne with meat and vegetable sauces. Keep an assortment of dried pastas in your cupboard so you'll be ready for a fast meal anytime.

Fusilli with Peppers

~

A colorful pasta dish you can prepare in minutes. Add a green salad, a loaf of crusty bread — and enjoy!

1/2 pound fusilli
1 teaspoon olive oil
1 medium sweet red pepper, cut into 1-inch pieces
1 medium sweet yellow pepper, cut into 1-inch pieces
1 medium bulb fennel, cut into strips
1 clove garlic, crushed
1 teaspoon dried oregano leaves, crushed
2/3 cup low-fat ricotta cheese
1/4 cup chopped fresh parsley
2 tablespoons grated Parmesan cheese
1/4 teaspoon freshly ground black pepper

1 • Cook the fusilli as the package label directs. Drain the fusilli, reserving 1/4 cup of the cooking liquid. Place the fusilli in a large bowl with the reserved liquid.

2 • Meanwhile, in a nonstick skillet, heat the olive oil over medium-high heat. Add the sweet red and yellow peppers, fennel, garlic, and oregano. Sauté about 5 minutes or until the vegetables are tender. Add the sweet pepper mixture, ricotta cheese, parsley, Parmesan, and black pepper to the fusilli. Toss to combine all the ingredients.

Makes 4 servings. Per serving: 167 calories, 9 g protein, 21 g carbohydrate, 6 g fat, 15 mg cholesterol, 99 mg sodium.

quick

Al Dente

No, this is not the name of a new dance but, rather, a description of properly cooked pasta. Cooked *al dente*, pasta should be tender but still firm to the bite. To test, snag a strand or piece of pasta from the boiling water. Hold the pasta under cold running water, and bite it to check its firmness. Then look at the bitten cross section — if you still see a whitish center, or core, the pasta is probably underdone. It should be just cooked through — not overcooked. Cooking pasta *al dente* also preserves some of the vitamins and minerals usually lost in the water if the pasta is overcooked.

Pasta with Pancetta

This pasta dish, with its classic bread crumb garnish, arrives at the table in short order. Serve with your favorite combination of greens and a loaf of good-quality bakery bread. You can find pancetta (see page 96) at Italian markets or at supermarkets with a separate butcher or deli section.

1 cup fresh coarse bread crumbs
$^1/_2$ teaspoon crushed red-pepper flakes
$^1/_4$ cup extra-virgin olive oil
$^1/_4$ pound thinly sliced pancetta, cut into 1-inch pieces
$^3/_4$ pound linguine
$^3/_4$ pound leeks, halved lengthwise, sliced crosswise into $^1/_2$-inch-thick pieces, and rinsed (2 cups)
1 pound sweet red peppers, quartered, cored, seeded, and sliced crosswise into thin strips
1 butternut squash (1 pound), peeled, seeded, and cut into 2 x $^1/_4$-inch sticks
$^3/_4$ pound broccoli, stalks trimmed, coarsely chopped
3 large cloves garlic, minced
$^3/_4$ teaspoon salt
$^1/_2$ teaspoon freshly ground black pepper

1 • Preheat the oven to 350°F. In a medium bowl, combine the bread crumbs, red-pepper flakes, and 1 tablespoon of the oil. Spread evenly over a baking sheet. Bake the bread crumbs for 5 minutes or until golden brown and toasted, stirring once. Set aside.

2 • In a large skillet, heat 1 tablespoon of the oil over medium heat. Add the pancetta and cook for 8 minutes or until crisp, stirring occasionally.

3 • Meanwhile, cook the linguine as the package label directs. Drain, reserving $^3/_4$ cup of the cooking liquid. Keep the pasta hot.

4 • With a slotted spoon, remove the pancetta to a bowl. To the drippings in the skillet, add the leeks; sauté for 10 minutes or until tender but not brown. With a slotted spoon, add the leeks to the pancetta in the bowl.

---

low-fat

quick

Give Bread a Whirl

Making your own bread crumbs is simple. One slice of bread makes approximately $^1/_2$ cup of crumbs. Use fresh bread to avoid a stale taste, and pulse lightly in a food processor or blender for a few seconds. For coarser crumbs, break the bread up by gently pulling it apart with a fork. If you're not going to use the crumbs right away, keep them stored in a tightly sealed container in the freezer. For variety and extra flavor, try making your bread crumbs with whole-wheat or multi-grain bread.

5 • To the skillet, add the remaining 2 tablespoons oil; heat over medium-high heat until hot. Add the sweet red peppers and butternut squash; sauté for 4 minutes. Add the broccoli, garlic, and $\frac{1}{4}$ cup of the reserved pasta water; cover. Over high heat, cook for 3 minutes or until the vegetables are tender but not soft.

6 • In a large serving bowl, combine the pasta, the remaining $\frac{1}{2}$ cup of the reserved pasta water, the vegetables, the pancetta mixture, and the salt and pepper; toss to mix. Sprinkle with the bread crumb mixture. Serve.

Makes 4 servings. Per serving: 718 calories, 23 g protein, 110 g carbohydrate, 23 g fat, 12 mg cholesterol, 738 mg sodium.

Pasta with Pancetta

Amatriciana

Rich with pancetta and sparked with hot red-pepper flakes, this dish comes from the city of Amatrice, northeast of Rome. A crisp green salad and a chilled glass of white wine are the perfect accompaniments.

2 tablespoons extra-virgin olive oil
6 ounces pancetta, diced (about 1 cup)
1 large Spanish onion, halved and sliced (about 1 pound)
1 (28-ounce) can Italian tomatoes, coarsely chopped
1/2 cup chopped sun-dried tomatoes in oil
1/2 cup water
1/2 teaspoon freshly ground black pepper
1/2 teaspoon salt
1/4 teaspoon crushed red-pepper flakes
1 pound perciatelli or bucatini pasta (long or short straight macaroni)
Grated pecorino Romano cheese

1 • In a large saucepan or Dutch oven, heat the extra-virgin olive oil over medium-high heat. Add the pancetta and sauté about 5 minutes or until the pancetta is lightly browned. Reduce the heat to medium. Add the Spanish onion and sauté about 8 to 9 minutes or until the onion is soft and translucent. Add the canned tomatoes, sun-dried tomatoes, water, ground black pepper, salt, and red-pepper flakes. Stir to mix the ingredients well. Reduce the heat to low and simmer the sauce, stirring occasionally, for 30 minutes.

2 • Cook the perciatelli or bucatini as the package label directs. Drain the pasta and place it in a serving bowl. Pour the sauce over the pasta. Pass the pecorino Romano cheese separately.

> Makes 6 servings. Per serving: 502 calories, 18 g protein, 73 g carbohydrate, 16 g fat, 16 mg cholesterol, 716 mg sodium.

---

low-fat

make ahead

preparation time:
5 minutes

cooking time:
45 minutes

Pancetta

Used in several of our recipes to flavor pasta dishes and sauces, pancetta is a salt-cured (not smoked) Italian bacon. Because of its strong flavor, a little goes a long way. Wrap pancetta well and store it in the refrigerator up to 3 weeks. You can substitute smoked ham or prosciutto for pancetta in most recipes.

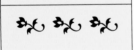

Three-Mushroom Fettuccine

If you like, you can use all regular mushrooms in this earthy pasta dish. Serve it with a tomato and zucchini salad.

> 1 ounce dried porcini mushrooms
> 3 tablespoons unsalted butter
> 2 large shallots, minced
> 8 ounces cremini or regular mushrooms, sliced
> 3 ounces oyster mushrooms or chanterelles, sliced
> 1 1/2 teaspoons grated gingerroot
> 1 teaspoon chopped fresh thyme leaves or 1/4 teaspoon dried thyme, crushed
> 3 tablespoons dry white vermouth
> 1 1/4 cups heavy cream
> 3/4 teaspoon salt
> 1/4 teaspoon freshly ground pepper
> 12 ounces fettuccine
> Chopped fresh parsley

1 • In a medium bowl, pour boiling water over the porcini mushrooms to cover; soak for 20 minutes. Strain the mushrooms, reserving the soaking liquid for another use. Discard the porcini stems and coarsely chop the caps.

2 • In a large skillet over medium-high heat, melt the butter. Add the shallots and sauté about 4 minutes or until the shallots are soft. Increase the heat to high; add the cremini and oyster mushrooms and sauté about 4 to 5 minutes or until the mushrooms are soft and slightly browned. Add the ginger, thyme, vermouth, and porcini mushrooms; sauté for 1 minute. Add the heavy cream, salt, and pepper, and stir until the ingredients are well mixed. Cook the sauce for 2 minutes.

3 • Meanwhile, cook the fettuccine as the package label directs; drain well. Place the fettuccine in a serving bowl and pour the sauce over the pasta. Sprinkle with the fresh parsley.

Makes 4 servings. Per serving: 716 calories, 15 g protein, 79 g carbohydrate, 38 g fat, 125 mg cholesterol, 444 mg sodium.

---

quick

Cream Conversion

To reduce the fat when your pasta recipe calls for cream to thicken the sauce, substitute the same amount of chicken broth with just a tablespoon of cream added.

Fusilli Primavera

Fusilli Primavera

~

This delicious version of pasta primavera is made with creamy, rich goat cheese.

6 ounces goat cheese, crumbled
1 cup fresh basil leaves, julienned
1 pound long fusilli
1$^1/_4$ cups low-sodium chicken broth
1 pound asparagus, trimmed and cut diagonally into 1-inch pieces
1 sweet yellow pepper, sliced into strips
$^1/_2$ cup sun-dried tomato halves (not in oil), diced
2 small yellow squash, halved lengthwise and sliced crosswise
1 cup frozen peas, thawed
6 plum tomatoes, seeded and diced

low-fat

quick

1 • In a large, shallow serving bowl, combine the goat cheese and fresh basil. Set aside the cheese mixture.

2 • Cook the fusilli as the package label directs; drain well. Meanwhile, in a large skillet over medium heat, bring the chicken broth to boiling. Add the asparagus, sweet yellow pepper, and sun-dried tomatoes. Cover the saucepan and cook for 2 minutes, stirring once. Stir in the yellow squash and cook, uncovered, for 2 minutes more. Remove the saucepan from the heat and stir in the peas.

3 • Add the vegetable mixture to the bowl with the cheese mixture. Add the fusilli and plum tomatoes, and toss to combine all the ingredients. Serve the pasta immediately.

> *Makes 8 servings. Per serving: 295 calories, 16 g protein, 55 g carbohydrate, 2 g fat, 1 mg cholesterol, 99 mg sodium.*

Tortellini with Gorgonzola Sauce

A crisp vegetable salad is the perfect partner for this rich pasta dish. If Gorgonzola cheese is unavailable, substitute another blue cheese.

❧ ❧ ❧
quick
❧ ❧ ❧

5 ounces mild domestic Gorgonzola cheese, crumbled
¹/₄ cup grated Parmesan cheese
¹/₃ cup heavy cream
1 teaspoon pepper
2 (9-ounce) packages tortellini or tortelloni
2 small zucchini, shredded

1 • In a small saucepan, combine the Gorgonzola and Parmesan cheeses and the heavy cream. Cook, stirring, over low heat until the cheeses have melted. Stir in the pepper. Keep the sauce warm.

2 • Cook the tortellini or tortelloni as the package label directs. Drain the pasta and place it in a serving bowl. Pour the cheese sauce over the pasta. Add the zucchini and toss to coat all the ingredients with the sauce. Serve immediately.

> *Makes 4 servings. Per serving: 400 calories, 19 g protein, 19 g carbohydrate, 27 g fat, 80 mg cholesterol, 1,059 mg sodium.*

Tortellini Primavera

By the time you finish the quick vegetable prep for this sinfully simple pasta dish, dinner will practically be on the table.

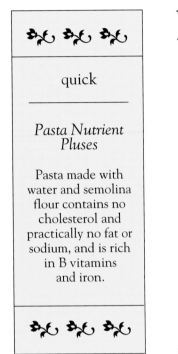

quick

Pasta Nutrient Pluses

Pasta made with water and semolina flour contains no cholesterol and practically no fat or sodium, and is rich in B vitamins and iron.

1 (16-ounce) package tricolor cheese tortellini
2 tablespoons olive oil
1 pound asparagus, cut into 2-inch pieces
$1/2$ pound fresh shiitake mushrooms, sliced
$1/2$ pound snow peas, trimmed
2 large carrots, pared and thinly sliced
1 onion, sliced crosswise and separated into rings
1 large clove garlic, crushed
$1/2$ teaspoon salt
1 cup heavy cream
$1/3$ cup freshly grated Parmesan cheese
$1/4$ cup butter or margarine
$1/4$ teaspoon freshly ground pepper

1 • Cook the tortellini as the package label directs. Drain the tortellini and keep it warm.

2 • In a large skillet over medium-high heat, heat the olive oil. Add the asparagus, shiitake mushrooms, snow peas, carrots, onion, garlic, and salt. Sauté until the vegetables are tender-crisp, about 3 minutes. Stir in the heavy cream, Parmesan cheese, butter or margarine, and pepper. Bring the mixture to boiling. Add the tortellini and toss gently until all the ingredients are mixed. Reduce the heat to medium and stir until the pasta mixture is heated through.

> *Makes 4 servings. Per serving: 594 calories, 17 g protein, 50 g carbohydrate, 38 g fat, 122 mg cholesterol, 647 mg sodium.*

Tortellini Primavera

Chicken, Asparagus, and Pasta with Lemon Cream

Celebrate the taste of spring with this luscious dish — which can be prepared in the amount of time it takes to boil the pasta. Serve with semolina bread.

2 tablespoons unsalted butter
1 (10-ounce) boneless, skinless chicken breast, cut into $^1/_4$-inch-wide
    strips
1 pound asparagus, trimmed and cut diagonally into $^1/_2$-inch pieces
$^1/_4$ cup chicken broth
3 tablespoons fresh lemon juice
$^1/_4$ cup heavy cream
3 green onions, thinly sliced diagonally
2 tablespoons chopped fresh parsley
2 teaspoons grated lemon zest (colored part of peel)
$^3/_4$ teaspoon salt
$^1/_2$ teaspoon freshly ground pepper
8 ounces farfalle (bow-tie pasta)

1 • In a large skillet over medium heat, melt the butter. Add the chicken and sauté about 5 minutes or until the chicken is golden brown around the edges. With a slotted spoon, remove the chicken to a plate.

2 • To the juices in the skillet, add the asparagus, chicken broth, and lemon juice. Reduce the heat to medium-low, partially cover the skillet, and cook about 5 minutes or just until the asparagus is tender. Return the chicken to the skillet. Stir in the heavy cream, green onions, parsley, lemon zest, salt, and pepper. Bring the mixture to boiling and cook about 3 minutes or until the liquid is slightly reduced.

3 • Meanwhile, cook the farfalle as the package label directs. Drain the pasta and add it to the skillet with the chicken mixture. Toss to combine all the ingredients and serve immediately.

> *Makes 4 servings. Per serving: 421 calories, 25 g protein, 50 g carbohydrate, 14 g fat, 72 mg cholesterol, 497 mg sodium.*

Sidebar

low-fat

quick

Citrus Zest

The zest of citrus fruits — oranges, lemons, limes, or grapefruits — is the outermost part of the rind. This part of the peel adds an intense, fruity flavor to many different dishes. Zest can be removed with a sharp knife, a vegetable peeler, a zesting tool (which removes the rind in thin strips), or a grater. Don't dig too deeply into the fruit or the bitter white pith (the white portion under the skin) will come off with the colored peel.

Chicken, Asparagus, and
Pasta with Lemon Cream

Five Speedy Pasta Sauces

Adjust the ingredients to suit your taste and the number of people you're feeding. When amounts are specified below, the recipe will yield 4 servings.

- Add chopped sun-dried tomatoes to your favorite homemade or purchased marinara sauce. Toss with penne, ziti, or other types of medium-sized pasta.

- For pesto with an Asian accent, combine 1 cup each of fresh basil and mint leaves, 2 tablespoons of peanuts, 1 clove of garlic, and $1/2$ cup of vegetable oil in a food processor. Process until the ingredients are blended. Toss with thin noodles, like vermicelli or spaghettini.

- Sauté 2 pounds of fresh greens (such as spinach, kale, or Swiss chard) in a garlic-flavored olive oil just until the greens are wilted. Pour the sauce over spaghetti and add $1/2$ teaspoon of crushed red-pepper flakes. Toss to combine the ingredients.

- Stir chopped, roasted sweet red and yellow peppers into your favorite spaghetti sauce; toss with orecchiette or rotelle.

- Toss 4 to 6 ounces of diced smoked salmon, chopped fresh dill, cracked black pepper, and a splash of cream with fettuccine.

Penne with Chicken Sausage and Broccoli

quick

We reduced the fat in this dish by substituting sausage made from chicken for the usual Italian pork sausage. You can also substitute regular cooked ham for the pancetta. Serve with 7-grain rolls or semolina bread.

Penne with Chicken Sausage and Broccoli

1 pound penne pasta
1¼ cups broccoli florets
2 ounces pancetta, diced
1 pound chicken sausage (about 8 links)
¼ cup olive oil
1 large red onion, cut lengthwise into quarters and thinly sliced
  lengthwise again
4 ounces fresh shiitake mushrooms, stems discarded and caps sliced
2 each sweet red and yellow peppers, roasted, peeled, seeded, and cut
  into thin 1- to 2-inch-long strips
¼ cup minced fresh parsley
¾ teaspoon salt
½ teaspoon crushed red-pepper flakes

1 • In a large pan of boiling, salted water, cook the penne as the package label directs, adding the broccoli for the last 3 minutes of cooking time. Drain the pasta and broccoli, place it in a large bowl, and keep it warm.

2 • Meanwhile, in a 12-inch nonstick skillet over medium heat, cook the pancetta about 5 minutes or until it is crisp. With a slotted spoon, transfer the pancetta to paper towels to drain.

3 • In the drippings in the skillet, cook the chicken sausages about 12 to 15 minutes or until they are well browned, turning the sausages often with tongs. Transfer the sausages to a plate to cool. Slice the sausages into ½-inch-thick pieces. Cover the plate and set aside the sausages.

4 • To the sausage drippings in the skillet, add 1 tablespoon of the olive oil. Add the red onion. Over medium-high heat, sauté the onion for 5 minutes. Stir in the shiitake mushrooms and sauté for 2 minutes more. Stir in the roasted sweet red and yellow peppers, fresh parsley, salt, red-pepper flakes, pancetta, chicken sausage, and the remaining olive oil, and heat through. Pour the mixture over the hot pasta and toss to mix the ingredients well.

Makes 8 servings. Per serving: 448 calories, 22 g protein, 48 g carbohydrate, 18 g fat, 49 mg cholesterol, 652 mg sodium.

Rigatoni with Sausage, Shiitake, and Spinach

~

For extra flavor, the pasta is cooked in the same water used to steam the spinach. To trim the fat, substitute turkey sausage for the Italian sausage. Serve with garlic toast.

> 2 tablespoons olive oil
> 3/4 pound sweet Italian sausage
> 1 (10-ounce) bag prewashed, torn and dried spinach leaves or 1 pound spinach, coarse stems removed, leaves washed and dried, and cut into 1-inch pieces
> 1 pound rigatoni
> 4 cloves garlic, minced
> 1 tablespoon chopped fresh sage leaves or 1 teaspoon dried sage, crumbled
> 1/2 teaspoon crushed red-pepper flakes
> 1 pound fresh shiitake mushrooms, stems removed and caps sliced
> 2/3 cup chicken broth
> Freshly grated pecorino Romano or Parmesan cheese

1 • In a large skillet over medium heat, heat the olive oil. Add the Italian sausage and cook, turning the sausage, about 12 to 14 minutes or until it is cooked through.

2 • Meanwhile, place the spinach in a colander. Place the colander in a large saucepan with 1 inch of boiling water. Cover the saucepan and steam about 3 to 5 minutes or until the spinach is wilted. Remove the colander from the pan and set aside the spinach. Add enough water to the saucepan to cook the rigatoni; bring the water to boiling. Cook the pasta as the package label directs. Drain the rigatoni and keep it warm.

3 • While the pasta cooks, finish the sauce: With tongs, remove the sausage to a cutting board. Slice the sausages diagonally into 1/4-inch slices. To the drippings in the skillet, add the garlic, sage, and red-pepper flakes. Sauté about 30 seconds to 1 minute or until the garlic mixture is very fragrant. Add the shiitake mushrooms and chicken broth. Stir the mixture with a wooden spoon, scraping up any browned bits from the bottom of the skillet. Cook the mushrooms about 4 to 5

❧ ❧ ❧

quick

Shiitake Mushrooms

Originally grown in Japan and Korea, these meaty mushrooms are now cultivated in the United States. They are large (up to 8 inches in diameter), with umbrella-shaped, dark brown caps. Shiitake mushrooms, which can be expensive, are available fresh and dried. Fresh mushrooms are most plentiful in the spring and autumn. They lend themselves well to grilling, broiling, sautéing, and baking.

❧ ❧ ❧

minutes or until they are tender. Add the sausage and spinach to the skillet and stir until the ingredients are mixed. Pour the sauce over the hot pasta and toss to combine the ingredients. Pass the pecorino Romano or Parmesan cheese.

Makes 4 servings. Per serving: 735 calories, 31 g protein, 94 g carbohydrate, 26 g fat, 45 mg cholesterol, 889 mg sodium.

Rigatoni with Sausage, Shiitake, and Spinach

Pasta with Ricotta and Swiss Chard

quick

A creamy delight of a dish. You can substitute kale, spinach, or escarole for the Swiss chard in this recipe. Serve with garlic bread.

1 pound Swiss chard, rinsed and cut into 1-inch pieces
1/2 pound slab bacon, diced
1 large yellow onion, chopped
1 (15-ounce) container part-skim ricotta cheese
1/2 cup grated Parmesan cheese
1/2 teaspoon freshly ground pepper
1/4 teaspoon salt
1 pound penne
1 cup frozen peas, thawed

1 • In a saucepan of boiling water, cook the Swiss chard for 1 minute. With a slotted spoon, transfer the Swiss chard to a colander set over a bowl to catch the cooking liquid.

2 • In a large skillet over medium-high heat, sauté the bacon about 5 minutes or until it is well browned and the fat has been rendered. Discard half of the bacon drippings. To the remaining drippings in the skillet, add the onion. Reduce the heat to medium-low and sauté the onion for 10 minutes. Reduce the heat to low and add the ricotta cheese, 1/4 cup of the Parmesan cheese, 3/4 cup of the reserved liquid from the Swiss chard, the pepper, and the salt. Stir to combine the ingredients, and keep the sauce warm.

3 • Meanwhile, cook the penne as the package label directs, adding the peas for the last minute of cooking. Drain the penne and peas and place them in a serving bowl. Add the sauce and remaining 1/4 cup of Parmesan to the bowl. Toss until the pasta is coated with the sauce.

Makes 6 servings. Per serving: 550 calories, 27 g protein, 68 g carbohydrate, 19 g fat, 46 mg cholesterol, 720 mg sodium.

Spaghetti Carbonara

For a dramatic presentation, this scrumptious favorite can be assembled right at the table. If you wish, omit the basil. Serve with a tossed green salad.

2 tablespoons unsalted butter
2 tablespoons extra-virgin olive oil
3 cloves garlic, crushed
$^1/_4$ pound pancetta, cut into thin strips
Pinch crushed red-pepper flakes
3 tablespoons dry white vermouth
12 ounces spaghetti
3 large egg yolks
$^1/_4$ cup heavy cream
$^1/_2$ cup grated Parmesan cheese
$^1/_4$ cup grated pecorino Romano cheese
$^1/_4$ cup chopped fresh parsley
$^1/_2$ teaspoon freshly ground black pepper
$^1/_4$ teaspoon salt
2 tablespoons julienned fresh basil leaves (optional)

quick

1 • In a large skillet over medium heat, melt the butter in the extra-virgin olive oil. Add the garlic and sauté about 2 minutes or until the garlic is lightly golden. Add the pancetta and sauté about 3 to 4 minutes, until the fat has been rendered but the pancetta is not crisp. Add the red-pepper flakes and vermouth, and cook for 2 minutes more. Remove the skillet from the heat and discard the garlic. Cover the skillet and keep the pancetta mixture warm.

2 • Cook the spaghetti as the package label directs.

3 • Meanwhile, in a large serving bowl, combine the egg yolks, heavy cream, Parmesan and pecorino Romano cheeses, parsley, ground black pepper, and salt. Stir to mix all the ingredients well.

4 • Drain the spaghetti. Add the spaghetti to the pancetta mixture and toss to coat the pasta with the sauce. Add the spaghetti-pancetta mixture to the cheese mixture and toss to coat the pasta with the cheese mixture. Sprinkle the pasta with the basil, if using, and serve immediately.

Makes 4 servings. Per serving: 773 calories, 24 g protein, 67 g carbohydrate, 44 g fat, 240 mg cholesterol, 724 mg sodium.

Spaghetti and Meatballs

Our meatballs, made from turkey sausage and ground turkey, are lower in fat than those made from beef or pork — but they're every bit as flavorful. The sweetness of the orange zest and the saltiness of the capers create a pleasing contrast in the sauce. If you like, prepare the meatballs and sauce a day ahead. Serve with a tomato and red-leaf lettuce salad.

$1/2$ *pound lean ground turkey*
$1/4$ *pound sweet or hot turkey sausage, removed from casing*
1 cup soft bread crumbs from reduced-calorie bread
1 large egg
$1/2$ *teaspoon salt*
$1/4$ *teaspoon freshly ground pepper*
2 tablespoons olive oil
$1/4$ *cup chicken broth, fat skimmed*
1 small onion, minced
2 cloves garlic, minced
$1/4$ *teaspoon fennel seeds*
*1 (28-ounce) can plus 1 (16-ounce) can Italian plum tomatoes,
    drained and chopped*
1 (8-ounce) can tomato sauce
2 × 1-inch piece orange zest (colored part of peel)
1 teaspoon minced fresh marjoram leaves
1 tablespoon drained capers
1 (17-ounce) package whole-wheat spaghetti
$1/3$ *cup grated Parmesan cheese*

1 • In a large bowl, combine the ground turkey, turkey sausage, bread crumbs, egg, $1/4$ teaspoon of the salt, and $1/8$ teaspoon of the pepper. Gently mix just until the ingredients are combined. Roll the meat mixture into 1-inch-diameter balls.

2 • In a large nonstick skillet over medium heat, heat the olive oil. Working in batches, cook the meatballs about 5 minutes or until they are browned on all sides, turning the meatballs with tongs. Return all the browned meatballs to the skillet. Cover the skillet and cook about 3 to 5 minutes more or until the meatballs are cooked through. Remove the meatballs to a plate.

3 • Add the chicken broth to the drippings in the skillet. Bring the broth mixture to boiling, scraping the pan with a spoon to loosen any browned bits. Add the onion, garlic, and fennel seeds; cook for 3 minutes, stirring occasionally. Add the plum tomatoes, tomato sauce, orange zest, marjoram, capers, and the remaining $1/4$ teaspoon of salt and $1/8$ teaspoon of pepper. Simmer the sauce over medium heat for 10 minutes, stirring occasionally.

4 • Meanwhile, cook the spaghetti as the package label directs. Drain the spaghetti and place it on a serving platter. Spoon the meatballs and sauce over the pasta, and toss to combine the ingredients. Sprinkle the pasta with the Parmesan cheese.

> *Makes 8 servings. Per serving: 409 calories, 20 g protein, 58 g carbohydrate, 11 g fat, 52 mg cholesterol, 624 mg sodium.*

"Grilled" Vegetable Lasagna (page 129) and Spaghetti and Meatballs

Capers

Ranging in size from very small beads to buds as large as a fingertip, capers are actually the buds of a bush found in Mediterranean regions. Sun-dried and pickled, they are usually packaged in brine and are available in bulk at specialty food shops and in small bottles in the condiment section of supermarkets. Capers add a distinctive salty tang to sauces and meat or pasta dishes. To eliminate some of the salt, rinse capers before using them.

Classic Bolognese

make ahead

preparation time:
25 minutes

cooking time:
2 hours

The rich meat and vegetable sauce can be prepared a day or two ahead and refrigerated.

1 pound skirt steak or chuck, cut into 1-inch pieces
$^1/_2$ pound pork shoulder, cut into 1-inch pieces
$^1/_2$ pound chicken or turkey giblets
$^1/_4$ cup unsalted butter
$^1/_4$ cup extra-virgin olive oil
2 cups finely chopped onions
$1^1/_2$ cups finely chopped carrots
1 cup finely chopped celery
$^1/_4$ pound pancetta, minced
$1^1/_2$ teaspoons salt
1 teaspoon freshly ground pepper
2 cups dry red wine
$^3/_4$ cup low-sodium beef broth
$^1/_2$ teaspoon ground nutmeg
$^1/_4$ teaspoon ground cloves
2 cups crushed fresh or canned Italian tomatoes
1 cup milk
2 pounds lasagnette noodles or fettuccine

1 • Working in batches in a food processor, coarsely grind the steak or chuck, pork shoulder, and chicken or turkey giblets. Set the meat mixture aside.

2 • In a large saucepan or Dutch oven over medium heat, melt the butter in the extra-virgin olive oil. Add the onions, carrots, celery, and pancetta, and sauté about 10 minutes or until the mixture is golden. Add the ground-meat mixture, salt, and pepper, and sauté about 15 minutes or until the meat is medium brown. Add the red wine; cook about 30 minutes or until the wine is reduced by half. Add the beef broth, nutmeg, and cloves, and simmer about 30 to 40 minutes or until the liquid is nearly evaporated. Add the Italian tomatoes and cook for 30 minutes. Add the milk and stir until all ingredients are well mixed.

3 • Meanwhile, cook the lasagnette noodles or fettuccine as the package label directs. Drain the pasta and place it in a serving bowl. Pour the sauce over the pasta and serve.

Makes 8 servings. Per serving: 586 calories, 26 g protein, 64 g carbohydrate, 22 g fat, 94 mg cholesterol, 529 mg sodium.

Ziti with Turkey and Prosciutto

A light main dish of turkey cutlets and escarole, plus a touch of prosciutto for flavor. Serve with an endive and orange salad.

1/2 pound ziti (half a 1-pound package)
1 teaspoon olive oil
3/4 pound turkey cutlets, cut into 1/2-inch-wide strips
1 ounce prosciutto, julienned
2 teaspoons chopped fresh sage
1/4 teaspoon freshly ground pepper
10 ounces escarole leaves, torn into 2-inch pieces (about 4 cups)
1/4 cup water
2 tablespoons grated Parmesan cheese

1 • Cook the ziti as the package label directs. Drain the ziti and place it in a serving bowl.

2 • Meanwhile, in a nonstick skillet over medium-high heat, heat the olive oil. Add the turkey, prosciutto, sage, and pepper, and sauté until the turkey is browned on all sides. With a slotted spoon, transfer the turkey mixture to the bowl with the ziti.

3 • To the drippings in the skillet, add the escarole and water. Bring the water to boiling. Reduce the heat, cover the skillet, and simmer about 2 minutes or until the escarole is wilted. Add the escarole with its cooking liquid to the ziti. Add the Parmesan cheese and toss to combine all the ingredients.

Makes 4 servings. Per serving: 227 calories, 24 g protein, 18 g carbohydrate, 6 g fat, 54 mg cholesterol, 205 mg sodium.

low-fat

quick

Prosciutto

Prosciutto is an Italian ham, air-dried and salt-cured, usually sliced paper thin. A flavorful addition to many recipes, prosciutto with melon or figs is a traditional Italian appetizer. Look for prosciutto in better supermarkets, Italian markets, and other specialty food shops.

Long Strands

Fettuccine, Bucatini, Spaghetti, Linguine: Substantial noodles such as these require hearty sauces such as pesto or Bolognese. Extra-firm fettuccine and bucatini can also stand up to thick sauces that call for vigorous tossing, like Alfredo and carbonara.

Medium Shapes

Ziti, Rigatoni, Conchiglie (shells), Fusilli: These shapely noodles have ridges and "cups" to catch chunky sauces and vegetables. Try fusilli with a sauce of fried eggplant and tomatoes; rigatoni with your favorite meat sauce. Cut vegetables to match the length and shape of the pasta; zucchini sticks with ziti, for example.

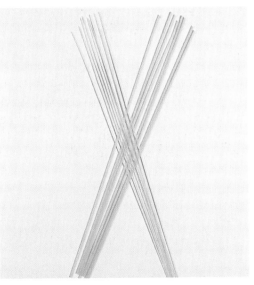

Tiny Shapes

Acini di Pepe, Small Shells, Tubetti, Orecchiette: For a balance of flavors, pair these petite pastas with sauces containing tiny chunks of chopped vegetables. The smallest noodles, like acini di pepe, will get lost in rich main-dish sauces and are best in soups or as side dishes.

Thin and Delicate

Spaghettini, Angel Hair: Fragile noodles such as these taste best with simple sauces that don't overwhelm the pasta, such as fresh herbs and cream or a light tomato sauce. Toss the noodles very gently to avoid tearing them.

Linguine and Clam Sauce

A luscious version of an all-time favorite dish. Bread sticks and an escarole salad are good matches.

3 dozen littleneck clams, shucked and coarsely chopped, liquor
  reserved
$^1/_3$ cup extra-virgin olive oil
4 shallots, thinly sliced
4 cloves garlic, minced
$^1/_4$ cup chicken broth
$^1/_4$ teaspoon crushed red-pepper flakes
2 tablespoons fresh lemon juice
$^1/_4$ teaspoon grated lemon zest (colored part of peel)
$^1/_2$ teaspoon salt
8 ounces linguine
$^1/_3$ cup minced parsley

low-fat

quick

1 • In a medium skillet over medium heat, cook the clams with their liquor about 3 to 5 minutes or just until the clams are cooked through. With a slotted spoon, transfer the clams to a small bowl and set them aside. Discard the cooking liquid and wipe out the skillet.

2 • In the same cleaned skillet over medium heat, heat the olive oil. Add the shallots and sauté about 2 minutes or until the shallots are translucent. Add the garlic and sauté until it is light golden. Pour in the chicken broth and add the red-pepper flakes; bring the mixture to boiling. Boil the sauce until the liquid is slightly reduced. Remove the skillet from the heat and stir in the clams, lemon juice, lemon zest, and salt.

3 • Cook the linguine as the package label directs. Drain the linguine and place it in a large bowl. Pour the clam sauce over the pasta and add the minced parsley. Toss to combine all the ingredients. Transfer the linguine to a serving platter and serve warm.

Makes 4 servings. Per serving: 418 calories, 16 g protein, 48 g carbohydrate, 18 g fat, 21 mg cholesterol, 357 mg sodium.

Fresh Tuna Vermicelli

～

Fresh tuna makes this pasta dish very special. A few salad greens, fresh from the garden, is all you need to complete this meal.

2 teaspoons olive oil
3/4 pound fresh tuna, cut into 1/2 -inch cubes
1 small onion, chopped
1 clove garlic, crushed
1 (14 1/2-ounce) can Italian plum tomatoes, drained (reserve juice) and chopped
1 (8-ounce) package vermicelli
1/4 cup fresh basil leaves, julienned
2 tablespoons chopped fresh parsley
1 tablespoon balsamic vinegar
1/4 teaspoon freshly ground pepper
1/4 teaspoon salt

1 • In a nonstick skillet over medium-high heat, heat 1 teaspoon of the olive oil. Add the tuna and sauté until it is golden, about 3 minutes. With a slotted spoon, transfer the tuna to a large bowl.

2 • To the drippings in the skillet, add the remaining teaspoon of olive oil, the onion, and garlic; sauté until the onion is tender, about 5 minutes. Add the plum tomatoes with their reserved juice; bring the mixture to boiling. Lower the heat, partially cover the skillet, and simmer for 15 minutes.

3 • Meanwhile, cook the vermicelli as the package label directs. Drain the vermicelli and add it to the bowl with the tuna.

4 • To the tomato mixture in the skillet, add the fresh basil, fresh parsley, balsamic vinegar, pepper, and salt. Cook the sauce for 1 minute. Pour the sauce over the vermicelli and tuna, and toss to combine all the ingredients.

Makes 4 servings. Per serving: 242 calories, 24 g protein, 21 g carbohydrate, 7 g fat, 32 mg cholesterol, 334 mg sodium.

Fusilli with Tuna, Roasted Peppers, and Lemon

~

To make it easy on you, this tuna-pasta combination uses canned tuna rather than fresh. You probably have all the ingredients on hand in your cupboard and refrigerator.

8 ounces long fusilli
2 tablespoons extra-virgin olive oil
1 large onion, thinly sliced
2 cloves garlic, minced
1 (7-ounce) jar roasted red peppers, julienned
1 (6^1/$_2$-ounce) can imported tuna in olive oil
Pinch crushed red-pepper flakes
2 teaspoons grated lemon zest (colored part of peel)
^{1}/$_2$ teaspoon freshly ground black pepper
^{1}/$_4$ teaspoon salt
1 tablespoon fresh lemon juice
Chopped fresh parsley (optional)

1 • Cook the fusilli as the package label directs. Drain the fusilli and place it in a large bowl.

2 • While the pasta is cooking, heat the extra-virgin olive oil in a medium skillet over medium-high heat. Add the onion and sauté about 5 minutes or until the onion is soft. Add the garlic, roasted red peppers, tuna, red-pepper flakes, lemon zest, ground pepper, salt, and lemon juice. Sauté about 2 to 3 minutes or until the mixture is warm.

3. Pour the tuna mixture over the vermicelli. If you wish, sprinkle the chopped parsley over the pasta.

> Makes 4 servings. Per serving: 409 calories, 23 g protein, 52 g carbohydrate, 12 g fat, 9 mg cholesterol, 316 mg sodium.

low-fat

quick

Linguine with Shrimp

~

This recipe makes a memorable dinner for two. Or double it to serve a party of four. Delicious with a watercress salad and dry white wine.

6 ounces linguine
2 tablespoons olive oil
$^1/_4$ cup sliced shallots
1 ($14^1/_2$-ounce) can diced tomatoes in olive oil, garlic, and spices
1 tablespoon chopped fresh basil or 1 teaspoon dried basil, crumbled
$^1/_3$ cup heavy cream
$^1/_2$ pound medium shrimp, shelled, deveined, tails intact, and cooked, or $^1/_2$ pound cooked lobster
$^1/_8$ teaspoon ground hot red pepper
$^1/_3$ cup fresh basil leaves, julienned

1 • Cook the linguine as the package label directs. Drain the linguine and place it in a large bowl; keep the pasta warm.

2 • Meanwhile, in a skillet over medium-high heat, heat the olive oil. Add the shallots and sauté about 4 to 5 minutes or until the shallots are tender. Add the tomatoes and the chopped or dried basil; bring the mixture to boiling. Lower the heat and simmer for 5 minutes. Add the heavy cream and return to boiling; boil about 2 to 3 minutes or until the liquid is slightly reduced. Add the shrimp or lobster and the ground hot red pepper. Heat the sauce through.

3 • Pour the sauce over the linguine. Add the julienned basil leaves and toss to combine the ingredients.

Makes 2 servings. Per serving: 733 calories, 37 g protein, 78 g carbohydrate, 31 g fat, 221 mg cholesterol, 524 mg sodium.

Perfectly Easy Pasta

1. Fill a large saucepan or Dutch oven with enough cold water to allow plenty of room for the pasta to move freely, about 6 to 8 quarts.

2. After the water has come to a rolling boil, add salt. (For optimum flavor, use about 1 tablespoon of salt per pound of dried pasta.)

3. Add the pasta to the rapidly boiling water, stirring constantly with a long-handled spoon. Continue stirring the pasta vigorously from the bottom of the pot to prevent the strands from sticking together.

4. When the water returns to a full boil, begin timing the pasta. As the pasta cooks, stir it occasionally. To determine doneness, scoop up a piece and bite into it. Pasta should be tender yet resilient to the bite — al dente. Never cook pasta until it is mushy.

5. Drain the pasta in a large colander in the sink. Do not rinse the pasta unless it is to be used in a salad. (The reason: Rinsing pasta draws away the surface starch, which helps to thicken the sauce.)

Stuffed Shells

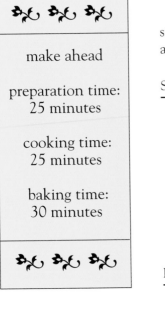

make ahead

preparation time:
25 minutes

cooking time:
25 minutes

baking time:
30 minutes

You can prepare the sauce and assemble the shells up to 2 days before serving, and refrigerate. To serve, bake for 45 minutes or until the stuffed shells are heated through. For a prettier presentation, use white and green pasta shells. This dish is perfect for a buffet table.

SAUCE

> 2 tablespoons extra-virgin olive oil
> 4 cloves garlic, crushed
> 1 (28-ounce) can Italian tomatoes with purée
> $^1/_2$ teaspoon salt
> $^1/_2$ teaspoon freshly ground black pepper
> 1 teaspoon dried basil leaves, crumbled
>
> 12 ounces jumbo pasta shells

FILLING

> 1 (1-pound) container ricotta cheese
> 2 (10-ounce) packages chopped frozen spinach, thawed and squeezed very dry
> 1 (7-ounce) jar roasted red peppers, drained well, patted dry, and chopped
> 1 cup shredded Italian fontina cheese (about 4 ounces)
> $^1/_2$ cup grated Parmesan cheese
> 1 teaspoon grated lemon zest (colored part of peel)
> 1 large egg yolk
> 1 teaspoon salt
> 1 $^1/_2$ teaspoons freshly ground black pepper

1 • Prepare the Sauce: In a large saucepan over medium-high heat, heat the olive oil. Add the garlic and sauté about 2 minutes or until the garlic is lightly golden. Stir in the Italian tomatoes with their purée, breaking up the tomatoes with a wooden spoon. Add the $^1/_2$ teaspoons of salt and pepper, and the basil. Stir to mix the ingredients well. Reduce the heat to low and simmer the Sauce for 20 minutes, stirring occasionally.

2 • Meanwhile, cook the pasta shells as the package label directs. Drain the pasta shells, rinse them under cold running water, and drain again.

3 • Prepare the Filling: In a large bowl, combine the ricotta cheese, spinach, roasted red peppers, fontina and Parmesan cheeses, lemon zest, egg yolk, the 1 teaspoon of salt, and the 1½ teaspoons of pepper. Stir to mix all the ingredients well.

4 • Preheat the oven to 350°F. Grease the bottom and sides of a 13 × 9-inch baking pan. Spoon the Filling into the pasta shells, dividing the Filling equally. Arrange the stuffed shells in the prepared pan. Spoon the Sauce over the shells. Cover the pan with aluminum foil and bake about 30 minutes or until the stuffed shells are heated through.

> *Makes 8 servings. Per serving: 427 calories, 22 g protein, 45 g carbohydrate, 19 g fat, 76 mg cholesterol, 904 mg sodium.*

Stuffed Shells

Four-Cheese Pasta

make ahead

preparation time:
15 minutes

cooking time:
10 minutes

baking time:
30 minutes

A marvelous melding of bow-tie pasta and four cheeses, including Italian fontina and smoked Dutch Gouda. Our version includes Swiss chard for added flavor and texture. Serve with a cucumber and tomato salad dressed with balsamic vinaigrette.

WHITE SAUCE

4 tablespoons butter or margarine
1 medium onion, chopped
$^1/_4$ cup all-purpose flour
1 teaspoon salt
$^3/_4$ teaspoon coarsely ground pepper
$1^1/_2$ cups milk
$^1/_2$ cup dry white wine

PASTA

1 pound Swiss chard or kale, tough ends trimmed
1 pound farfalle (bow-tie, or butterfly, pasta)
8 ounces Italian fontina cheese, shredded
4 ounces smoked Gouda cheese, shredded
8 ounces fresh mozzarella cheese, cut into $^1/_2$-inch cubes

PARMESAN BREAD CRUMBS

1 cup fresh bread crumbs, made from Italian bread
$^1/_4$ cup freshly grated Parmesan cheese
2 tablespoons butter or margarine, melted

1 • Grease a 13 × 9-inch baking dish or a 4-quart gratin dish. Prepare the White Sauce: In a medium saucepan over medium heat, melt the 4 tablespoons butter or margarine. Add the onion and sauté about 5 minutes or until the onion is soft. Stir in the flour, salt, and pepper until the ingredients are blended. Cook the mixture until it is bubbly, about 1 minute. Gradually add the milk and white wine, stirring until the mixture is blended. Cook, stirring, until the White Sauce boils and thickens, and the texture is smooth.

2 • Prepare the Pasta: Preheat the oven to 350°F. In a large saucepan, in 4 quarts boiling, salted water, cook the Swiss chard for 2 minutes. With tongs, transfer the Swiss chard to a colander and rinse under cold running water. In the same boiling water, cook the farfalle as the package label directs. Drain the farfalle and return it to the saucepan. Pour the White Sauce over the pasta; add the fontina, Gouda, and mozzarella cheeses, and the Swiss chard. Stir all the ingredients until they are well mixed. Pour the mixture into the prepared baking dish.

3 • Prepare the Parmesan Bread Crumbs: In a small bowl, combine the bread crumbs, Parmesan cheese, and the 2 tablespoons melted butter or margarine. Stir until the ingredients are well mixed. Sprinkle the Parmesan Bread Crumbs over the pasta in the baking dish. Bake the pasta mixture for 30 minutes.

> *Makes 8 servings. Per serving: 624 calories, 29 g protein, 55 g carbohydrate, 31 g fat, 103 mg cholesterol, 1,037 mg sodium.*

Four-Cheese Pasta

Macaroni and Cheese

make ahead

preparation time:
5 minutes

cooking time:
20 minutes

baking time:
25 minutes

Accompany this family favorite with a cold vegetable salad.

1 pound ziti pasta
4 tablespoons butter
$^1/_2$ cup fine dry bread crumbs
10 ounces extra-sharp Cheddar cheese, shredded ($2^1/_2$ cups)
$^3/_4$ cup grated Parmesan cheese (3 ounces)
3 tablespoons all-purpose flour
3 cups milk
$^1/_2$ teaspoon salt
$^1/_2$ teaspoon freshly ground black pepper

Macaroni and Cheese

1 • Preheat the oven to 400°F. Grease a 13 × 9 × 2-inch baking dish.

2 • Cook the pasta as the package label directs. Drain; rinse with cold water. Drain again. Place in a large bowl.

3 • Meanwhile, in a medium saucepan, over medium heat, melt the butter. Pour 1 tablespoon of the melted butter into a small bowl. Add the bread crumbs, $^1/_2$ cup of the Cheddar, and $^1/_4$ cup of the Parmesan.

4 • To the remaining butter in the saucepan, add the flour; whisk to blend. Cook for 1 minute, whisking. Add the milk gradually, whisking until blended after each addition. Heat to boiling, whisking occasionally. Simmer for 2 minutes. Add the remaining cheeses, the salt, and the pepper. Add the cheese mixture to the bowl with the pasta and toss to coat. Spread the pasta in the prepared baking dish. Sprinkle with the bread crumb mixture.

5 • Bake for 25 minutes or until browned and bubbly.

> Makes 8 servings. Per serving: 536 calories, 24 g protein, 54 g carbohydrate, 25 g fat, 73 mg cholesterol, 676 mg sodium.

Baked Macaroni and Cheese Primavera

~

A low-fat version of the family favorite, using skim milk and reduced-fat Cheddar cheese. Team it with crunchy iceberg-lettuce salad and your favorite bottled low-fat salad dressing.

Nonstick cooking spray
1 pound macaroni
$^1/_2$ cup chicken broth
1 cup diced onion (1 large onion)
3 large cloves garlic, finely chopped
3 large plum tomatoes, diced (1$^1/_2$ cups)
1 $^1/_2$ teaspoons dried basil leaves, crumbled
1 medium carrot, pared and grated
1 (10-ounce) package frozen chopped spinach, thawed and squeezed dry

low-fat

make ahead

preparation time:
15 minutes

cooking time:
20 minutes

baking time:
40 minutes

SAUCE

¹/₃ cup all-purpose flour
3 cups skim milk
6 ounces reduced-fat Cheddar cheese, grated (about 1³/₄ cups)
2 tablespoons grated Parmesan cheese
1 tablespoon Dijon mustard
1 teaspoon salt
¹/₂ teaspoon freshly ground pepper

TOPPING

1 slice white bread
2 tablespoons grated Parmesan cheese

1 • Preheat the oven to 350°F. With the nonstick cooking spray, grease a shallow, 3-quart baking dish or a 13 × 9-inch baking dish. Set aside the prepared pan.

2 • In a large saucepan of boiling, salted water, cook the macaroni as the package label directs. Drain the macaroni, rinse it under cold running water, and set it aside to drain.

3 • In a large saucepan, combine the chicken broth, onion, and garlic; bring the broth to boiling. Reduce the heat and simmer about 7 minutes or until the onion is tender and the broth has evaporated. Add the plum tomatoes and basil, and cook about 3 minutes or until the tomatoes are hot. Add the carrot and spinach. Stir to mix the ingredients well, and set aside the vegetable mixture.

4 • Prepare the Sauce: Place the flour in a small bowl. Gradually add ¹/₄ cup of the milk, stirring until the mixture is blended. Pour the remaining milk into a medium saucepan. Whisk the flour mixture into the milk until they are well blended. Over low heat, bring the milk mixture to boiling, whisking constantly. Reduce the heat and simmer for 2 minutes. Add the Cheddar cheese, the 2 tablespoons of Parmesan cheese, the Dijon mustard, salt, and pepper. Cook until the cheeses melt, stirring to blend all the ingredients.

5 • In a large bowl, combine the macaroni, vegetable mixture, and the Sauce. Stir gently until the ingredients are well mixed. Pour the macaroni mixture into the prepared baking dish.

6 • Prepare the Topping: Tear the bread slice in half and place the halves in a food processor. Using the pulse action, process until crumbs form. In a cup, combine the bread crumbs with the 2 tablespoons of Parmesan cheese until they are well mixed. Sprinkle the Topping over the macaroni mixture. Cover the baking dish with aluminum foil and bake for 20 minutes. Uncover the dish and bake about 20 minutes more or until the casserole is browned and bubbly.

Makes 8 servings. Per serving: 374 calories, 21 g protein, 59 g carbohydrate, 6 g fat, 19 mg cholesterol, 575 mg sodium.

Baked Macaroni and Cheese Primavera

Vegetable Lasagna with Escarole

A fantastic dish for easy, casual entertaining, this lasagna can be assembled earlier in the day. If moving directly from the refrigerator to the oven, allow a little extra baking time. Also, the fresh basil can be replaced with $1/2$ teaspoon of dried basil; add to the food processor in step 4.

> 1 large eggplant, pared
> Nonstick cooking spray
> 1 large Spanish onion, chopped
> 2 large cloves garlic, crushed
> 2 heads escarole, washed and broken into 1-inch pieces
> $1/8$ to $1/4$ teaspoon crushed red-pepper flakes
> 24 fresh basil leaves
> 1 cup low-fat cottage cheese
> $1/2$ teaspoon salt
> 1 (15-ounce) container marinara sauce
> 6 cooked lasagna noodles
> $1/2$ cup shredded part-skim mozzarella cheese (about 2 ounces)

1 • Slice the eggplant crosswise into $1/2$-inch-thick slices. Arrange the eggplant slices in a single layer on 1 or 2 large baking sheets. Broil the eggplant 6 inches from the heat source about 4 minutes on each side, until the slices are browned. Set aside the eggplant slices.

2 • With the nonstick cooking spray, grease a large, deep skillet. Place the skillet over medium heat until it is hot. Add the Spanish onion and garlic, and sauté about 5 minutes or until the onion is tender. With a slotted spoon, remove half of the onion mixture to a blender or food processor.

3 • To the remaining onion mixture in the skillet, add the escarole and red-pepper flakes; stir to combine all the ingredients. Cover the skillet and cook about 5 minutes or until the escarole is wilted and tender.

4 • Reserve 8 basil leaves. To the onion mixture in the blender or food processor, add the remaining basil leaves, the cottage cheese, and the salt. Process until all the ingredients are blended.

5 • Preheat the oven to 375°F. Spread one third of the marinara sauce over the bottom of an 11 × 8-inch baking dish. Place half of the eggplant slices over the sauce, overlapping the slices if necessary. Spread half of the escarole mixture over the eggplant slices and cover with 3 of the lasagna noodles. Spread half of the cottage-cheese mixture over the noodles. Repeat the layering: one third of the sauce, the remaining eggplant, escarole mixture, noodles, and cottage-cheese mixture. Spread the remaining third of the sauce over all.

6 • Cover the baking dish with aluminum foil and bake the lasagna for 40 minutes. Remove the foil. Arrange the reserved fresh basil leaves over the lasagna and sprinkle with the mozzarella cheese. Bake, uncovered, for 5 minutes more, until the top is bubbly and the cheese is melted. Let the lasagna stand for 10 minutes before cutting.

Makes 6 to 8 servings. Per serving: 165 calories, 11 g protein, 29 g carbohydrate, 2 g fat, 5 mg cholesterol, 822 mg sodium.

"Grilled" Vegetable Lasagna

The roasted vegetables lend a wonderful smoky quality to this lasagna (shown on page 111). During the warm months, grill the vegetables outdoors for extra flavor. In winter, use the broiler.

TOMATO SAUCE

Nonstick cooking spray
1 large red onion, chopped
6 cloves garlic, crushed
2 (28-ounce) cans Italian plum tomatoes, drained and chopped
1/4 cup lightly packed fresh basil leaves, chopped
1/2 teaspoon salt
1/4 teaspoon crushed red-pepper flakes

LASAGNA

1 eggplant
2 medium zucchini
Salt
Nonstick cooking spray
1 roasted sweet red pepper, seeded and skinned
1 roasted sweet yellow pepper, seeded and skinned
1/4 cup lightly packed fresh basil leaves
1 cup low-fat cottage cheese
1 1/2 cups part-skim shredded mozzarella cheese (about 6 ounces)

low-fat

make ahead

preparation time:
25 minutes

eggplant and
zucchini
standing time:
30 minutes

broiling time:
10 minutes

cooking time:
18 minutes

baking time:
30 minutes

9 cooked lasagna noodles
2 tablespoons grated Parmesan cheese
Fresh basil leaves (optional)

1 • Prepare the Tomato Sauce: With the nonstick cooking spray, grease a large nonstick skillet. Add the red onion. Over medium heat, cook about 5 minutes or until the onion is tender. Add the garlic and cook for 1 minute more. Remove half of the red onion mixture to a medium bowl.

2 • To the red onion mixture remaining in the skillet, add the plum tomatoes, the 1/4 cup of basil leaves, the 1/2 teaspoon of salt, and the red-pepper flakes. Bring the mixture to boiling. Reduce the heat and simmer about 10 minutes or until the Tomato Sauce is slightly thickened. Remove 2 cups of the sauce to a small saucepan and set it aside.

3 • Prepare the Lasagna: Cut the eggplant and the zucchini lengthwise into 1/4-inch-thick slices. Sprinkle the slices with salt. Place the slices in a colander set on a large plate and let the slices stand about 30 minutes. Rinse the slices and pat them dry.

4 • With the nonstick cooking spray, grease a large baking sheet. Working in batches, arrange the eggplant and zucchini slices in a single layer on the prepared baking sheet and broil 4 inches from the heat source about 3 to 5 minutes on each side or until the slices are cooked. Remove the cooked slices to a cutting board. Slice the cooked eggplant and zucchini slices, and the roasted sweet red and yellow peppers crosswise into 1/2-inch-wide strips. Place the vegetable strips in the bowl with the red onion mixture. Toss to combine all the vegetables.

5 • Preheat the oven to 400°F. In a blender or food processor, chop the 1/4 cup basil leaves. Add the cottage cheese and process until the mixture is puréed. Place the cottage cheese mixture in a bowl and stir in the mozzarella cheese.

6 • Over the bottom of a 13 × 9-inch baking dish, spread one fourth of the Tomato Sauce. Place 3 lasagna noodles over the sauce. Spread one third of the cheese mixture over the noodles and top with one third of the vegetable mixture. Repeat the layering 2 more times, ending with a layer of Tomato Sauce. Sprinkle the Parmesan cheese over all. Bake about 30 minutes or until the mixture is bubbly. Let the lasagna stand for 10 minutes before cutting. Meanwhile, heat the reserved Tomato Sauce in the small saucepan and serve with the lasagna. If desired, garnish the lasagna with the fresh basil leaves.

Makes 9 servings. Per serving: 325 calories, 18 g protein, 54 g carbohydrate, 5 g fat, 13 mg cholesterol, 624 mg sodium.

Three-Mushroom Lasagna

This lasagna, a favorite with both children and adults, can be assembled up to two days ahead. Vary the kinds of mushrooms, depending on what's available in your market.

FILLING

1 1/2 ounces dried porcini mushrooms
3/4 cup boiling water
1/4 cup butter or margarine
1 large onion, chopped
1 pound white mushrooms, sliced
1/2 pound fresh shiitake mushrooms, stems removed and caps sliced
1/2 pound cooked ham, diced
1 (7-ounce) jar roasted red peppers, drained and chopped

SAUCE

6 tablespoons butter or margarine
5 tablespoons all-purpose flour
1 3/4 cups milk
1/2 teaspoon salt
1/8 to 1/4 teaspoon crushed red-pepper flakes

9 cooked lasagna noodles
1 (15-ounce) container part-skim ricotta cheese
1 cup shredded part-skim mozzarella cheese (about 4 ounces)

make ahead

preparation time:
25 minutes

cooking time:
30 minutes

baking time:
50 minutes

1 • Prepare the Filling: Place the porcini mushrooms in a small bowl. Pour the boiling water over the mushrooms and let them soak for 15 minutes.

2 • Meanwhile, in a large, deep skillet, over medium heat, melt the 1/4 cup of butter or margarine. Add the onion and sauté about 4 minutes or until the onion is tender. Add the white and shiitake mushrooms, and sauté for 10 minutes. Drain the porcini mushrooms, pouring the soaking liquid through a fine sieve lined with a double thickness of cheesecloth into a small bowl, reserving the liquid for the Sauce. Rinse the porcini mushrooms to remove any grit and coarsely chop the mushrooms. Add the porcini mushrooms to the skillet. Cook, stirring, about 5 minutes or until all of the liquid in the skillet evaporates. Stir in the

Dried Porcini Mushrooms

Porcini mushrooms are available fresh, but dried mushrooms can be stored longer and have a very intense flavor when reconstituted. The dried mushrooms are sold at specialty food shops and better supermarkets.

To reconstitute: Rinse the mushrooms, then soak them in hot water to cover, for 15 minutes or until softened. Strain the mushrooms through a sieve lined with a double thickness of dampened cheesecloth or dampened paper towels or a dampened coffee filter set over a bowl to catch the liquid. Save the soaking liquid to use in soups, sauces, or salad dressings. Before adding them, rinse the mushrooms again to remove any lingering grit.

ham and roasted red peppers. Place the Filling in a medium bowl and set it aside. Wipe out the skillet.

3 ⋅ Prepare the Sauce: In the same, cleaned skillet over medium heat, melt the 6 tablespoons of butter or margarine. With a wooden spoon, blend in the flour. Cook, stirring, until the mixture is bubbly. Blend in the milk and the porcini soaking liquid, and bring the mixture to boiling, stirring constantly. Cook, stirring, about 4 minutes or until the mixture thickens. Stir in the salt and red-pepper flakes.

4 ⋅ Assemble the lasagna: Over the bottom of a 13 × 9-inch baking dish, spread 1/2 cup of the Sauce. Place 3 noodles on top of the sauce and spread 2 cups of the Filling over the noodles. Top with half of the ricotta cheese and sprinkle half of the mozzarella cheese over all. For the next layer, use 1/2 cup of Sauce, 3 more noodles, 2 cups of Filling, then the remaining ricotta cheese. Then layer 1/4 cup of the Sauce, the remaining noodles, Filling, Sauce, and the remaining mozzarella cheese. (The lasagna may be prepared ahead to this point, covered, and refrigerated for up to 2 days.)

5 ⋅ To serve: Preheat the oven to 400°F. Cover the baking dish with aluminum foil. Bake the lasagna for 50 minutes, removing the foil for the last 10 minutes of baking time. If you refrigerated the lasagna before baking, add 10-15 minutes to the cooking time. Let the lasagna stand for 10 minutes before cutting.

Makes 8 servings. Per Serving: 493 calories, 24 g protein, 38 g carbohydrate, 28 g fat, 88 mg cholesterol, 811 mg sodium.

Three-Mushroom Lasagna

Creole Mushroom Lasagna

Creole cooking meets Italian cuisine in this special lasagna. Meaty shiitake mushrooms and zucchini rounds provide the rich vegetable base. For extra heat, serve with red-pepper bread sticks, found in better supermarkets or gourmet shops.

TOMATO SAUCE

1 tablespoon olive oil
4 shallots, minced
2 large cloves garlic, minced
1 (28-ounce) can whole tomatoes in thick purée
$^1/_2$ cup dry white wine
1 bay leaf
1 teaspoon dried thyme leaves, crumbled
$^1/_2$ teaspoon salt
$^1/_4$ teaspoon ground hot red pepper

VEGETABLE FILLING

1 tablespoon olive oil or safflower oil
4 shallots, thinly sliced
$^1/_2$ pound fresh shiitake mushrooms, stems removed and caps sliced
    $^1/_4$ inch thick
4 medium zucchini (7 to 8 ounces each), trimmed and thinly sliced
    crosswise
$^1/_4$ cup chopped fresh parsley
1 teaspoon dried basil leaves, crumbled
$^1/_2$ teaspoon salt
$^1/_4$ teaspoon freshly ground black pepper

9 cooked lasagna noodles
$1^1/_2$ cups shredded reduced-fat mozzarella cheese (about 6 ounces)
1 (15-ounce) container reduced-fat ricotta cheese

make ahead

preparation time:
25 minutes

cooking time:
50 minutes

baking time:
40 minutes

1 • Prepare the Tomato Sauce: In a 2-quart nonstick saucepan over medium heat, heat the olive oil. Add the 4 shallots and garlic, and sauté about 4 to 5 minutes or until the shallots are tender. Add the tomatoes with their purée, white wine, bay leaf, thyme, the $^1/_2$ teaspoon of salt, and the ground red pepper. Stir until the ingredients are well mixed. Bring the sauce to boiling. Reduce the heat to low and simmer about 30 minutes, stirring occasionally, until the sauce is reduced to about $3^1/_2$ cups. Cool the sauce slightly and remove the bay leaf.

2 • Meanwhile, prepare the Vegetable Filling: Preheat the oven to 400°F. In a large, deep nonstick skillet over medium heat, heat the olive or safflower oil. Add the 4 shallots and sauté about 5 minutes or until the shallots are tender. Add the sliced shiitake mushroom caps and sauté about 2 to 3 minutes or until the mushrooms are wilted. Add the zucchini, parsley, basil, the 1/2 teaspoon of salt, and the ground black pepper. Stir until the ingredients are well mixed. Cover the skillet and cook about 5 minutes or until the zucchini is tender-crisp. Remove the skillet from the heat and let the filling cool slightly.

3 • Over the bottom of a 13 × 9-inch baking pan, spread one third of the Vegetable Filling. Place 3 noodles on top of the filling. Reserve 1/4 cup of the mozzarella cheese; in a medium bowl, stir together the remaining mozzarella cheese and the ricotta cheese. Spread one third of the cheese mixture over the noodles in the baking dish. Top with one third of the Tomato Sauce. Repeat the layering: one third of the filling, 3 noodles, one third of the cheese mixture, and one third of the sauce. For the final layer, spread the final third of the filling, noodles, cheese mixture, and sauce. Sprinkle the reserved mozzarella cheese over all. Cover the baking dish tightly with aluminum foil. Bake the lasagna about 40 to 45 minutes or until the lasagna is bubbly. Let the lasagna stand for 10 minutes before cutting.

Makes 12 servings. Per serving: 223 calories, 13 g protein, 27 g carbohydrate, 8 g fat, 14 mg cholesterol, 397 mg sodium.

Creole Mushroom Lasagna

Sesame Noodles

~

This speedy Asian noodle dish is a favorite in restaurants — now you can make it at home. Serve it for a summer lunch, or an easy supper on a busy day. Shredded bok choy tossed with balsamic vinegar makes a nice accompaniment.

SAUCE

2 tablespoons dark brown sugar
1 tablespoon grated gingerroot
Pinch ground hot red pepper
5 tablespoons low-sodium soy sauce
$^1/_4$ cup creamy peanut butter
2 tablespoons dark sesame oil
2 tablespoons balsamic vinegar
1 clove garlic, crushed

PASTA

12 ounces spaghettini
$^1/_2$ European cucumber, cut into 4 × $^1/_4$-inch strips
2 green onions, cut into 2-inch-long strips
1 bunch radishes, julienned
1 tablespoon toasted sesame seeds

1 • Prepare the Sauce: In a medium bowl, combine the dark brown sugar, ginger, ground red pepper, soy sauce, peanut butter, dark sesame oil, balsamic vinegar, and garlic. Whisk until the mixture is well blended. Set aside the Sauce.

2 • Prepare the Pasta: Cook the spaghettini as the package label directs. Drain the spaghettini, rinse it under cold running water, and drain it again. Place the spaghettini in a serving bowl. Pour the Sauce over the spaghettini and toss to coat the pasta. Add the cucumber, green onions, and radishes, and sprinkle the toasted sesame seeds over all.

> Makes 6 servings. Per serving: 354 calories, 11 g protein, 53 g carbohydrate, 12 g fat, 0 mg cholesterol, 745 mg sodium.

quick

Chapter Five

~

Vegetables

$$\maltese \quad \maltese \quad \maltese$$

Quick — what do you do if you don't have any asparagus on hand for the Asparagus Tofu "Quiche" (page 141)? Just substitute sweet red pepper or broccoli florets — or almost any other vegetable. One of the reasons we love vegetable dishes is for their interchangeability of ingredients. Reason number two: Vegetables combined with grains, pasta, legumes, eggs, cheese, and other dairy products provide a nutritionally sound meal, without the added expense of meat or fish.

What's more, pasta, rice, and other grains are a natural backdrop for vegetables, since their neutral taste lets all the flavors of the vegetables shine. One of our favorites is quick-cooking couscous, as in Couscous with Vegetables (page 147). Dishes from the southwest and Mexico often mix beans and vegetables, and our selection includes Vegetable and Cheese Enchiladas (page 150) and Vegetable Burritos (page152) as well as Chiles Rellenos (page 143).

There's just one rule of thumb we have to offer: When preparing any vegetable dish, select only the best raw ingredients, and don't compromise on quality. If a recipe calls for broccoli and the broccoli at the store doesn't look great, then hold off on preparing the recipe or go for a substitution.

Eggplant Sandwiches

The flavors of the Mediterranean enliven this main-dish sandwich. The Marinara Sauce can be made a day ahead, and the sandwiches themselves can be prepared earlier in the day and refrigerated until ready to cook. Serve with a shredded carrot salad.

2 (1-pound) eggplants, trimmed and cut crosswise into
    ¼-inch-thick slices
1 tablespoon coarse (kosher) salt

MARINARA SAUCE

1 tablespoon olive oil
2 small cloves garlic, flattened slightly with side of broad knife
2 (35-ounce) cans Italian plum tomatoes, drained and finely chopped
¼ teaspoon freshly ground black pepper
¼ teaspoon salt
¼ cup finely julienned fresh basil leaves

About 2¼ cups olive oil

FILLING

1 cup fresh basil leaves, chopped
½ cup bottled roasted red peppers, drained and finely chopped
10 flat anchovies, rinsed, patted dry, and minced
2 tablespoons capers, drained and chopped
½ teaspoon freshly ground black pepper
8 ounces mozzarella, thinly sliced

½ cup all-purpose flour
3 large eggs, lightly beaten
3 cups fresh soft Italian bread crumbs
¼ cup freshly grated Parmesan cheese

1 • Sprinkle the eggplant slices with the coarse salt. Place the slices in a colander set over a bowl or in the sink and let the eggplant drain for 1 hour.

make ahead

preparation time:
25 minutes

eggplant
standing time:
1 hour

baking time:
18 minutes

cooking time:
25 minutes

2 • Meanwhile, prepare the Marinara Sauce: In a large skillet over medium heat, combine the 1 tablespoon of olive oil and the garlic. Cook until the garlic is very aromatic but is not browned. Stir in the Italian tomatoes, the ¼ teaspoon of pepper, and the ¼ teaspoon of salt. Reduce the heat to medium-low and cook about 20 minutes or until the liquid is reduced and the mixture is thickened. Remove the skillet from the heat and let the Marinara Sauce cool to room temperature. Remove and discard the garlic. Just before serving, reheat the sauce and stir in the julienned basil leaves.

3 • Preheat the oven to 375°F. Pat the eggplant slices dry with paper towels. Brush both sides of each slice with some of the olive oil. Place the eggplant slices in a single layer over 2 large baking sheets. Bake about 18 minutes or until the slices are tender. Let the eggplant slices cool.

4 • Meanwhile, prepare the Filling: In a small bowl, combine the chopped basil leaves, roasted red peppers, anchovies, capers, and the ½ teaspoon of black pepper. Stir until the ingredients are well mixed. Spoon some of the Filling onto half of the eggplant slices; top with the mozzarella cheese, trimming the cheese slices to fit, if necessary. Place a plain eggplant slice on top of each filled eggplant slice; try to keep the top and bottom slices the same size. Press the eggplant slices together firmly to set the sandwiches. (The eggplant sandwiches can be refrigerated at this point until ready for frying.)

Eggplant Sandwiches

5 • Place the flour in one pie plate and the eggs in another pie plate. In a medium bowl, stir together the bread crumbs and Parmesan cheese until they are well mixed.

6 • In a large cast-iron skillet, heat ½ inch of the olive oil to 375°F. Preheat the oven to 300°F. One at a time, dip the eggplant sandwiches in the flour until completely coated, shaking off the excess flour. Then dip the sandwiches into the egg, letting the excess drain off. Finally, dip the sandwiches into the bread crumb mixture until completely coated, shaking off the excess crumbs. Fry the sandwiches, a few at a time, in the hot olive oil about 1½ to 2 minutes on each side or until the sandwiches are golden; add more olive oil to the skillet as needed. With tongs, transfer the sandwiches to a jelly-roll pan lined with paper towels. Keep the cooked sandwiches warm in the oven while frying the remaining sandwiches. Serve the eggplant sandwiches warm or at room temperature with the Marinara Sauce.

> *Makes 6 servings (18 sandwiches, 3½ cups sauce). Per serving: 565 calories, 22 g protein, 45 g carbohydrate, 35 g fat, 145 mg cholesterol, 1,659 mg sodium.*

Asparagus Tofu "Quiche"

Set to star at your next brunch, this eggless "quiche" uses tofu as the base. Tender fresh asparagus lends its incomparable flavor — and a visual extra — to the finished dish. Serve with a radish and tomato salad.

½ (15-ounce) package refrigerated all-ready pie crust (1 crust)
2 cups water
¾ pound asparagus, trimmed
2 (10½-ounce) packages firm tofu
¾ cup shredded Monterey Jack cheese (about 3 ounces)
3 green onions, sliced
2 cloves garlic, crushed
1 teaspoon lemon pepper
1 teaspoon dried thyme leaves, crushed
¾ teaspoon salt
1 tablespoon grated Parmesan cheese

preparation time:
25 minutes

crust baking
time:
13 minutes

cooking time:
4 minutes

quiche baking
time:
50 minutes

Tofu

Tofu, or bean curd, is made from soybean milk in a process similar to cheese making. Cholesterol-free, high in protein, and low in calories, tofu is available as cakes packed in water or vacuum-packed. Somewhat bland in taste, tofu adds texture to a dish and absorbs the flavors of other ingredients. If you purchase tofu in water, drain it, then refrigerate the tofu in fresh water for up to a week. Look for it in specialty Asian food shops or your supermarket produce section.

1 • Preheat the oven to 450°F. Roll out the pie crust into a 12-inch round. Place the dough round in a 9½-inch quiche pan with a removable bottom; trim off the excess dough. Line the crust with a sheet of aluminum foil. Using a fork, prick the crust several times through the foil. Bake the crust for 10 minutes. Remove the foil lining and bake about 3 minutes more or until the crust is lightly golden. Place the crust on a wire rack to cool.

2 • Reduce the oven heat to 350°F. In a 2-quart saucepan, bring the water to boiling. Add the asparagus and cook about 4 minutes or until the asparagus is tender-crisp. Drain the asparagus and rinse it under cold running water until the asparagus is cool. Cut 9 asparagus spears into 2½-inch-long pieces and set them aside. Cut the remaining spears into ½-inch pieces.

3 • In a blender or food processor, process the tofu until it is puréed. Pour the puréed tofu into a large bowl. Stir in the ½-inch asparagus pieces, the Monterey Jack cheese, green onions, garlic, lemon pepper, thyme, and salt until the mixture is blended. Spoon the tofu mixture into the cooled crust. Arrange the 9 reserved asparagus spears spoke fashion on top of the tofu mixture. Sprinkle the Parmesan cheese over all. Bake about 50 minutes or until the quiche is golden and firm.

> *Makes 12 servings. Per serving: 147 calories, 8 g protein, 9 g carbohydrate, 10 g fat, 7 mg cholesterol, 141 mg sodium.*

Asparagus Tofu "Quiche"

Chiles Rellenos

Sharp Cheddar and creamy Monterey Jack form the cheese duo inside these traditional batter-coated mild chili peppers. The hot red pepper–spiked Roasted Tomato Sauce lends a touch of fire; the crunchy Jícama Salsa, enlivened with the tang of fresh lime juice, adds a cool counterpoint — and both can be made a day ahead.

JÍCAMA SALSA

1/2 pound jícama, pared and diced (about 1 1/2 cups)
2 large carrots, pared and diced
3 green onions, trimmed and chopped
2 tablespoons minced fresh cilantro
2 tablespoons fresh lime juice
1 tablespoon vegetable oil
1/8 teaspoon salt

ROASTED TOMATO SAUCE

2 medium plum tomatoes
1/4 teaspoon ground cumin
1/8 teaspoon ground hot red pepper
1/8 teaspoon salt

CHILES RELLENOS

4 poblano chili peppers
3/4 cup shredded Cheddar cheese
3/4 cup shredded Monterey Jack cheese
1 large egg yolk
1/3 cup all-purpose flour
1/4 cup beer
2 large egg whites
1/4 teaspoon salt
Vegetable oil for frying

make ahead

preparation time:
25 minutes

broiling time:
15 minutes

cooking time:
8 minutes

Poblano Chilies

These are the fresh peppers of choice for Chiles Rellenos, mostly because of their size. Stuffed, poblano peppers present an ample single-serving portion. Poblano peppers are dark green and are usually about 3 inches wide and 4 inches long.

1 • Prepare the Jícama Salsa: In a medium bowl, combine the jícama, carrots, green onions, and cilantro. Stir until the ingredients are well mixed. In a small bowl, whisk together the lime juice, the 1 tablespoon of vegetable oil, and the 1/8 teaspoon of salt until they are well blended. Pour the lime-juice mixture over the jícama mixture

Jícama

Available in shops specializing in Mexican foods and produce, and in some supermarkets, the jícama is a somewhat round root vegetable with crunchy, juicy flesh. Jícama is delicious raw in salads or as a snack, or lightly cooked (sautéed, steamed, or braised) for a side dish.

and toss to coat the vegetables with the dressing. Cover the bowl and set aside the Jícama Salsa.

2 • Prepare the Roasted Tomato Sauce: Preheat the broiler. Place the plum tomatoes on a rack in a broiler pan. Broil 4 to 5 inches from the heat source, turning the tomatoes frequently, until the skin is charred and blistered on all sides. Remove the broiled tomatoes to a bowl and let them stand until they are cool enough to handle. Remove and discard the skins, seeds, and watery juice from the tomatoes. Place the tomato pulp in a blender or food processor. Add the cumin, ground hot red pepper, and the $1/8$ teaspoon of salt. Process until the tomato mixture is puréed. Pour the sauce into a bowl. Cover the bowl and set aside the tomato sauce.

3 • Prepare the Chiles Rellenos: Place the poblano chili peppers on the rack in the broiler pan. Broil 4 to 5 inches from the heat source, turning the peppers frequently, until the skin is charred and blistered on all sides. Remove the chili peppers to a paper bag, close the bag, and let the peppers stand about 10 minutes or until they are cool enough to handle. Remove the skins from the peppers. With a small knife, make a lengthwise slit in each pepper, leaving the stem intact. Carefully remove the seeds and ribs from each pepper.

4 • In a bowl, combine the Cheddar and Monterey Jack cheeses until they are well mixed. Stuff each pepper with the cheese mixture. Carefully close each stuffed pepper to seal the opening.

5 • In a medium bowl, with a fork, beat the egg yolk, flour, and beer until the mixture is well blended. In a large bowl, with an electric mixer at high speed, beat the egg whites and the $1/4$ teaspoon of salt until stiff peaks form when the beaters are raised. With a rubber spatula, gently fold the egg-yolk mixture into the egg whites until no white streaks remain.

6 • In a 5-quart saucepan, heat $1\frac{1}{2}$ inches of the vegetable oil to 375°F. One at a time, dip the stuffed peppers into the batter until the pepper is completely coated. Fry the coated peppers in the hot oil, turning once, until the peppers are puffy and golden brown, about $1\frac{1}{2}$ to 2 minutes. Drain the fried peppers on paper towels.

7 • To serve: Spoon some of the Roasted Tomato Sauce onto each of 4 plates. Place a fried chili pepper in the sauce on each plate. Pass the Jícama Salsa.

Makes 4 servings. Per serving: 576 calories, 17 g protein, 25 g carbohydrate, 46 g fat, 94 mg cholesterol, 700 mg sodium.

*Chiles
Rellenos*

Is It Ripe?

Asparagus: Choose medium-green, firm, straight spears with tightly closed buds. Skin should be wrinkle-free and unblemished. Size and width do not affect the taste.

Broccoli: Bunches should have firm stalks with no yellowing, and heads should have tight florets.

Cabbage: Choose heads that are heavy in proportion to size, with no blemished leaves.

Carrots: Look for firm, bright orange carrots without any root hairs.

Corn: Select ears with even rows of plump kernels, fresh-looking green husks, and moist silk.

Eggplant: Shiny purple skin and firm flesh are sure signs of a healthy, ripe eggplant. Stay away from soft eggplants, as well as those with scars, cuts, or dark spots.

Green Beans: Select beans that are blemish-free and bright in color, with smooth skin, that give a slight snap when broken.

Sweet Peppers: Skin should be firm, smooth, and glossy.

Potatoes: Skin should be firm, clean, and smooth, with no sprouting or bruised spots. Also, there should be no green discoloration, which is a result of too much exposure to light.

Zucchini: This vegetable should have a shiny, deep green surface and be firm and blemish-free. Yellow patches mean the zucchini is overripe.

Fennel Risotto with Peas and Carrots

Risotto, a divinely creamy, rich rice dish made with Arborio rice, takes a little time and patience to prepare, but the extraordinary result is its own reward.

2 (14-ounce) cans chicken broth
1/4 cup unsalted butter or margarine
2 large bulbs fennel (about 1 pound), trimmed, cored, and cut into
   1/4-inch dice; chop and reserve 2 tablespoons fernlike leaves from top
2 shallots, chopped
1 1/2 cups Arborio rice (available at Italian grocery stores)
1 large carrot, pared and shredded
1 cup frozen peas, thawed
1/4 cup freshly grated Parmesan cheese, plus extra for passing

1 • In a 2-quart glass measure, combine the chicken broth with enough water to make 6 1/2 cups of liquid. Pour the broth mixture into a medium saucepan and heat just to simmering.

2 • Meanwhile, in a large heavy saucepan, melt the butter or margarine over medium heat. Add the diced fennel and the shallots, and sauté about 10 minutes or until the vegetables are tender. Add the Arborio rice and carrot, and sauté for 3 minutes. Stir in about 3/4 cup of the hot broth. Cook, stirring constantly, about 4 to 5 minutes or until the rice has absorbed almost all of the liquid. Repeat, adding 3/4 cup of the hot broth at a time, and cooking and stirring the rice mixture until almost all liquid is absorbed before adding more broth.

3 • When almost all of the broth has been added and the rice begins to pull away from the sides of the pan when stirred, add the remaining broth. Cook, stirring, until the rice is creamy and firm but not chalky in the center; the total cooking time will be about 30 to 40 minutes. Stir in the peas and cook for 1 minute more.

4 • Remove the saucepan from the heat and stir in the Parmesan cheese and the reserved chopped fennel top. Pass extra Parmesan cheese separately.

Makes 6 servings. Per serving: 330 calories, 10 g protein, 49 g carbohydrate, 10 g fat, 24 mg cholesterol, 577 mg sodium.

Couscous with Vegetables

An easy-to-prepare grain dish with lots of vegetables, which you can vary according to the season. This really is a meal in itself. Serve the couscous warm or at room temperature, with the Onion Relish and, if you like, a loaf of semolina bread.

ONION RELISH

1 tablespoon butter
1 tablespoon olive oil
4 large onions, halved and sliced
1 teaspoon honey
1/2 teaspoon salt
3/4 cup raisins
1/2 cup toasted almonds

COUSCOUS

2 1/2 cups chicken broth
1 tablespoon butter
1 (10-ounce) box couscous

VEGETABLES

1 tablespoon olive oil
2 large cloves garlic, finely chopped
2 teaspoons ground cumin
1 teaspoon ground coriander
1/2 teaspoon ground ginger
3/4 teaspoon crushed red-pepper flakes
1/2 butternut squash, peeled, seeded, and cut into 3/4-inch cubes
2 large carrots, pared and cut crosswise into 1/4-inch-thick slices
1 cup chicken broth
1/2 pound green beans, trimmed and cut into 2-inch lengths
1 large zucchini (about 8 ounces), cut into 3/4-inch cubes
1 large sweet red pepper, cut into 3/4-inch cubes
1 (15-ounce) can chickpeas, drained and rinsed

low-fat

quick

Onion Relish can be made ahead

Couscous

Couscous, which is granular in form, is processed from the hard heart of durum wheat. It can be found in some supermarkets and in health food stores, and the quick-cooking variety requires just a brief steeping in boiling water.

1 • Prepare the Onion Relish: In a large skillet over medium-high heat, melt the 1 tablespoon of butter in the 1 tablespoon of olive oil. Add the onions, honey, and salt, and stir until the ingredients are well mixed. Reduce the heat to medium and cook, stirring frequently, about 25 minutes or until the onions are browned; add the raisins for the last 5 minutes of cooking time. Remove the skillet from the heat and add the toasted almonds. Stir until all the ingredients are well mixed. Set aside.

2 • Meanwhile, prepare the Couscous: In a medium saucepan, combine the 2½ cups of chicken broth and the 1 tablespoon of butter. Bring the mixture to boiling. Add the couscous and stir until the ingredients are well mixed. Cover the saucepan and remove it from the heat.

3 • Prepare the Vegetables: In a Dutch oven over medium heat, heat the 1 tablespoon of olive oil. Add the garlic, cumin, coriander, ginger, and red-pepper flakes; stir until the ingredients are well mixed. Add the butternut squash, carrots, and the 1 cup of chicken broth. Stir until all the ingredients are well mixed. Increase the heat to medium-high, cover the Dutch oven, and cook the mixture for 3 minutes. Stir in the green beans, zucchini, sweet red pepper, and the chickpeas. Cover the Dutch oven again and cook about 5 to 6 minutes or until the Vegetables are tender, stirring once.

Couscous with Vegetables

4 • To serve: With a fork, fluff the Couscous. Spoon the Couscous around the edges of a large serving platter. With a slotted spoon, place the Vegetables in the center of the platter. Place the Onion Relish in a small bowl and serve on the side. Pass the cooking juices from the Vegetables for drizzling over the Couscous.

Makes 6 servings. Per serving: 641 calories, 22 g protein, 105 g carbohydrate, 18 g fat, 10 mg cholesterol, 698 mg sodium.

Enjoying Healthy Foods

Just knowing that a meal is "healthy" can sometimes make you feel as though you're missing something. The following are strategies for increasing the enjoyment of foods that are good for you.

- Set the scene: When placed against the proper background, anything can look dazzling. Set the table with a boldly patterned tablecloth, matching cloth napkins, and a pretty bowl filled with fruit as a colorful centerpiece.

- Make a pleasing presentation: If you take the time to arrange food attractively on the plate, the visual stimulation will add to your sense of satisfaction at meal's end.

- Less is more: Trompe l'oeil isn't just for art! Fool your eyes into thinking the portion is larger by serving your main course on smaller dessert plates (or plates with wide borders).

- "If music be the food . . .": Studies have shown that music with a slow tempo (such as classical works or romantic ballads) makes you eat at a more leisurely pace. Why is this so important? It takes 20 minutes for the brain to tell the stomach that eating has begun. So if you finish your entrée in less than 20 minutes, you'll feel like eating more. But if you make your meal last longer, you'll feel full before you've cleaned your plate.

Vegetable and Cheese Enchiladas

make ahead

preparation time:
30 minutes

cooking time:
12 minutes

baking time:
18 minutes

This entire dish can be assembled earlier in the day and refrigerated. If you transfer the dish directly from the refrigerator to the oven, allow a little extra baking time.

TOMATO SAUCE

1 (16-ounce) can crushed tomatoes
2 tablespoons chopped fresh cilantro
1 teaspoon chili powder
$1/2$ teaspoon ground cumin
$1/2$ teaspoon salt
$1/4$ teaspoon freshly ground black pepper

CHEESE FILLING

1 cup ricotta cheese
2 cups shredded Monterey Jack cheese or Monterey Jack cheese with jalapeños (about 8 ounces)

VEGETABLE FILLING

1 tablespoon vegetable oil
1 medium yellow onion, chopped
1 large carrot, pared and thinly sliced crosswise
1 sweet yellow pepper, cut into $3/4$-inch dice
1 small zucchini, halved lengthwise and thinly sliced crosswise
1 large clove garlic, crushed
2 tablespoons chopped fresh cilantro
1 (4-ounce) can whole green chilies, chopped, drained, and patted dry
$3/4$ teaspoon salt
$1/4$ teaspoon freshly ground black pepper

6 ($6 1/4$-inch-diameter) corn tortillas
Cooked white rice

1 • Prepare the Tomato Sauce: In a medium bowl, combine the crushed tomatoes, the 2 tablespoons of cilantro, the chili powder, the cumin, the $1/2$ teaspoon of salt, and the $1/4$ teaspoon of pepper. Stir until all the ingredients are well mixed. Set aside.

2 • Prepare the Cheese Filling: In a blender or food processor, process the ricotta cheese until it is puréed. Pour the ricotta purée into a medium bowl. Reserve $1/2$ cup of the Monterey Jack cheese; add the remaining Monterey Jack cheese to the ricotta. Stir until the cheeses are well blended. Set aside.

3 • Preheat the oven to 425°F. Prepare the Vegetable Filling: In a large, nonstick skillet over medium heat, heat the vegetable oil. Add the yellow onion and sauté about 3 minutes or just until the onion is tender. Stir in the carrot and sauté for 3 minutes more. Stir in the sweet yellow pepper, zucchini, and garlic, and cook about 6 minutes or just until the vegetables are tender. Stir in the 2 tablespoons of cilantro, the green chilies, the $3/4$ teaspoon of salt, and the $1/4$ teaspoon of pepper. Stir gently just until all the ingredients are blended. Remove the skillet from the heat.

4 • Assemble the enchiladas: Spoon $1/4$ cup of the Tomato Sauce over the bottom of a 12 × 8-inch, $2^1/2$-quart baking dish. Dip one tortilla in the remaining sauce to soften it slightly. Spoon a scant $1/3$ cup of the Cheese Filling and then $1/2$ cup of the Vegetable Filling over the tortilla. Roll up the tortilla jelly-roll fashion. Place the filled tortilla, seam side down, on top of the sauce in the baking dish. Repeat with the remaining tortillas, sauce, and fillings. Pour the remaining sauce over the filled tortillas and sprinkle the reserved Monterey Jack over all.

5 • Cover the baking dish with aluminum foil. Bake the enchiladas for 15 minutes. Remove the foil and bake about 3 to 5 minutes more or until the cheese melts. Serve the enchiladas with the cooked rice.

Makes 6 servings. Per serving (without rice): 341 calories, 18 g protein, 24 g carbohydrate, 20 g fat, 54 mg cholesterol, 1,122 mg sodium.

Chili Hands

While cleaning and seeding fresh, canned, or pickled chili peppers, wear rubber gloves. If you don't have rubber gloves available, wash your hands thoroughly with soap and water after working with the chilies. Never touch your hand, even gloved, to your face, or you may wind up with a smarting eye or a burning nose. Remember to wash the gloves after you've finished.

Vegetable Burritos

make ahead

preparation time:
20 minutes

tortilla baking
time:
10 minutes

cooking time:
8 minutes

burrito baking
time:
15 minutes

You can prepare these burritos as early as two days ahead and reheat them in a warm oven or in the microwave—the vegetables will retain their crunchy texture.

8 (7-inch-diameter) flour tortillas
1 medium yellow squash
1 medium zucchini
2 tablespoons vegetable oil
1 small onion, sliced
2 medium cloves garlic, crushed
1 medium carrot, pared and thinly sliced
1 medium sweet green pepper, julienned
1 teaspoon ground cumin
$1/2$ teaspoon dried basil leaves, crushed
$1/2$ teaspoon dried oregano leaves, crushed
$1/2$ teaspoon salt
2 plum tomatoes, seeded and chopped
$1/2$ cup sliced, pitted canned black olives
1 (1-pound) can refried beans
2 cups shredded Monterey Jack cheese (about 8 ounces)
Prepared salsa, sour cream, avocado slices, and sliced black olives
  (optional)

1 • Preheat the oven to 425°F. Wrap the tortillas in aluminum foil. Bake the tortillas about 10 minutes or until they are warm.

2 • Meanwhile, cut the yellow squash and zucchini in half lengthwise; cut each half crosswise into $1/4$-inch-thick slices. In a large skillet over medium heat, heat the vegetable oil. Add the onion and garlic, and sauté about 3 minutes or until the onion is tender. Add the yellow squash, zucchini, carrot, sweet green pepper, cumin, basil, oregano, and salt. Increase the heat to high; cook the mixture, stirring, for 3 minutes. Add the plum tomatoes and cook for 1 minute. Stir in the olives.

3 • Assemble the burritos: Working with one tortilla at a time (keep remaining tortillas covered), spread one half of each tortilla with 3 tablespoons of the refried beans. Top with $1/2$ cup of the vegetable mixture and sprinkle with $1/4$ cup of the Monterey Jack cheese. Roll up the tortilla jelly-roll fashion. Place the rolled tortillas, seam side down, in a

$13 \times 9 \times 2$-inch baking pan. Cover the baking pan with aluminum foil and bake for 15 minutes. If desired, serve the burritos with salsa, sour cream, avocado slices, and sliced black olives.

> *Makes 4 servings. Per serving: 662 calories, 28 g protein, 71 g carbohydrate, 32 g fat, 50 mg cholesterol, 1,428 mg sodium.*

Vegetables Stuffed with Cheese and Olives

Serve these home-style stuffed vegetables for a weekend lunch or a weekday supper. The vegetables can be stuffed earlier in the day and refrigerated. Allow a little extra baking time if transferring the veggies directly from the refrigerator to the oven.

2 (12-ounce) Spanish onions
2 large sweet red peppers
2 medium zucchini
2 tablespoons olive oil
$\frac{1}{2}$ cup uncooked orzo (rice-shaped pasta)
1 cup chicken broth
$1\frac{1}{2}$ cups shredded mozzarella cheese (about 6 ounces)
$\frac{1}{2}$ cup sun-dried tomatoes, chopped
$\frac{1}{2}$ cup calamata olives, pitted and chopped
$\frac{1}{2}$ cup chopped parsley
1 teaspoon dried oregano leaves, crushed
$\frac{1}{4}$ teaspoon freshly ground black pepper
$\frac{1}{4}$ cup fine, dry, seasoned bread crumbs
2 tablespoons grated Parmesan cheese

make ahead

preparation time:
25 minutes

cooking time:
18 minutes

baking time:
45 minutes

1 • Cut off and reserve one $\frac{1}{4}$-inch-thick slice from the stem end of each Spanish onion and sweet red pepper, and from one long side of each zucchini. With a melon-ball scoop, hollow out the vegetables, leaving a $\frac{1}{2}$-inch-thick shell on the onions, removing the seeds from the sweet red peppers, and leaving a $\frac{1}{4}$-inch-thick shell on the zucchini. Chop enough of the reserved tops and scooped-out insides of the onions to measure $1\frac{1}{2}$ cups. Chop the trimmings from the sweet peppers and zucchini.

2 • In a large saucepan of boiling water, cook the vegetable shells for 5 minutes. Drain the vegetable shells and let them cool slightly. Pat the shells dry with paper towels.

3 • In a large skillet over medium-high heat, cook 1 tablespoon of the olive oil until it is hot. Add the chopped onion, sweet red pepper, and zucchini, and sauté until the vegetables are tender-crisp, about 5 minutes. Stir in the orzo. Reduce the heat to medium and sauté for 1 minute. Stir in ³/₄ cup of the chicken broth. Bring the mixture to boiling. Lower the heat, cover the skillet, and simmer the mixture about 10 minutes, stirring occasionally, until the liquid is absorbed and the orzo is cooked. Remove the skillet from the heat. Add the mozzarella cheese, sun-dried tomatoes, calamata olives, parsley, oregano, and pepper, and stir until well mixed. Spoon the mixture into the onion, sweet red pepper, and zucchini shells, mounding the mixture slightly.

4 • Preheat the oven to 350°F. Place the stuffed vegetables in a 13 × 9 × 2-inch baking dish. Add the remaining chicken broth to the baking dish. In a cup, with a fork, mix the bread crumbs with the Parmesan cheese and the remaining 1 tablespoon of olive oil; sprinkle the bread-crumb mixture over the top of the filling in the vegetable shells. Bake about 45 minutes or until the vegetables are tender and the topping is browned. Cool the stuffed vegetables slightly before serving.

> *Makes 6 servings. Per serving: 224 calories, 10 g protein, 20 g carbohydrate, 12 g fat, 24 mg cholesterol, 251 mg sodium.*

Tomatoes: A Global Love Affair

Christopher Columbus may be best known for "discovering America," but his greatest contribution might well be his assistance in popularizing the tomato. Introduced to the Spanish explorers by the Aztecs and Mayans, tomatoes were brought back to Europe in the 1500s, where they caused quite a stir. Botanists of the time accused them of being poisonous, while other, more enlightened souls considered the juicy red vegetables aphrodisiacs. Once their edibility was confirmed, the popularity of tomatoes skyrocketed.

Today, tomatoes are grown all over the world. Look for those grown locally, because tomatoes are most flavorful just after they've been picked. To keep tomatoes tasting their freshest, never refrigerate them, and always store them in the same position in which they grow — stem-side up.

Brie Custard
and Vegetable Tart

~

A luscious combination of flavorful Brie cheese, eggplant, leeks, and roasted red pepper, baked in a tender pastry crust. Serve this as a special light supper or for a weekend brunch. The tart can be made ahead and served warm or at room temperature.

PASTRY

1 cup all-purpose flour
1/2 teaspoon salt
6 tablespoons butter, cut into bits
2 to 3 tablespoons ice water

VEGETABLES

1/2 eggplant, cut into 1/2-inch pieces
1 tablespoon coarse (kosher) salt
2 tablespoons olive oil
2 large leeks (white part only), sliced crosswise and rinsed well
2 cloves garlic, minced
1 large sweet red pepper, roasted, skinned, and sliced into strips

CUSTARD

4 ounces Brie cheese
1/2 cup freshly grated Parmesan cheese
1 cup milk
2 large eggs, lightly beaten
2 tablespoons all-purpose flour
1/8 teaspoon freshly ground black pepper
1/4 cup snipped fresh chives
3 to 4 whole fresh chives for garnish

❧ ❧ ❧
make ahead
preparation time: 50 minutes
crust baking time: 17 minutes
cooking time: 14 minutes
tart baking time: 30 minutes
❧ ❧ ❧

1 • Preheat the oven to 400°F. Prepare the Pastry: In a food processor, combine the 1 cup of flour, salt, and butter. Using a pulse motion, process until the mixture resembles coarse crumbs. With the motor running, add the ice water, 1 tablespoon at a time, through the feed tube. Process just until the pastry dough holds together.

2 • Turn out the pastry dough onto a lightly floured work surface. Gently pat the dough into a disk. With a lightly floured rolling pin, roll the dough disk into a 14-inch-diameter round. Gently lift the dough round and place it into an 11-inch tart pan with a removable bottom. Freeze the pastry for 10 minutes. Place a sheet of aluminum foil over the pastry and press gently to fit. With a fork, prick the pastry through the foil in several places. Bake the pastry shell for 12 minutes. Remove the foil and bake the shell about 5 minutes more or until the pastry is lightly browned. Cool the pastry shell completely on a wire rack. Reduce the oven heat to 350°F.

3 • Meanwhile, prepare the Vegetables: Place the eggplant pieces in a colander set over a plate. Sprinkle the coarse salt over the eggplant and let it stand for 10 minutes. Rinse the eggplant well and pat dry with paper towels. In a large nonstick skillet over medium-high heat, heat the olive oil. Add the leeks and sauté for 5 minutes. Add the eggplant pieces and sauté about 6 minutes or until the eggplant is tender. Stir in the garlic and roasted red pepper strips, and sauté for 2 minutes. Arrange the Vegetables over the bottom of the prepared pastry shell.

4 • Prepare the Custard: Remove and discard the rind from the Brie cheese. Cut the Brie into pieces. Place the Brie pieces and the Parmesan cheese in a food processor. Using the pulse motion, process just until the Brie is finely chopped. With the motor running, add the milk, eggs, the 2 tablespoons of flour, and the pepper through the feed tube. Process until the mixture is blended. Stir in the snipped chives.

5 • Pour the custard mixture over the Vegetables in the prepared pastry shell. Arrange the whole chives over the top of the Custard. Bake the tart about 30 minutes or until the Custard is set; do not overbake. Cool the tart slightly before serving; serve warm or at room temperature.

Makes 6 main-course or 12 appetizer servings. Per main-course serving: 368 calories, 14 g protein, 28 g carbohydrate, 23 g fat, 133 mg cholesterol, 617 mg sodium.

Chapter Six

Chicken and Turkey

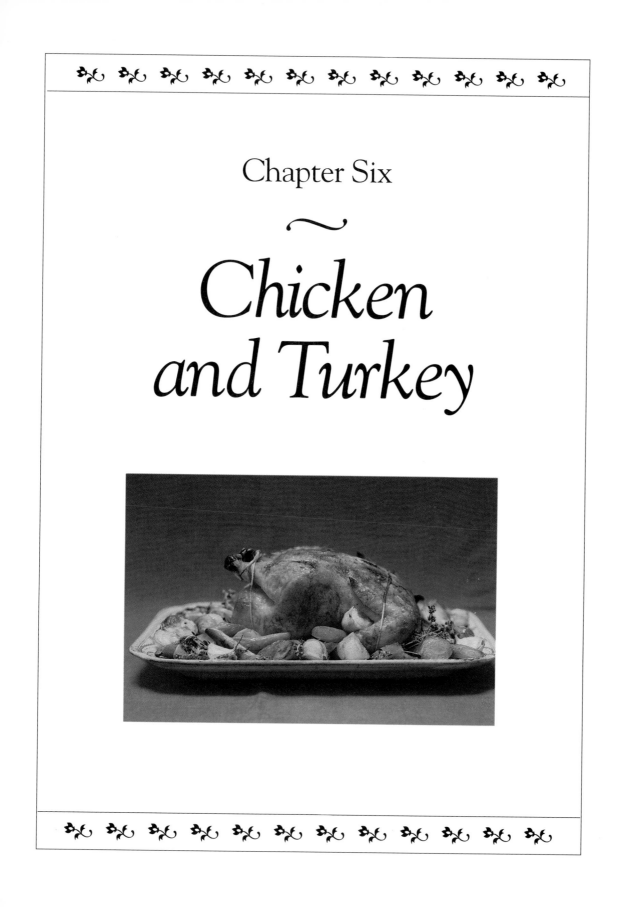

W̲e all know that chicken is versatile, nutritious, relatively inexpensive — and a one-dish meal that includes chicken is guaranteed to be satisfying.

First, a quick review of the basics. Nutritionally, a 3½-ounce serving of broiled chicken provides about 52 percent of the average adult daily requirement of protein, but at one-half to two-thirds less fat than other meats. And as we all know, if you remove the skin, you remove even more fat.

We've selected recipes that take advantage of readily available chicken parts and give you a sampling of different cuisines, such as a whole chicken cut up for Tunisian Orange Chicken (page 163); chicken breasts for Chicken Cacciatore Pie (page 176); and chicken thighs for Paella with Chicken Thighs (page 184).

Leftover chicken, especially from a whole bird, is very much at home in casseroles such as our Chicken Pot Pies (page 193), or in a quick-to-fix Southwest specialty, Chicken and Black Bean Tostadas (page 187). Remember, whole chicken usually runs about six to ten cents less per pound than packaged chicken parts. To make your life even simpler, whenever you serve a whole bird, freeze the leftovers so you always have some on hand for quick-to-fix dinners anytime.

Our selection of turkey recipes uses turkey breast, turkey sausage, and that post-holiday special, leftover turkey, and gives a new taste twist to some familiar dishes.

Whole Roasted Chicken with Roasted Root Vegetables

~

Our recipe for oven-roasted chicken (shown on page 157), baked with carrots, parsnips, potatoes, and shallots, is a surprisingly easy — and economical — way to enjoy the whole bird.

1 (3½- to 4-pound) roasting chicken, giblets removed
1 lemon, cut into 8 wedges
14 sprigs fresh thyme
1 bay leaf
4 tablespoons unsalted butter
³/4 teaspoon salt
¹/2 teaspoon freshly ground pepper
8 large carrots, trimmed, pared, halved, and cut into 2-inch lengths
1 pound small red potatoes
2 large turnips, trimmed, pared, and cut into 1-inch chunks
4 small parsnips, pared and cut into 2-inch lengths
4 whole large shallots, peeled
1 whole head garlic (about 4 ounces), cloves separated but left unpeeled
2 tablespoons olive oil
¹/4 cup minced fresh parsley

preparation time:
20 minutes

baking time:
1¹/4 hours

1 • Preheat the oven to 400°F. Tie the wings to the chicken breast with kitchen string. Place the lemon wedges, 10 of the thyme sprigs, the bay leaf, and 2 tablespoons of the butter in the cavity. Tie the legs together and then to the breast with kitchen string. Place the trussed chicken on a rack in a shallow roasting pan. Slice the remaining butter and place the pieces over the breast. Sprinkle the chicken with about half of the salt and pepper.

2 • In a large bowl, combine the carrots, red potatoes, turnips, parsnips, shallots, and whole garlic cloves. Add the olive oil, the remaining 4 thyme sprigs, and the remaining salt and pepper. Toss to coat the vegetables with the oil and seasonings. Arrange the oil-coated vegetables under the roasting rack and around the chicken.

3 • Roast the chicken for 1 hour and 15 minutes or just until the chicken is cooked through and the juices of the thigh run clear when pierced with a fork. Baste the chicken with the pan juices and toss vegetables frequently during the cooking time.

4 • Transfer the chicken to a serving platter and let it stand for 10 minutes before carving. Sprinkle the vegetables with 2 tablespoons of the parsley and toss to distribute the parsley evenly. Place the vegetables around the chicken on the platter. Sprinkle the chicken and vegetables with the remaining parsley.

Makes 6 servings. Per serving: 502 calories, 40 g protein, 48 g carbohydrate, 18 g fat, 132 mg cholesterol, 227 mg sodium.

Four Steps to Safer Chicken

Low in fat and calories, chicken has become the "health food" of choice for many Americans. But because it may carry the bacteria that causes food poisoning, follow these simple but vital rules when preparing, cooking, and storing chicken.

- Handle with care. Using hot, soapy water, thoroughly wash your hands and all surfaces that have come into contact with raw chicken after each step of preparation.

- Store safely. Refrigerate chicken as soon as you bring it home, and store it in the coldest part of the refrigerator. If you won't be cooking the chicken within two days, freeze it. Never defrost chicken at room temperature — it's the ideal breeding ground for bacteria. Thaw chicken on a plate in the refrigerator overnight or in a microwave oven following the manufacturer's instructions.

- Cook thoroughly. Chicken should be cooked until it is no longer pink. Using an instant-read meat thermometer, cook chicken parts with bones to 180°F and boneless parts to 160°F. Remember to wash the thermometer in warm soapy water after use.

- Don't leave leftovers out. Refrigerate leftover parts of chicken within two hours of eating and don't let cooked chicken sit in the refrigerator for more than three days. Thoroughly reheat leftover chicken before serving.

Chicken with Pear and Apple

Chicken with Pear and Apple

Pears, apples, and apple brandy combine to create a sensuous sauce for this chicken dish. Our secret ingredient, vanilla, enhances the flavor of the fruit. Serve with white or basmati rice for soaking up the delicious sauce.

2 tablespoons olive oil
1 broiler-fryer chicken (about 3 pounds), cut into 8 pieces
2 ripe firm pears, pared, cored, and cut into $^{1}/_{2}$-inch wedges
1 Granny Smith apple, pared, cored, and cut into $^{1}/_{2}$-inch wedges
2 tablespoons butter or margarine
2 celery stalks, cut into 1-inch pieces
1 large onion, cut into wedges
1 cup chicken broth
$^{1}/_{3}$ cup apple brandy
2 tablespoons sugar
$^{1}/_{2}$ cup heavy cream
$^{1}/_{2}$ teaspoon vanilla extract
$^{1}/_{3}$ cup chopped hazelnuts, toasted

preparation time:
15 minutes

cooking time:
45 minutes

1 • In a large skillet over medium-high heat, heat the olive oil. Working in batches, cook the chicken pieces until they are browned on all sides, about 15 minutes. Remove the chicken pieces to a plate.

2 • In the drippings left in the skillet, sauté the pear and apple wedges for 3 minutes. With a slotted spoon, remove the pear and apple wedges to a small bowl.

3 • Add the butter or margarine to the drippings in the skillet. When the butter has melted, add the celery and onion, and sauté for 5 minutes. Return the chicken pieces to the skillet. Add the chicken broth and the apple brandy. Bring the mixture to boiling. Lower the heat, cover the skillet, and simmer for 20 minutes. Add the pear and apple wedges with any juices that have accumulated in the bowl. Heat the mixture through.

4 • Transfer the chicken, vegetables, and fruit to a large serving platter, and keep warm. Stir the sugar and heavy cream into the liquid remaining in the skillet. Bring the liquid to boiling; cook, uncovered, about 3 minutes or until the liquid has thickened. Remove the skillet from the heat and stir in the vanilla. Spoon the sauce over the chicken, fruit, and vegetables. Sprinkle the chopped hazelnuts over all.

Makes 4 servings. Per serving: 731 calories, 51 g protein, 36 g carbohydrate, 41 g fat, 197 mg cholesterol, 393 mg sodium.

Chicken Nutrition Facts

- A 3-ounce serving of roast chicken provides about 180 calories while supplying about half of the recommended daily allowance of protein.

- Removing the skin before cooking chicken lowers the amount of fat by half.

- Dark meat chicken contains about twice as much fat per serving as white meat.

- The amount of cholesterol in chicken meat is about 70 to 80 mg per 3-ounce serving, regardless of whether the meat is dark or white.

Tunisian Orange Chicken

$\sim$

Couscous makes a speedy — and sensational — side dish: just pour hot water over the grain and let it stand briefly.

2 tablespoons safflower oil
1 (3-pound) chicken, cut into 8 pieces
1 large onion, cut crosswise into $^1/_4$-inch-thick slices, separated into rings
1 cup sliced celery
1 small clove garlic, crushed
$1^1/_2$ tablespoons all-purpose flour
$^1/_2$ teaspoon sugar
1 tablespoon ground cumin
2 teaspoons paprika
1 teaspoon salt
$^1/_4$ teaspoon freshly ground black pepper
$^1/_4$ teaspoon ground hot red pepper
1 large tomato, chopped
1 cup orange juice
2 large navel oranges, peeled and cut crosswise into $^1/_2$-inch-thick slices
$^1/_2$ cup small black olives
4 servings hot, cooked couscous

low-fat

preparation time:
15 minutes

cooking time:
1 hour

1 • In a Dutch oven or large, deep skillet, over medium-high heat, heat the safflower oil until it is hot. Working in batches, cook the chicken pieces until they are browned on all sides, about 15 minutes. Transfer the chicken pieces to a platter.

2 • Spoon off all but 2 tablespoons of the drippings remaining in the pan. To the hot drippings, add the onion, celery, and garlic; sauté the mixture about 5 minutes or until the vegetables are tender. Stir in the flour, sugar, cumin, paprika, salt, black pepper, and hot red pepper until the mixture is blended. Add the tomato. Gradually stir in the orange juice. Bring the mixture to boiling, stirring constantly; boil for 2 minutes, stirring.

3 • Reduce the heat and return the chicken pieces to the pan. Cover the pan and simmer until the chicken is tender, about 30 minutes, turning the chicken pieces once. Add the orange slices and the olives. Simmer, uncovered, for 5 minutes more. Spoon off any visible fat from the surface of the sauce. Serve the chicken with the couscous.

Makes 4 servings. Per serving (without couscous): 578 calories, 75 g protein, 24 g carbohydrate, 19 g fat, 239 mg cholesterol, 926 mg sodium.

Chicken and Cheese Mole Burritos

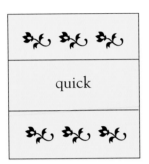

quick

Mole (pronounced "moe-lay"), a savory Mexican sauce, contains unsweetened chocolate. Serve with a cold vegetable salad.

MOLE SAUCE

3 dried ancho chilies, cored and seeded
1 tablespoon sesame seeds
$1/2$ teaspoon ground coriander
$1/2$ teaspoon ground cumin
$1/2$ teaspoon dried oregano leaves, crumbled
$1/2$ teaspoon salt
$1/4$ teaspoon ground cinnamon
$1/4$ teaspoon fennel seeds
$1/4$ teaspoon crushed red-pepper flakes
1 tablespoon vegetable oil
$1/2$ cup chopped onion
2 medium cloves garlic, minced
1 (8-ounce) can tomato sauce
1 tablespoon raisins
$1/2$ ounce ($1/2$ square) unsweetened chocolate
2 tablespoons creamy peanut butter
$3/4$ cup chicken broth

1 deli-roasted chicken (3 pounds), bones and skin discarded, and
    meat shredded ($3 1/2$ cups meat)
1 (16-ounce) package flour tortillas
1 tablespoon vegetable oil
1 Spanish onion, halved and sliced
1 sweet yellow pepper, cored, seeded, and julienned
$1/2$ teaspoon salt
$1/2$ teaspoon ground black pepper
6 ounces queso blanco or Monterey Jack cheese, shredded ($1 1/2$ cups)

1 • Make the Mole Sauce: In a small bowl, combine the chilies with enough hot water to cover. Set aside.

2 • In a medium skillet, over medium heat, toast the sesame seeds for 3 minutes or until golden, shaking the pan frequently. Add the coriander, cumin, oregano, salt, cinnamon, fennel seeds, red-pepper flakes, and 1 tablespoon of the oil; sauté until hot. Add the onion and garlic; sauté for 5 minutes or until the onion is softened.

3 • Drain the chilies; add the chilies to the sesame mixture. Add the tomato sauce, raisins, chocolate, and peanut butter; sauté for 3 to 5 minutes or until the chocolate and peanut butter melt and the sauce is smooth and thick. Place in a food processor; purée. Return to the skillet; add the chicken broth. Over low heat, mix until smooth and hot.

4 • Add the chicken; heat through.

5 • Preheat the oven to 300°F. Wrap the tortillas in aluminum foil. Heat them in the oven until warm.

6 • In a large skillet, heat the 1 tablespoon of oil over medium-high heat. Add the onion and sweet yellow pepper; sauté for 5 minutes or until the vegetables begin to brown and are soft. Sprinkle with the ½ teaspoon salt and the black pepper.

7 • To serve: In separate serving bowls, place the chicken mole, onion mixture, and cheese. Unwrap the tortillas and place on a serving plate. Let each person make his or her own burritos, wrapping some chicken mole, onion mixture, and cheese in each tortilla.

> *Makes 6 servings. Per serving: 611 calories, 39 g protein, 56 g carbohydrate, 28 g fat, 93 mg cholesterol, 1,206 mg sodium.*

Chicken and Cheese Mole Burritos

Chicken and Rice Casserole

low-fat

preparation time:
15 minutes

cooking time:
55 minutes

*S*hown on our cover, this wonderful one-dish meal is just as tasty reheated.

1 chicken (3 pounds), cut up and skinned
1¹/₂ teaspoons dried thyme leaves, crumbled
1 teaspoon paprika
1¹/₄ teaspoons salt
¹/₂ teaspoon ground black pepper
2 tablespoons vegetable oil
1 pound yellow onions, halved and sliced
2 carrots, halved lengthwise and sliced
2 tablespoons minced fresh gingerroot
4 large cloves garlic, minced
³/₄ pound shiitake or regular mushrooms, stemmed and quartered
¹/₂ pound green beans, trimmed
1 sweet red pepper, cored, seeded, and diced
1 cup frozen green peas
3 cups chicken broth
1¹/₂ cups jasmine rice or regular white rice

1 • Preheat the oven to 375°F. Place chicken pieces in a large bowl.

2 • In a small bowl, combine the thyme, paprika, ¹/₂ teaspoon of the salt, and ¹/₄ teaspoon of the black pepper. Sprinkle the thyme mixture over the chicken; turn to coat.

3 • In a large Dutch oven, heat the oil over medium-high heat. Add the chicken in batches and brown, 3 to 4 minutes each batch; remove the chicken to a plate after browning. To the drippings in the pan, add the onions and carrots and sauté for 1 minute. Add the ginger, garlic, mushrooms, green beans, sweet red pepper, peas, chicken broth, jasmine rice or regular rice, and the remaining salt and black pepper. Top with the chicken. Cover.

4 • Bake the chicken for 35 to 40 minutes or until the chicken and rice are cooked and the liquid is absorbed.

Makes 6 servings. Per serving: 561 calories, 48 g protein, 57 g carbohydrate, 16 g fat, 113 mg cholesterol, 973 mg sodium.

Chicken and Rice Casserole

Chicken in Tomato-Vinegar Sauce

Garlic and rosemary enhance the marinara sauce, made slightly tart by the addition of red-wine vinegar. The flavor of this dish improves if it is made a day or two ahead.

1 tablespoon olive oil
4 large whole chicken breasts on the bone (1 pound), split
3 celery stalks, cut into 2-inch pieces
4 medium cloves garlic, crushed
1/2 pound medium mushrooms, quartered
1 medium yellow squash, cut crosswise into 3/4-inch pieces
1 (15-ounce) container marinara sauce
1 1/2 teaspoons chopped fresh rosemary leaves or 1/2 teaspoon dried rosemary
1/4 teaspoon freshly ground pepper
1/4 teaspoon salt
2 teaspoons red-wine vinegar
Fresh rosemary sprigs (optional)

1 • In a large, deep skillet over medium-high heat, heat the olive oil until it is hot. Add half of the chicken breasts and cook until they are browned on all sides. Transfer the cooked chicken to a plate and keep warm. In the hot drippings remaining in the skillet, brown the remaining chicken breasts. Spoon off and discard half of the drippings remaining in the skillet.

2 • To the hot drippings in the skillet, add the celery, garlic, mushrooms, and yellow squash. Sauté about 5 minutes or until the vegetables are tender-crisp. Stir in the marinara sauce, rosemary, pepper, and salt. Bring the sauce mixture to boiling.

3 • Return the chicken breasts to the skillet, skin side down. Lower the heat, cover the skillet, and simmer for 20 minutes, stirring occasionally. Turn over the chicken breasts and stir in the red-wine vinegar. Cook, covered, about 20 minutes more or until the chicken is tender. Spoon off and discard any visible fat from the surface of the sauce. If desired, garnish the chicken with fresh rosemary sprigs.

Makes 8 servings. Per serving: 439 calories, 49 g protein, 7 g carbohydrate, 23 g fat, 144 mg cholesterol, 545 mg sodium.

make ahead

preparation time:
15 minutes

cooking time:
60 minutes

Sensible Saucing

Don't cover grilled or broiled chicken with a heavy cream sauce. Instead, top the chicken with a low-calorie salsa — only about 5 calories per tablespoon, with no cholesterol or fat.

Herbed Chicken with Mozzarella

Herbed Chicken with Mozzarella

In our variation of a favorite recipe, Chicken Parmesan, the chicken is lightly dusted with flour and sautéed in olive oil. The meltable topping is part-skim mozzarella cheese. Plus, this entire dish is ready in less than 25 minutes! Serve with a broccoli salad.

quick

3 tablespoons extra-virgin olive oil
2 tablespoons chicken broth
1 small onion, finely chopped
2 cloves garlic, minced
1 cup crushed Italian tomatoes
1 tablespoon minced fresh basil, plus extra for garnish
1 teaspoon minced fresh oregano
$\frac{1}{2}$ teaspoon salt
$\frac{1}{8}$ teaspoon crushed red-pepper flakes
$\frac{1}{4}$ cup all-purpose flour
4 boneless, skinless chicken breast halves (about 1 pound)
4 slices part-skim mozzarella cheese (about 2 ounces)

1 • In a medium saucepan over medium heat, heat 1 tablespoon of the olive oil and the chicken broth. Add the onion and cook for 3 minutes. Add the garlic and cook for 1 minute. Add the Italian tomatoes, 1 tablespoon of the basil, the oregano, salt, and red-pepper flakes, and cook for 5 minutes, stirring occasionally. Keep the sauce warm.

2 • Place the flour in a plastic food-storage bag. Add the chicken breasts and shake to coat the chicken with the flour.

3 • In a large nonstick skillet over medium-high heat, heat the remaining 2 tablespoons of olive oil. Add the chicken breasts and cook for 4 minutes on one side. Turn over the chicken and cook for 2 minutes more. Place one slice of the mozzarella cheese on each chicken breast. Cover the skillet and cook about 2 to 3 minutes more or until the chicken is cooked through.

4 • To serve: Spoon the warm sauce over a serving platter. Arrange the chicken breasts, cheese side up, over the sauce. Sprinkle additional minced basil over all.

Makes 4 servings. Per serving: 345 calories, 34 g protein, 20 g carbohydrate, 15 g fat, 76 mg cholesterol, 476 mg sodium.

Chicken Manchamantel

The name of this dish translates as "tablecloth stainer" because of the dark chili peppers used in the classic Mexican version. Serve with warm tortillas or rice.

make ahead

preparation time:
15 minutes

cooking time:
2¼ hours

¹/₃ cup whole almonds, chopped
2 teaspoons sesame seeds
1¹/₂ teaspoons salt
1 teaspoon ground cinnamon
¹/₂ teaspoon ground cloves
¹/₂ teaspoon ground cumin
2 tablespoons vegetable oil
3 pounds chicken breast halves, on bone
1¹/₂ pounds boneless pork shoulder, cut into 1¹/₂-inch pieces

3 medium jalapeño peppers, seeded and finely chopped
2 large cloves garlic, crushed
1 (28-ounce) can whole tomatoes in purée
1 large plantain, peeled and sliced crosswise into $1/2$-inch pieces
2 cups fresh pineapple cubes
1 medium jícama (about $3/4$ pound), pared and cut into 2 × $1/2$-inch slices
1 large sweet green or red pepper, chopped

1 • In a Dutch oven over medium heat, roast the almonds, sesame seeds, salt, cinnamon, cloves, and cumin about 1 to 2 minutes or until the mixture is fragrant and the nuts and seeds are slightly browned. Transfer the almond mixture to a small bowl.

2 • In the same pan over medium-high heat, heat the vegetable oil. Working in batches, cook the chicken breasts until they are browned on all sides, about 8 minutes. With tongs, transfer the chicken to a large bowl. In the hot drippings remaining in the pan, cook the pork until it is browned on all sides, about 8 minutes. Transfer the pork to the bowl with the chicken.

3 • In the drippings remaining in the pan, sauté the jalapeño peppers and the garlic for 1 minute. Stir in the almond mixture and the tomatoes with their purée. Bring the mixture to boiling. Add the chicken and pork, and any juices that have accumulated in the large bowl. Stir in the plantain. Reduce the heat, cover the pan, and simmer for 45 minutes. Stir in the pineapple cubes, jícama, and sweet green or red pepper. Simmer, covered, until all the meats and the vegetables are tender, about 15 minutes.

> Makes 6 servings. Per serving: 644 calories, 69 g protein, 34 g carbohydrate, 26 g fat, 192 mg cholesterol, 1,050 mg sodium.

Plantains

A plantain is a large, tough, firm relative of the banana that must be cooked before it is eaten. Plantains have a thick skin that must be peeled or cut away. The fruit itself has a different flavor at every stage of ripeness. When the skin is green, the plaintain is hard and starchy and can be cooked like a potato. Yellow-ripe plantains, once cooked, have a creamy texture and a banana aroma. They can be used in soups, stews, and casseroles, and are delicious grilled. When cooked, the black, overripe plantains are the most flavorful — wonderfully sweet with a taste approaching the banana. Often fried, roasted, or sautéed, the fruit is used in many Latin American dishes.

Chicken Milanese with Arugula Salad

This updated version of an Italian classic can be made in less than 15 minutes and features an intriguing mixture of breaded chicken cutlets and garden-fresh vegetables.

DRESSING

3 tablespoons olive oil
1 tablespoon balsamic vinegar
1 teaspoon Dijon mustard
1 large clove garlic, minced
1/4 teaspoon freshly ground pepper
1/4 teaspoon salt

1/2 large red onion, thinly sliced
1 large tomato, cut into 3/4-inch dice
8 cups arugula leaves (about 2 bunches), torn into 2-inch pieces
1/2 cup all-purpose flour
2 large eggs, lightly beaten
2 cups coarse fresh bread crumbs
4 boneless, skinless chicken breast halves (about 1 pound), pounded slightly
3 tablespoons olive oil

1 • Prepare the Dressing: In a small jar with a tight-fitting lid, combine the 3 tablespoons of olive oil, the balsamic vinegar, Dijon mustard, garlic, pepper, and salt. Cover the jar and shake it until the Dressing is blended.

2 • In a large bowl, combine the red onion and tomato. Pour the Dressing over the tomato mixture and toss to coat the vegetables with the Dressing. Place the arugula over the tomato mixture. Cover the bowl with plastic wrap and refrigerate the mixture until it is well chilled.

3 • Just before serving, place the flour in a shallow pie plate. Place the eggs in a second plate and the bread crumbs in a third. One at a time, dip the chicken breasts into the flour until completely coated, then into the eggs, and finally into the bread crumbs, shaking off the excess after each dipping.

---

quick

Overcooked Chicken?

The thickness of your skillet and the type of stove you use will influence how quickly your boneless chicken breast cooks. For that reason you need to begin testing chicken for doneness about 3 minutes before the recommended cooking time is up. (If a range is given, start checking at the shortest time.) A perfectly cooked chicken breast should feel springy to the touch and no longer be pink on the inside.

4 • In a 12-inch nonstick skillet over medium heat, heat 2 tablespoons of the olive oil. Working in batches, add the coated chicken breasts to the skillet and cook about 3 to 4 minutes on each side or until the chicken is cooked through, adding the remaining oil as needed.

5 • To serve: Place 1 cooked chicken breast on each of 4 dinner plates. Toss the arugula mixture until all of the ingredients are coated with the Dressing. Place some of the salad on top of the chicken on each plate.

Makes 4 servings. Per serving: 472 calories, 28 g protein, 29 g carbohydrate, 27 g fat, 3 mg cholesterol, 353 mg sodium.

Low-Fat Coating

If you're covering chicken with a crumb coating, use just the egg whites as the "glue" — you'll save 58 calories and 5 grams of fat per egg.

Chicken Milanese with Arugula Salad

Chicken with Oranges, Leeks, and Olives

Chicken with Oranges, Leeks, and Olives

~

low-fat

quick

Citrus fruits are at their peak during the winter months — they taste sweeter and fresher because they're in season, and they're less expensive than at any other time. Serve with a little rice or orzo on the side, if you like.

2 tablespoons all-purpose flour
3 teaspoons grated orange zest (colored part of peel)
1 teaspoon salt
4 boneless, skinless chicken breast halves (about 1 pound)
2 tablespoons olive oil
4 leeks, sliced and rinsed well (about 2 cups)
1 teaspoon ground cumin
$\frac{1}{4}$ teaspoon crushed red-pepper flakes
2 medium tomatoes, chopped
$\frac{1}{2}$ cup chicken broth
2 medium oranges, peeled, sliced, and pitted, white pith removed
$\frac{1}{3}$ cup niçoise olives, pitted

1 • In a shallow pie plate, combine the flour, 2 teaspoons of the orange zest, and ½ teaspoon of the salt. Dip each chicken breast half into the flour mixture until the chicken is completely coated; shake off the excess mixture.

2 • In a large skillet over medium-high heat, heat the olive oil. Add the chicken breasts and sauté about 5 minutes on each side or until the chicken is just cooked through. Transfer the chicken to a serving platter and keep warm.

3 • In the drippings remaining in the skillet, sauté the leeks, cumin, red-pepper flakes, and the remaining salt about 4 minutes or until the leeks are softened. Add the tomatoes, chicken broth, and the remaining 1 teaspoon of orange zest. Simmer the mixture for 5 minutes. Stir in the orange slices and niçoise olives, and heat the mixture through. Pour the mixture over the chicken.

Makes 4 servings. Per serving: 321 calories, 36 g protein, 22 g carbohydrate, 10 g fat, 82 mg cholesterol, 830 mg sodium.

Niçoise Olives

Grown in France, these small black olives are cured in brine before being packed in oil or vinegar. Extraordinary for eating as an hors d'oeuvre, niçoise olives are also marvelous in salads and in chicken and fish dishes.

A Basic Guide to Rice

Move over pasta: Rice is the hot "new" dish of the nineties. Easy to prepare, inexpensive, and incredibly versatile, this ancient grain is also a dream food for dieters: It's low in calories and virtually fat-free. And now even the most exotic varieties of rice are available in supermarkets and specialty shops. There's basmati (with a nutty flavor and aroma that's perfect for pilafs), jasmine (its grains work well in warm rice salad), Arborio (the rice of choice for risotto), wehani (reddish brown, chewy, and wonderful tossed with a little butter), and rizcous (quick-cooking and great stirred into soups), to name just a few.

Chicken Cacciatore Pie

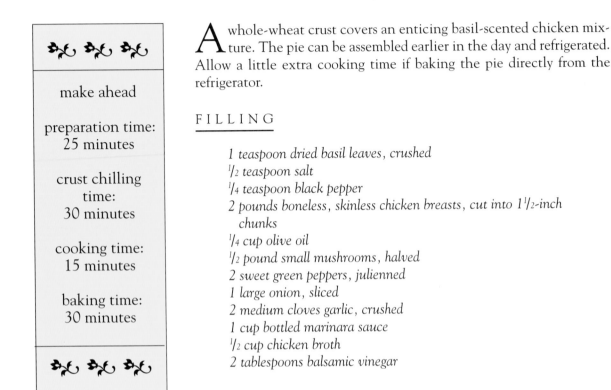

A whole-wheat crust covers an enticing basil-scented chicken mixture. The pie can be assembled earlier in the day and refrigerated. Allow a little extra cooking time if baking the pie directly from the refrigerator.

FILLING

- 1 teaspoon dried basil leaves, crushed
- 1/2 teaspoon salt
- 1/4 teaspoon black pepper
- 2 pounds boneless, skinless chicken breasts, cut into 1 1/2-inch chunks
- 1/4 cup olive oil
- 1/2 pound small mushrooms, halved
- 2 sweet green peppers, julienned
- 1 large onion, sliced
- 2 medium cloves garlic, crushed
- 1 cup bottled marinara sauce
- 1/2 cup chicken broth
- 2 tablespoons balsamic vinegar

PASTRY

- 1/2 cup all-purpose flour
- 1/2 cup whole-wheat flour
- 1/2 teaspoon salt
- 1/3 cup lard or solid vegetable shortening
- 2 to 3 tablespoons ice water

1 • Prepare the Filling: In a medium bowl, combine the basil, the 1/2 teaspoon of salt, and the black pepper. Add the chicken chunks and toss to coat them with the basil mixture. In a large skillet over medium-high heat, heat the olive oil. Add the chicken and sauté about 5 minutes or until the chicken is golden on all sides. With a slotted spoon, transfer the chicken to a small bowl.

make ahead

preparation time:
25 minutes

crust chilling
time:
30 minutes

cooking time:
15 minutes

baking time:
30 minutes

2 • In the drippings remaining in the skillet, sauté the mushrooms, sweet green peppers, onion, and garlic until the vegetables are tender-crisp, 4 to 5 minutes. Return the chicken to the skillet. Stir in the marinara sauce, chicken broth, and balsamic vinegar until all the ingredients are combined. Bring the mixture to boiling. Lower the heat and simmer for 10 minutes. Spoon the Filling into a deep, 2½-quart casserole dish. Set aside to cool slightly.

3 • Meanwhile, prepare the Pastry: In a medium bowl, combine the all-purpose and whole-wheat flours and the ½ teaspoon of salt. With a pastry blender or 2 knives, cut in the lard or shortening until the mixture resembles coarse crumbs. Sprinkle the ice water, 1 tablespoon at a time, over the flour mixture, tossing the mixture lightly with a fork after each addition until the pastry dough is moist enough to hold together but is not sticky. Shape the pastry dough into a disk, wrap it in plastic wrap, and refrigerate the disk for 30 minutes.

4 • Assemble the pie: Preheat the oven to 400°F. On a lightly floured surface, roll out the dough to a ¼-inch thickness; the shape of the rolled dough should be about 2 inches larger all around than the top of the casserole dish (allow for extra pastry to make decorations). Place the rolled pastry loosely over the chicken mixture. Fold the pastry edges under and crimp them decoratively. With the tip of a knife, cut several slits in the pastry to allow steam to escape. From the remaining pastry, cut out decorative shapes with cookie cutters. Brush the pastry shapes with water and place them over the top of the pie. Bake the pie for 30 minutes or until the pastry is golden brown.

Makes 8 servings. Per serving: 410 calories, 35 g protein, 20 g carbohydrate, 21 g fat, 93 mg cholesterol, 550 mg sodium.

Chicken Broccoli Stir-Fry

Chicken Broccoli Stir-Fry

A speedy stir-fry that's full of flavor. Spoon the fragrant chicken mixture over wide noodles, or white or brown rice.

3 tablespoons vegetable oil
1 tablespoon dark sesame oil
1½ pounds boneless, skinless chicken breasts, cut into 2-inch pieces
3 medium cloves garlic, crushed
1 tablespoon minced gingerroot
¾ teaspoon crushed red-pepper flakes
3 green onions, thinly sliced
1 cup chicken broth
¼ cup low-salt soy sauce
1 pound broccoli florets
2 tablespoons sugar
1 tablespoon cornstarch
3 tablespoons red-wine vinegar

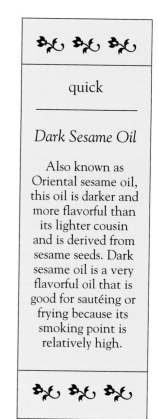

quick

Dark Sesame Oil

Also known as Oriental sesame oil, this oil is darker and more flavorful than its lighter cousin and is derived from sesame seeds. Dark sesame oil is a very flavorful oil that is good for sautéing or frying because its smoking point is relatively high.

1 • In a large skillet or wok over medium-high heat, combine and heat the vegetable and sesame oils. Add the chicken pieces and sauté about 5 minutes or until the chicken is tender. With a slotted spoon, transfer the chicken to a medium bowl.

2 • To the drippings remaining in the skillet, add the garlic, ginger, red-pepper flakes, and green onions. Stir-fry about 2 minutes or until the mixture is very fragrant. Stir in the chicken broth and soy sauce. Bring the mixture to boiling and add the broccoli florets. Stir-fry about 5 minutes or until the broccoli is tender-crisp. With a slotted spoon, remove the broccoli to the bowl with the chicken.

3 • In a cup, combine the sugar, cornstarch, and red-wine vinegar. Stir until the mixture is well blended. Stir the cornstarch mixture into the broth mixture in the skillet. Bring the combined mixtures to boiling; boil for 1 minute. Return the chicken-broccoli mixture to the skillet and toss to coat the meat and vegetables with the sauce. Heat the mixture through.

Makes 4 servings. Per serving: 403 calories, 33 g protein, 14 g carbohydrate, 24 g fat, 95 mg cholesterol, 834 mg sodium.

Cashew-Chicken Stir-Fry

As a super time-saver, prepare the Sauce and the Vegetable Mixture for this dish the night before. Then assemble and stir-fry the chicken with its accompaniments in just 15 minutes. Serve with steaming bowls of white or brown rice.

SAUCE

4 teaspoons cornstarch
1/2 teaspoon crushed red-pepper flakes
1 cup low-sodium chicken broth
3 tablespoons low-sodium soy sauce
1 tablespoon rice vinegar
1 teaspoon dark sesame oil

CHICKEN MIXTURE

1 1/2 pounds boneless, skinless chicken breasts, cut into 1-inch pieces
2 teaspoons cornstarch
1 tablespoon low-sodium soy sauce
2 tablespoons vegetable oil

VEGETABLE MIXTURE

3 large cloves garlic
1 (1 × 1-inch) piece gingerroot, pared
4 small green onions, cut into 1-inch pieces
2 (6-ounce) bags cleaned spinach (about 8 cups)
1 tablespoon vegetable oil
2 carrots, pared and thinly sliced crosswise
1 celery stalk, thinly sliced crosswise
1 large sweet red pepper, cut into thin strips
2 cups small broccoli florets
3/4 cup toasted unsalted cashews

1 • Prepare the Sauce: In a small bowl, combine the 4 teaspoons of cornstarch and the red-pepper flakes. Gradually add the chicken broth, stirring until the mixture is well blended. Add the 3 tablespoons of soy sauce, the rice vinegar, and sesame oil. Stir until the ingredients are well blended. Set aside.

2 • Prepare the Chicken Mixture: In a medium bowl, combine the chicken pieces, the 2 teaspoons of cornstarch, and the 1 tablespoon of soy sauce. Stir until the ingredients are well blended. Let stand for 5 minutes.

3 • In a wok or large skillet over high heat, heat 1 tablespoon of the vegetable oil. Add half of the Chicken Mixture. Stir-fry about 4 minutes or until the chicken is cooked through. With a slotted spoon, transfer the chicken to a medium bowl. Repeat with the remaining 1 tablespoon of vegetable oil and the remaining Chicken Mixture.

4 • Prepare the Vegetable Mixture: In a blender or food processor, combine the garlic, ginger, and green onions. Using a pulse motion, finely chop the mixture, scraping down the work bowl as necessary. In the wok over medium-high heat, combine 2 teaspoons of the garlic mixture and one bag of spinach. Toss to coat the spinach with the garlic mixture. Cover the wok and cook until the spinach wilts, stirring once. Transfer the cooked spinach to a serving platter. Repeat with 2 more teaspoons of the garlic mixture and the remaining bag of spinach.

5 • Spread the cooked spinach over the platter. Cover the platter and keep the spinach warm. In the wok, heat the 1 tablespoon of vegetable oil. Add the remaining garlic mixture and the carrots, celery, sweet red pepper, and broccoli florets. Stir-fry about 3 minutes or until the vegetables are tender-crisp.

6 • Increase the heat to high. Stir the Sauce to recombine the mixture. Add the Sauce to the vegetables in the wok, stirring to coat the vegetables with the Sauce. Cook, stirring, until the Sauce boils and thickens. Add the Chicken Mixture and the cashews, and stir to mix the ingredients well. Heat the mixture through. Serve the stir-fry over the spinach on the platter.

Makes 6 servings. Per serving: 341 calories, 33 g protein, 16 g carbohydrate, 17 g fat, 66 mg cholesterol, 678 mg sodium.

Chicken Lo Mein

low-fat

quick

An old family favorite ready in less than 20 minutes! (A package of mixed frozen vegetables is what makes the time difference.)

1 tablespoon dark sesame oil
1 pound boneless, skinless chicken breasts, cut into strips
1 (14-ounce) can chicken broth
1 cup water
1 tablespoon minced gingerroot
$\frac{1}{8}$ teaspoon crushed red-pepper flakes
3 tablespoons teriyaki sauce
1 large clove garlic, minced
1 (8-ounce) package spaghetti
1 (1-pound) package frozen broccoli, carrot, sweet red pepper, and
    water chestnut combination
2 green onions, sliced

1 • In a 12-inch skillet over medium-high heat, heat the sesame oil. Add the chicken strips and sauté about 3 minutes or until the chicken is browned. With a slotted spoon, transfer the chicken to a plate.

2 • In the same skillet, combine the chicken broth, water, ginger, red-pepper flakes, teriyaki sauce, and garlic. Bring the broth mixture to boiling; add the spaghetti. Reduce the heat, cover the skillet, and simmer for 8 minutes, stirring occasionally to separate the spaghetti strands.

3 • Stir in the vegetable combination and the chicken strips. Bring the mixture to boiling. Reduce the heat, cover the skillet, and simmer about 4 minutes more or until the spaghetti is al dente and the vegetables are tender. Stir in the green onions.

*Makes 4 servings. Per serving: 302 calories, 28 g protein, 26 g carbohydrate,
10 g fat, 61 mg cholesterol, 1,230 mg sodium.*

Chicken Aromatic

preparation time:
15 minutes

marinating time:
30 minutes

cooking time:
50 minutes

The Moroccan influence on this chicken casserole is revealed by the piquant seasonings — cumin, ginger, saffron, and coriander — as well as by the bed of couscous.

2 teaspoons ground cumin
1 large clove garlic, crushed
1 teaspoon ground ginger
1 teaspoon ground coriander
3/4 teaspoon salt
1/2 teaspoon ground hot red pepper
Large pinch ground saffron
8 chicken thighs (about 1 1/2 pounds)
2 tablespoons olive oil
1 very large red onion, halved lengthwise and thinly sliced
1-inch piece cinnamon stick
1 cup chicken broth
18 pitted prunes (about 4 ounces)
4 servings hot, cooked couscous
3 tablespoons minced fresh cilantro

1 • In a small bowl, combine the cumin, garlic, ginger, coriander, salt, ground hot red pepper, and saffron. Stir until the spice mixture is well blended. Place the chicken thighs on a baking sheet. Rub the spice mixture all over the chicken thighs. Let the chicken stand for 30 minutes.

2 • In a Dutch oven over medium heat, heat the olive oil. Working in batches, add the chicken and cook about 5 minutes on each side or until the chicken is browned all over. Transfer the chicken to a small bowl.

3 • To the drippings remaining in the skillet, add the red onion and the cinnamon stick. Sauté about 5 minutes or until the onion softens. Return the chicken to the skillet and add the chicken broth. Reduce the heat to medium-low, cover the skillet, and simmer for 30 minutes, adding the prunes for the last 3 minutes of cooking time. Serve the chicken mixture over the couscous. Sprinkle the minced cilantro over all.

Makes 4 servings. Per serving (without couscous): 515 calories, 35 g protein, 33 g carbohydrate, 28 g fat, 114 mg cholesterol, 695 mg sodium.

Paella with Chicken Thighs

preparation time:
30 minutes

cooking time:
30 minutes

baking time:
30 minutes

An ethnic seafood classic that's perfect for a large and hungry crowd. This one-dish wonder is a colorful mixture of clams, mussels, shrimp, chicken, spicy chorizo sausage, fresh green beans, and rice, all tinted a vivid yellow by a pinch of saffron.

24 small littleneck clams, scrubbed
12 small mussels, scrubbed and beards removed
5 cups chicken broth
1 teaspoon saffron threads or $^1/_4$ teaspoon powdered saffron
5 tablespoons olive oil
$^3/_4$ pound chorizo sausage, cut into $^1/_2$-inch-thick pieces
$1^1/_2$ pounds boneless chicken thighs, skinned, halved
1 pound medium shrimp, peeled, deveined, and tails intact
2 medium onions, thinly sliced
1 large sweet red pepper, cut into thin strips
4 large cloves garlic, finely chopped
2 large ripe tomatoes, peeled, seeded, and chopped
3 cups Arborio rice (see Note)
$^1/_2$ pound small green beans
$^1/_2$ cup frozen peas

1 • In a Dutch oven, bring $^1/_2$ inch of water to boiling. Add the clams. Cover the pan and cook about 3 to 5 minutes or until the clams open, removing the clams to a large bowl as they open. Discard any unopened clams. Using the same water, repeat with the mussels. Strain the cooking liquid through a double thickness of cheesecloth into a glass measure. If necessary, add enough water to measure 1 cup of liquid. Set aside the cooking liquid.

2 • Preheat the oven to 350°F. In a medium saucepan, heat the chicken broth to simmering. Crumble the saffron threads or add the saffron powder to the simmering broth. Cover the saucepan and remove it from the heat. Set aside the broth mixture to steep.

3 • In a 17-inch paella pan (available in gourmet shops and specialty kitchenware stores) or a very large, ovenproof skillet over medium-high heat, heat 2 tablespoons of the olive oil. Add the chorizo sausage and sauté about 3 minutes or until the sausage is browned. With a slotted spoon, transfer the sausage to a medium bowl. Add the chicken thighs to the pan and sauté about 5 minutes or until the chicken is browned on all sides. Transfer the chicken to the bowl with the chorizo. Add 1

more tablespoon of the olive oil to the pan. Add the shrimp and sauté about 1 minute or just until the shrimp are pink. Transfer the shrimp to a second medium bowl. Add the remaining 2 tablespoons of olive oil to the pan. Add the onions and sweet red pepper. Over medium heat, sauté about 5 minutes or until the onions are golden. Add the garlic and tomatoes, and sauté for 5 minutes more.

4 • Add the Arborio rice to the vegetable mixture in the pan. Stir in the broth mixture and the reserved cooking liquid. Increase the heat to high and bring the mixture to boiling. Return the chorizo and chicken to the pan, and add the green beans. Stir until the ingredients are well mixed in the broth.

5 • Cover the pan tightly with heavy-duty aluminum foil or an oven-proof lid. Bake the rice mixture in the 350°F oven for 20 minutes.

6 • Remove the pan from the oven; do not turn off the oven. Carefully remove the foil and add the clams, mussels, shrimp, and peas to the rice mixture. Bake the paella, uncovered, about 10 minutes more or until the seafood is hot and the rice is just tender.

NOTE: Arborio rice is available in some supermarkets, specialty food shops, and Italian food stores.

Makes 8 servings. Per serving: 615 calories, 31 g protein, 69 g carbohydrate, 23 g fat, 123 mg cholesterol, 1,096 mg sodium.

Paella with Chicken Thighs

Ginger Fried Rice with Chicken Wings

A one-skillet wonder, these spicy chicken wings are combined with a fresh vegetable and rice mixture that is out of this world.

preparation time:
20 minutes

cooking time:
35 minutes

¹/₄ cup vegetable oil
1 (2-inch) piece gingerroot, pared and finely slivered
¹/₄ cup all-purpose flour
¹/₂ teaspoon ground hot red pepper
¹/₂ teaspoon salt
1¹/₂ pounds chicken wings, separated at joints, and tips discarded
1 tablespoon minced gingerroot
¹/₄ pound thin asparagus stalks, pared, trimmed, and cut diagonally into 2-inch lengths
1 generous cup small broccoli florets
1 small sweet red pepper, seeded and diced
1 large carrot, pared and julienned
¹/₂ cup chicken broth
¹/₄ pound shiitake or button mushrooms, stems discarded and caps thinly sliced
2 large eggs, beaten
3 cups cooked long-grain white rice, cooled
2 slices Canadian bacon (about 2 ounces), diced
¹/₂ cup frozen peas, thawed
2 green onions, trimmed and minced
1 tablespoon soy sauce
1 teaspoon hot-pepper sesame oil
¹/₄ cup minced fresh cilantro leaves
Additional fresh cilantro leaves for garnish

1 • In a large nonstick skillet over medium-high heat, heat the vegetable oil. Add the slivered ginger and stir-fry about 30 to 45 seconds or until the ginger is golden brown and frizzled. With a slotted spoon, transfer the ginger slivers to paper towels to drain. Remove and reserve 2 tablespoons of the oil from the skillet.

2 • On a sheet of waxed paper, combine the flour, ground hot red pepper, and salt. Stir until the flour mixture is well blended. One at a time, dip the chicken wings into the flour mixture until the wings are completely coated; shake off the excess flour mixture. Reheat the oil

remaining in the skillet. Over medium-high heat, working in 2 batches, add the chicken wings and cook about 3 to 5 minutes on each side or until the wings are well browned and crisp. Keep the chicken wings warm.

3 • Add 1 tablespoon of the reserved oil back to the skillet; cook the oil over medium-high heat. Add the minced ginger and stir-fry about 30 seconds to 1 minute. Add the asparagus, broccoli florets, sweet red pepper, carrot, and $^1/_4$ cup of the chicken broth. Stir-fry about 2 to 4 minutes or until the vegetables are tender-crisp. Add the mushrooms and cook for 1 minute. Add the eggs and cook about 1 minute more, stirring, just until the eggs are set. Transfer the vegetable-egg mixture to a plate.

4 • Add the cooked rice, the remaining chicken broth, the Canadian bacon, peas, green onions, soy sauce, and sesame oil to the skillet. Stir-fry for 3 minutes. Add the reserved vegetable-egg mixture and stir-fry until all the ingredients are heated through. Stir in the minced cilantro. Serve the rice mixture with the chicken wings. Garnish with cilantro leaves.

Makes 6 servings. Per serving: 433 calories, 21 g protein, 42 g carbohydrate, 20 g fat, 128 mg cholesterol, 586 mg sodium

---

Chicken and Black Bean Tostadas

A tostada is a crisply fried tortilla topped with just about anything you'd like. Here, we use a fresh salsa, chicken, and black beans.

SALSA

make ahead

quick

2 ripe plum tomatoes, seeded and chopped
$^1/_2$ cup chopped green onions
2 pickled jalapeño peppers, seeded and minced
1 small clove garlic, minced
2 tablespoons chopped fresh cilantro
2 tablespoons fresh lime juice
2 tablespoons vegetable oil
2 tablespoons tomato paste
$^1/_2$ teaspoon salt

FILLING

3 cups shredded cooked chicken
1 (15-ounce) can black beans, rinsed and drained
1 cup shredded Monterey Jack cheese (about 4 ounces)
2 tablespoons chopped fresh cilantro
$^1/_4$ teaspoon freshly ground black pepper

$^1/_3$ cup vegetable oil
6 (about 8-inch-diameter) flour tortillas
3 cups shredded romaine lettuce
1 ripe avocado, peeled, pitted, and sliced
6 tablespoons sour cream

1 • Prepare the Salsa: In a medium bowl, combine the plum tomatoes, green onions, jalapeño peppers, garlic, the 2 tablespoons of chopped cilantro, lime juice, the 2 tablespoons of vegetable oil, tomato paste, and salt. Gently stir until the ingredients are well mixed. Let the Salsa stand at room temperature to allow the flavors to blend.

2 • Prepare the Filling: In another medium bowl, combine the shredded cooked chicken, black beans, Monterey Jack cheese, the 2 tablespoons of cilantro, the ground black pepper, and 1 cup of the Salsa. Stir until the ingredients are well mixed. Set aside.

3 • In a large skillet over medium-high heat, heat the $^1/_3$ cup of vegetable oil. Add 1 tortilla and cook for 30 seconds or until the tortilla is browned and crisp. With tongs, transfer the tortilla to paper towels to drain. Repeat with the remaining tortillas.

4 • Assemble the tostadas: On each of 6 dinner plates, place 1 tortilla. Sprinkle some of the romaine around the edge of each tortilla; spoon some of the Filling into the centers. Serve the tostadas with the avocado, sour cream, and remaining Salsa.

Makes 6 servings. Per serving: 569 calories, 36 g protein, 46 g carbohydrate, 29 g fat, 85 mg cholesterol, 852 mg sodium.

Chicken Hash

A terrific special brunch dish, or an easy supper when served with a tossed salad.

2 baking potatoes (about 1^1/$_2$ pounds), scrubbed and cut into ^{3}/$_4$-inch dice
2 teaspoons salt
2 teaspoons chopped fresh rosemary leaves or ^{1}/$_2$ teaspoon dried rosemary
1 teaspoon freshly ground black pepper
4 tablespoons unsalted butter
1^1/$_2$ cups Vidalia or other sweet onions, cut into ^{3}/$_4$-inch dice
1 sweet red pepper, cut into ^{3}/$_4$-inch dice
3^1/$_2$ cups cooked chicken, cut into bite-sized pieces
1 tablespoon olive oil
^{1}/$_3$ cup heavy cream

make ahead

preparation time:
15 minutes

cooking time:
25 minutes

1 • Place the potatoes in a medium saucepan with enough water to cover the potatoes. Add 1 teaspoon of the salt. Bring the water to boiling. Reduce the heat, cover the saucepan, and simmer about 4 to 5 minutes or just until the potatoes are cooked through but are not mushy. Drain the potatoes and rinse them under cold running water until the potatoes are thoroughly cooled. Drain the potatoes well.

2 • In a cup, combine the remaining salt, the rosemary, and the ground pepper. Stir until the ingredients are blended. Set aside the herb mixture.

3 • In a 12-inch cast-iron skillet over medium to medium-high heat, melt 2 tablespoons of the butter. Add the Vidalia onion and sweet red pepper, and sauté about 5 minutes or until the vegetables are tender. With a slotted spoon, transfer the vegetables to a large bowl. Add 1 tablespoon of the remaining butter to the skillet. Over medium-high heat, when the butter is foaming, add the chicken and half of the herb mixture. Cook about 2 minutes, turning the chicken with a pancake turner only a few times. Transfer the chicken to the bowl with the vegetable mixture. Add the remaining tablespoon of butter and the olive oil to the skillet. When the butter is foaming, add the potatoes and the remaining herb mixture to the skillet. Cook about 6 to 8 minutes or until the potatoes begin to brown, turning the potatoes with the pancake turner twice during the cooking time.

4 • Add the chicken-vegetable mixture to the potatoes in the skillet. Toss until all the ingredients are well mixed. Lightly pat down the hash mixture with the pancake turner. Pour the heavy cream around the edges of the skillet and over the center of the hash. Cook for 5 minutes, turning the hash occasionally, until it is crusty.

Makes 6 servings. Per serving: 225 calories, 28 g protein, 8 g carbohydrate, 8 g fat, 136 mg cholesterol, 717 mg sodium.

Chicken Hash

Chicken Dumplings with Orange Dipping Sauce

~

Low in fat, high in taste, this dish is done in 45 minutes. Here, won ton wrappers encase a ginger-spiced chicken filling to create savory dumplings, which are served with a sweet-sour orange sauce. Serve with a shredded carrot salad.

FILLING

2 cups finely shredded napa cabbage
1/4 cup shiitake mushrooms, minced
1/2 pound ground chicken
1 green onion, minced
1 teaspoon minced gingerroot
3 tablespoons water
1/2 teaspoon salt

30 (3 1/2-inch-diameter) round won ton wrappers
Nonstick cooking spray
1 cup chicken broth

ORANGE DIPPING SAUCE

1/3 cup orange marmalade
3 tablespoons rice vinegar
1/4 cup chicken broth

1 • Prepare the Filling: In a large nonstick skillet over medium-high heat, sauté the cabbage and the shiitake mushrooms about 2 minutes or until the cabbage wilts. Remove from the heat and let the mixture cool for 5 minutes. Stir in the ground chicken, green onion, ginger, water, and salt.

2 • Place 1 teaspoon of the Filling in the center of one won ton wrapper. Moisten the edges of the wrapper with some water and bring the edges together, encasing the Filling; pleat the edges of the wrapper as needed to seal the dumpling. Repeat with the remaining Filling and won ton wrappers.

low-fat

preparation time:
20 minutes

cooking time:
25 minutes

3 • With cooking spray, grease the skillet. Over medium heat, cook half of the dumplings about 6 minutes or until the dumplings are browned on one side. Turn over the dumplings and increase the heat to medium-high. Add $^1/_2$ cup of the chicken broth. Cover the skillet and cook about 3 minutes or until almost all of the broth evaporates and the dumplings are cooked. Transfer the cooked dumplings to a platter and keep them warm. Repeat with the remaining dumplings and the remaining $^1/_2$ cup of chicken broth.

4 • Prepare the Orange Dipping Sauce: In a small serving bowl, combine the orange marmalade, rice vinegar, and the $^1/_4$ cup of chicken broth. Stir until the mixture is well blended. Serve the sauce with the hot dumplings.

Makes 6 servings, with about $^1/_2$ cup sauce. Per serving: 205 calories, 13 g protein, 34 g carbohydrate, 2 g fat, 31 mg cholesterol, 388 mg sodium.

Chicken Dumplings with Orange Dipping Sauce

Chicken Pot Pies

Tender cubes of chicken, yams, corn, and peas — all nestled beneath a flaky pastry crust. The crust is especially easy since it's made with packaged puff pastry.

SAUCE

6 tablespoons butter or margarine
7 tablespoons all-purpose flour
2 1/4 cups chicken broth
2 cups half-and-half
1/2 teaspoon poultry seasoning
1/2 teaspoon salt
1/4 teaspoon freshly ground pepper

FILLING

1 large yam (about 12 ounces), pared and cut into 3/4-inch dice
2 large carrots, pared and cut into 3/4-inch dice
1 large celery stalk, cut into 3/4-inch dice
1 cup frozen corn kernels
1/2 cup frozen peas
5 cups cubed cooked chicken

1/2 (17 1/4-ounce) package frozen puff pastry, thawed (1 sheet)
1 large egg, beaten
1 teaspoon water

preparation time:
25 minutes

cooking time:
25 minutes

baking time:
20 minutes

1 • Prepare the Sauce: In a medium saucepan over medium heat, melt the butter or margarine. Stir in the flour and cook for 1 minute. Gradually add the chicken broth, whisking constantly, until the ingredients are well blended. Whisk in the half-and-half, poultry seasoning, salt, and pepper. Over medium-high heat, bring the mixture to boiling, whisking frequently. Reduce the heat and simmer about 3 to 4 minutes or until the Sauce is very thick. Set aside and let it cool.

2 • Prepare the Filling: To a large saucepan of boiling water, add the yam and carrots. Cover the saucepan and cook for 12 minutes. Add the celery; cover and cook for 3 minutes. Add the corn and peas. Drain the vegetable mixture. In a large bowl, combine the Sauce, cooked vegetables, and chicken cubes. Gently stir until the ingredients are well mixed. Place 1 heaping cup of the mixture into each of 8 (8- to 10-ounce, 4-inch-diameter) individual soufflé dishes.

3 • Preheat the oven to 375°F. On a lightly floured surface, roll out the puff pastry to a 20 × 14-inch rectangle. Cut the pastry into 8 equal rectangles. In a cup, stir together the egg and water until they are blended. Brush the egg mixture over the pastry. Cut a 2-inch cross in the center of each pastry rectangle; carefully fold back the inner corners of the cut cross. Brush the pastry corners with the egg mixture.

4 • Place one pastry rectangle over the chicken mixture in each soufflé dish. With a floured fork, squash the rectangular edges of the pastry into a rustic, circular shape, pressing the pastry onto the rim of each dish to attach the crusts firmly. Bake about 20 to 25 minutes or until the pastry crusts are browned and the filling is bubbly. Cool the pot pies for 10 minutes before serving.

> *Makes 8 servings. Per serving: 590 calories, 32 g protein, 38 g carbohydrate, 34 g fat, 176 mg cholesterol, 560 mg sodium.*

Turkey Sausage and Peppers

A one-skillet supper, bursting with robust flavor and lively with the red and yellow colors of sweet peppers. Spoon the sausage mixture over Texmati rice or noodles.

preparation time:
20 minutes

cooking time:
35 minutes

$^3/_4$ pound sweet turkey sausage
$^1/_3$ cup reduced-sodium chicken broth, fat removed
2 tablespoons olive oil
1 large bulb fennel, trimmed and thinly sliced
1 large red onion, sliced
3 cloves garlic, minced
1 large sweet red pepper, thinly sliced
1 large sweet yellow pepper, thinly sliced
$1^1/_2$ teaspoons minced fresh oregano leaves or $^1/_4$ teaspoon dried oregano
$^1/_4$ teaspoon salt
$^1/_4$ teaspoon freshly ground black pepper
1 tablespoon balsamic vinegar

1 • In a medium nonstick skillet over medium heat, cook the turkey sausages, covered, about 10 minutes or until the turkey is browned on all sides, shaking the pan occasionally to turn the sausages. Add the chicken broth. Reduce the heat to medium-low, cover the skillet again, and cook about 10 minutes more or until the turkey is cooked through. Transfer the turkey sausages to a plate and keep them warm. Wipe out the skillet.

2 • In the same cleaned skillet over medium heat, heat the olive oil. Add the fennel, red onion, and garlic, and sauté about 6 to 7 minutes or until the vegetables are soft. Add the sweet red and yellow peppers and the oregano. Sauté about 4 to 5 minutes or until the sweet peppers are tender.

3 • Cut the turkey sausages diagonally into thick slices. Add the sausage slices to the vegetable mixture in the skillet. Cook, stirring occasionally, about 3 minutes more. Stir in the salt, black pepper, and balsamic vinegar.

Makes 4 servings. Per serving: 296 calories, 20 g protein, 9 g carbohydrate, 20 g fat, 69 mg cholesterol, 821 mg sodium.

Turkey Sausage and Peppers

Turkey Tacos

~

Fast and easy and the whole family will love them. Serve with Mexican beer or iced tea.

❧ ❧ ❧
quick
❧ ❧ ❧

1 tablespoon vegetable oil
8 green onions, trimmed and cut into $^1/_2$-inch pieces
$^1/_2$ large sweet red pepper, cored, seeded, and diced
$1^1/_2$ teaspoons chili powder
$^1/_2$ teaspoon ground cumin
$^1/_2$ teaspoon salt
$^1/_2$ teaspoon freshly ground black pepper
2 cups shredded cooked turkey
2 tablespoons fresh lime juice
1 (15-ounce) can pinto beans, rinsed and drained
1 ($4^1/_2$-ounce) package taco shells (12 shells), heated as package
   label directs
$^1/_2$ cup shredded reduced-fat Cheddar cheese (about 2 ounces)
3 cups shredded romaine lettuce
1 cup prepared salsa

1 • In a large skillet over medium-high heat, heat the vegetable oil. Add the green onions and sweet red pepper, and sauté about 3 minutes or until the vegetables are tender. Add the chili powder, cumin, salt, and black pepper. Stir until the ingredients are well mixed, and cook until the mixture is fragrant.

2 • Add the turkey, lime juice, and pinto beans to the skillet. Stir until the ingredients are well mixed. Cook about 2 minutes or until the mixture is heated through.

3 • To serve: Spoon some of the meat mixture into each taco shell. Top with some of the Cheddar cheese, romaine lettuce, and the salsa.

Makes 6 servings. Per serving: 298 calories, 22 g protein, 30 g carbohydrate, 11 g fat, 37 mg cholesterol, 736 mg sodium.

Turkey Chili

A fabulous recipe for leftover turkey. If you don't have leftovers, buy a ¾-pound cooked turkey breast and cut it into chunks.

2 medium zucchini, quartered lengthwise
5 teaspoons vegetable oil
½ teaspoon dried oregano, crushed
Salt
Pinch freshly ground black pepper
½ pound poblano chilies (about 4 to 5), halved lengthwise and seeded, or 2 (4-ounce) cans diced green chilies
1 (19-ounce) can cannellini beans, rinsed and drained
1¼ cups chicken broth
¾ pound cooked turkey breast, cut into 1-inch cubes (about 2 cups)
¾ cup finely chopped yellow onion
1 teaspoon minced garlic
1 tablespoon ground cumin
Pinch ground hot red pepper
2 tablespoons chopped fresh cilantro
¼ cup finely chopped red onion

low-fat

preparation time:
20 minutes

cooking time:
35 minutes

1 • Preheat the broiler. In a small bowl, combine the zucchini, 2 teaspoons of the vegetable oil, the oregano, a pinch of the salt, and the black pepper. Toss to coat the zucchini with the oil and seasonings. Arrange the zucchini and the poblano chilies over the rack of a broiler pan. Broil 5 inches from the heat source about 8 minutes or until the zucchini is well browned and the skins of the chilies are charred, turning the zucchini every 2 minutes. Place the chilies in a paper bag and seal the bag. Let the chilies cool for 10 minutes. Remove the chilies from the bag; remove the skin and cut the chilies into ½-inch dice. Cut the zucchini into 1-inch pieces. Place the chilies and zucchini in a large bowl.

2 • Add 1 cup of the cannellini beans to the zucchini mixture. In another bowl, place the remaining beans and ½ cup of the chicken broth. With a fork, mash the beans and the broth together.

3 • In a large saucepan over medium heat, heat the remaining 3 teaspoons of vegetable oil. Add the turkey cubes and the yellow onion. Cover the saucepan and cook about 7 minutes or until the onion is golden, stirring occasionally. Add the garlic, cumin, and ground hot red pepper, and sauté for 1 minute. Add the mashed bean mixture, the remaining $^3/_4$ cup of chicken broth, and $^1/_4$ teaspoon of the salt. Bring the mixture to boiling. Cover the saucepan and simmer for 5 minutes. Stir in the zucchini-chili mixture and simmer for 2 minutes more. Add the chopped cilantro and stir until the ingredients are well mixed. Sprinkle the red onion over the chili before serving.

> *Makes 4 servings. Per serving: 380 calories, 40 g protein, 37 g carbohydrate, 8 g fat, 73 mg cholesterol, 566 mg sodium.*

Chapter Seven

~

Beef, Pork, and Lamb

❧ ❧ ❧

For many, a meal isn't complete without meat. Combining small amounts of meat with vegetables and other ingredients is a terrific one-dish dinner strategy because not only does it cut your cost but it makes nutritional sense — you're using less meat per person.

When entertaining a large crowd, a roast cooked with vegetables is an excellent one-dish option — with the bonus of yummy leftovers. Our Cajun-Spiced Pot Roast (page 201) is a rib-sticking concoction with potatoes, sweet red peppers, okra, and tomatoes. Since few one-dish wonders can compete with chili, we offer several potfuls: Black Bean (page 212), El Paso (page 214), Cincinnati (page 211), and Chili-Lover's Chili (page 208). And don't forget to check out Szechuan Beef with Broccoli (page 207) for a fast, easy, and economical dinner.

The pork and lamb recipes we've gathered read as a celebration of the diverse ethnic cultures that make up America. From the bayous of Louisiana comes a mouth-watering Jambalaya (page 220). An Italian favorite, Ossobuco (page 215), features tender veal shanks; Pork with Soba Noodles (page 225) is a delicious Japanese dish. There's a Greek-inspired Moussaka (page 228), a piquant Lamb Curry (page 230), and even a few entrées, such as Polenta with Pork-Shiitake Sauce (page 224), that are true "melting pot" originals.

Cajun-Spiced Pot Roast

For a change of taste, try our spicy variation on a traditional pot roast. Leftover slices of the roast can be reheated in the cooking liquid.

1½ tablespoons all-purpose flour
1 teaspoon ground cumin
½ teaspoon ground hot red pepper
¼ teaspoon ground nutmeg
1 (2¾-pound) rump roast
2 tablespoons vegetable oil
1 large onion, cut into wedges
½ pound carrots, pared and cut crosswise into 1-inch pieces
1 (28-ounce) can whole tomatoes
1 cup beef broth
1 bay leaf
2 large potatoes, pared, cut in half lengthwise, and then cut crosswise into quarters
1 large sweet red pepper, cut into 1-inch pieces
1 (10-ounce) package frozen whole okra
1 teaspoon salt
½ teaspoon hot-pepper sauce

low-fat

preparation time:
20 minutes

cooking time:
2½ hours

1 • On a sheet of waxed paper, combine the flour, cumin, ground hot red pepper, and nutmeg. Roll the rump roast in the flour mixture until the roast is completely coated.

2 • In a 5-quart Dutch oven over medium-high heat, heat the vegetable oil until it is hot. Add the roast and cook, turning often, until the roast is browned on all sides, 10 to 15 minutes. With 2 large spoons, transfer the roast to a plate. In the hot drippings remaining in the pan, sauté the onion and carrots for 5 minutes. Stir in the tomatoes and their liquid, breaking up the tomatoes with a spoon. Stir in the beef broth and bay leaf. Return the roast to the pan.

3 • Bring the mixture to boiling. Lower the heat, cover the Dutch oven, and simmer for 1 hour and 30 minutes, turning the roast once during the cooking time.

4 • Add the potatoes and sweet red pepper to the Dutch oven. Bring the mixture to boiling. Lower the heat, cover the pan, and simmer for 30 minutes. Add the okra, salt, and hot-pepper sauce. Bring the mixture to boiling again. Lower the heat and simmer, uncovered, about 5 minutes or until the okra is cooked and the remaining vegetables and the meat are tender.

Makes 8 servings. Per serving: 359 calories, 39 g protein, 26 g carbohydrate, 12 g fat, 81 mg cholesterol, 613 mg sodium.

Is It Done?

Use an instant-read thermometer to determine whether the meat is completely cooked or not — it takes only about 10 seconds for the temperature to register.

For Beef:	Rare	140°F
	Medium-Rare	150°F
	Medium	160°F
	Well-Done	170°F
	Ground Beef	160–170°F
For Pork:	Medium	160°F
	Well-Done	170°F
For Lamb:	Rare	140°F
	Medium	160°F
	Well-Done	170°F

Beef Bourguignon

For the best flavor — and less fuss for the cook — make this classic French-style beef stew a day ahead, and then gently reheat it before serving. The caramelized shallots contribute a special flavor.

1 (6-ounce) slab bacon, diced
12 large shallots, peeled and halved
2 medium carrots, pared and diced
1/2 pound shiitake mushrooms, sliced
1 tablespoon olive oil
2 pounds chuck steak, cut into 1 1/4-inch cubes
1/4 cup all-purpose flour
1/2 teaspoon dried thyme leaves, crushed
1 teaspoon dried marjoram leaves, crushed
1/2 teaspoon salt
1/2 teaspoon freshly ground pepper
2 cups dry red wine
1 (14 1/2-ounce) can beef broth, plus more if needed
1/4 cup chopped parsley
Cooked spätzle or egg noodles

make ahead

preparation time:
15 minutes

cooking time:
2 3/4 hours

Shallots

A member of the onion family, shallots resemble a clove of garlic. Their mild onion flavor is particularly suited to delicate sauces, but shallots can be substituted for onions in most other dishes as well.

1 • In a Dutch oven over medium heat, sauté the bacon until it is browned and the fat has rendered. With a slotted spoon, transfer the browned bacon to paper towels to drain.

2 • Reduce the heat to low. In the bacon drippings remaining in the Dutch oven, sauté the shallots about 25 to 30 minutes or until the shallots are very soft and caramelized, adding the carrots for the last 8 to 10 minutes of cooking time. With the slotted spoon, transfer the shallot mixture to a medium bowl. Add the shiitake mushrooms to the drippings in the pan and sauté about 3 to 5 minutes or until the mushrooms are tender. With the slotted spoon, transfer the mushrooms to the bowl with the shallot mixture.

3 • Add the olive oil to the drippings in the Dutch oven and raise the heat to medium-high. Working in batches, add the beef cubes and brown the meat on all sides, about 4 to 5 minutes per batch; with the slotted spoon, remove the browned beef cubes to a large bowl. Sprinkle the beef cubes with the flour, thyme, marjoram, salt, and pepper. Gently stir until the ingredients are well mixed.

4 • Return the beef cubes to the Dutch oven and stir to coat the meat with the drippings in the pan. Over medium-high heat, cook about 1 to 2 minutes until the flour browns.

5 • Add the wine and beef broth to the beef cubes. Bring the mixture to boiling, stirring to loosen any browned bits from the bottom of the pan. Reduce the heat and partially cover the Dutch oven; simmer, stirring occasionally and adding more broth if necessary, about 2 hours or until the beef is very tender and the sauce is thickened. Stir in the shallot mixture, mushrooms, and bacon. Gently heat the mixture through. Sprinkle the stew with the chopped parsley. Serve with the spätzle or egg noodles.

> *Makes 6 servings. Per serving (without spätzle or egg noodles): 598 calories, 40 g protein, 14 g carbohydrate, 36 g fat, 152 mg cholesterol, 732 mg sodium.*

Pot Roast with Vegetables

low-fat

make ahead

preparation time:
30 minutes

baking time:
4 hours

Until now, making a perfect pot roast meant browning the meat in oil first, then simmering it for hours, checking constantly to make sure it didn't overcook. Our method eliminates all the fuss, as the brisket roasts in the oven, steeping in its own juices.

1 first-cut beef brisket (4 pounds) (see Note), fat trimmed to ¼ inch
2 cloves garlic, minced
1½ teaspoons salt
1 teaspoon freshly ground pepper, plus additional to taste
2 pounds onions, halved and sliced crosswise
½ cup sun-dried tomatoes packed in oil, drained and coarsely chopped
1 cup dry red wine
2 tablespoons balsamic vinegar
2 pounds large red potatoes, scrubbed, unpeeled, and cut into 1¼-inch chunks
1 pound large thick carrots, peeled and cut diagonally into ½-inch-thick slices
¾ pound parsnips, peeled and cut into ½-inch-thick slices
½ pound celery, cut diagonally into 1-inch-thick slices
2 tablespoons butter, melted
½ teaspoon dried thyme leaves, crumbled

Pot Roast with Vegetables

1 • Preheat the oven to 350°F. Line a large shallow roasting pan with heavy-duty aluminum foil, extending the foil over the sides of the pan by at least 4 inches.

2 • Rub the brisket with the garlic, 1 teaspoon of the salt, and ½ teaspoon of the pepper. Spread half of the onions over the foil-lined bottom of the roasting pan; sprinkle with the tomatoes. In a 2-cup glass measure, combine the wine and vinegar. Pour into the roasting pan with the onions and tomatoes. Top with the beef, fat side up. Spread the remaining onions over the beef. Crimp the foil loosely around the sides of the beef but not over the top.

3 • Cover the pan tightly with another piece of heavy-duty aluminum foil, crimping the foil tightly to seal to the pan edges. (Or, instead of using a foil-lined roasting pan, use a large Dutch oven with a heavy lid and ovenproof handles; lining with foil is not necessary.)

4 • Bake the brisket in the 350°F oven for 4 hours.

5 • Meanwhile, in a large bowl, combine the potatoes, carrots, parsnips, celery, butter, thyme, and remaining $1/2$ teaspoon each of the salt and pepper. Spread the vegetables evenly in a jelly-roll pan. Cover with heavy-duty aluminum foil, crimping the foil to seal the pan edges. After the beef has roasted for 2 hours, place the pan with the vegetables in the oven with the beef.

6 • Bake for 1 hour. Uncover the vegetables. Bake for 1 hour more, or until the vegetables are tender and are beginning to brown lightly in spots; stir the vegetables once or twice during the cooking.

7 • When the beef is done, scrape the onions from the top of the beef into the cooking juices in the bottom of the foil. Place the beef on a cutting board; cover with aluminum foil to keep warm.

8 • Prepare the gravy: With a slotted spoon, remove 1 cup of the onion-tomato mixture from the foil; set aside. Remove $1/2$ cup of the cooking juices; set aside. In a food processor or blender, combine the remaining onions, tomatoes, and cooking juices; process or blend until smooth. Pour into a medium saucepan. Add the reserved 1 cup onion-tomato mixture and pepper to taste. Keep the gravy hot over low heat.

9 • Thinly slice the brisket on a slight diagonal across the grain into $3/8$-inch-thick pieces. With a spatula, transfer the slices to a large serving platter in the order sliced to keep the shape of the brisket intact. Spoon the reserved $1/2$ cup of the cooking juices over the top of the sliced brisket. Spoon the vegetables around the brisket. Pour the gravy into a large sauce boat and pass with the brisket and vegetables.

NOTE: The brisket is usually sold in halves called the first cut (or thin cut, flat cut, or square cut) and the point cut (or front cut or thick cut). The first cut is flatter, thinner, and leaner than the point cut.

Makes 8 servings, 4 cups gravy. Per serving: 607 calories, 50 g protein, 60 g carbohydrate, 17 g fat, 138 mg cholesterol, 573 mg sodium.

Szechuan Beef with Broccoli

A colorful, quick stir-fry (shown on page 208) with lots of flavor. Use leftover beef in this dish and serve with fried noodles or rice.

1 tablespoon cornstarch
3 tablespoons dry sherry
1/2 cup oyster sauce
1/4 cup water
1/2 teaspoon crushed red-pepper flakes
2 tablespoons peanut or vegetable oil
1 tablespoon pared, slivered, gingerroot
1 large clove garlic, crushed
1 bunch broccoli (about 1 pound), cut into florets, stalks pared and
  sliced
1 large sweet red pepper, cut into julienne strips
2 celery stalks, diagonally sliced
6 green onions, cut into 1 1/2-inch pieces
2 cups cooked beef, cut into 2 1/2 × 1-inch strips

1 • In a small bowl, combine the cornstarch and sherry, and stir until the cornstarch is dissolved. Add the oyster sauce, water, and red-pepper flakes. Stir until the ingredients are well blended.

2 • In a wok or large skillet over medium-high heat, heat the peanut or vegetable oil. Add the ginger and garlic, and stir-fry for 1 minute. Add the broccoli florets and stir-fry for 3 minutes. Add the sweet red pepper, celery, and green onions, and stir-fry for 3 minutes. Stir in the cornstarch mixture and the beef strips. Stir-fry about 3 minutes or until the sauce thickens. Transfer the meat and vegetable mixture to a serving platter and spoon the sauce over all.

Makes 4 servings. Per serving: 344 calories, 29 g protein, 14 g carbohydrate, 19 g fat, 68 mg cholesterol, 2,174 mg sodium.

quick

Keeping Cooked Meat Fresh

To prevent cooked meat or poultry from becoming dried out when it's cooked a second time, follow these tips: Whenever possible, cut leftover meat into small pieces. This allows them to be reheated quickly, which will keep the meat from getting tough. Sautéing or stir-frying leftover meats will also help keep them from drying out, as each of these methods requires only a few minutes of cooking time.

Chili-Lover's Chili and Szechuan Beef with Broccoli

Chili-Lover's Chili

preparation time:
10 minutes

cooking time:
25 minutes

This quick chili uses cooked beef, so it makes an ideal easy-on-you supper late in the workweek.

2 tablespoons vegetable oil
2 celery stalks, chopped
1 large onion, chopped
1 large sweet red pepper, chopped
2 medium cloves garlic, crushed
2 tablespoons chili powder
1 teaspoon ground cumin
1/4 teaspoon dried oregano leaves, crushed
1/2 teaspoon salt
1 (28-ounce) can crushed tomatoes
3/4 cup beef broth
2 cups cubed cooked beef
2 (15-ounce) cans red kidney beans, drained
Shredded lettuce, shredded Cheddar or Monterey Jack cheese, and hot cooked rice (optional)

1 • In a 5-quart Dutch oven over medium-high heat, heat the vegetable oil. Add the celery, onion, sweet red pepper, and garlic, and sauté for 3 minutes. Add the chili powder, cumin, oregano, and salt; sauté for 1 minute more. Stir in the crushed tomatoes and the beef broth. Bring the mixture to boiling. Lower the heat and simmer the mixture for 15 minutes.

2 • Add the beef cubes and red kidney beans. Cook, stirring, until all the ingredients are heated through. If desired, serve the chili with the shredded lettuce, shredded cheese, and rice.

Makes 8 servings. Per serving: 248 calories, 18 g protein, 22 g carbohydrate, 10 g fat, 34 mg cholesterol, 735 mg sodium.

Beef Sukiyaki

A spirited mixture of beef tenderloin, mushrooms, and spinach — with a cooking time of less than 15 minutes. Accompany each serving with a small bowl of rice.

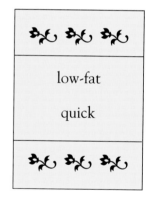

low-fat

quick

1 tablespoon reduced-calorie margarine
³/4 pound beef tenderloin, thinly sliced
1 (10-ounce) package mushrooms, sliced
4 large green onions, thinly sliced on the diagonal
1 large onion, thinly sliced
1 tablespoon sugar
1 teaspoon cornstarch
¹/4 cup soy sauce
¹/4 cup water
2 tablespoons dry sherry
1 (10-ounce) package fresh spinach, washed and stems removed
1 (8-ounce) can sliced water chestnuts, drained
2 cups hot cooked white rice

1 • In a large skillet over medium-high heat, melt the margarine. Add the beef slices and sauté just until the meat is browned. With a slotted spoon, remove the beef slices to a plate.

2 • To the liquid remaining in the skillet, add the mushrooms, the green onions, and the onion. Sauté about 5 minutes or until the vegetables are tender.

3 • In a small glass measure, combine the sugar, cornstarch, soy sauce, water, and sherry. Stir until the mixture is well blended. Add the cornstarch mixture to the skillet, stirring constantly. Continue to stir while adding the beef slices, spinach, and water chestnuts. Bring the mixture to boiling, stirring; boil for 1 minute. Cover the skillet, lower the heat, and simmer about 5 minutes or until the spinach is tender. Serve immediately over the rice.

Makes 4 servings. Per serving: 408 calories, 33 g protein, 49 g carbohydrate, 9 g fat, 59 mg cholesterol, 1,175 mg sodium.

Beef Sukiyaki

Cincinnati Chili

~

Chili is to Cincinnati what cheesesteak sandwiches are to Philadelphia and barbecue is to Texas — a time-honored tradition. But this is a unique take on "classic" chili: The meat mixture contains a small amount of chocolate and is served over spaghetti. A variety of toppings are served on the side, such as beans, onion, cheese, and oyster crackers.

3 pounds ground chuck
2 medium onions, chopped
3 cloves garlic, crushed
2 (15-ounce) cans tomato sauce
2 cups beef broth
1/4 cup red-wine vinegar
1/4 cup Worcestershire sauce
1/4 cup chili powder
2 teaspoons dried oregano leaves, crushed
1 1/2 teaspoons ground cinnamon
1 1/2 teaspoons ground cumin
1 teaspoon salt
1/2 teaspoon freshly ground pepper
1/4 teaspoon ground cloves
1 ounce unsweetened chocolate, chopped
1 pound spaghetti, cooked

CONDIMENTS

1 (15-ounce) can kidney beans, drained
1 small red onion, chopped
2 cups shredded Cheddar cheese (about 8 ounces)
Small oyster crackers

preparation time:
10 minutes

cooking time:
1 3/4 hours

1 • In a large saucepan or Dutch oven over medium-low heat, combine the ground chuck, onions, and garlic. Sauté the mixture about 12 to 15 minutes or until the meat is no longer pink and the vegetables are tender, stirring occasionally to break up the meat.

2 • Add the tomato sauce, beef broth, red-wine vinegar, and Worcestershire sauce. Stir until the ingredients are well mixed. Bring the mixture to simmering. Add the chili powder, oregano, cinnamon, cumin, salt, pepper, cloves, and chopped chocolate. Stir until all the ingredients are well mixed. Cook, uncovered, for 1 hour and 30 minutes, stirring often, until the chili is thick.

3 • To serve: Place some of the spaghetti on each of 8 dinner plates. Top with the chili. Place the kidney beans, red onion, Cheddar cheese, and oyster crackers in separate serving bowls. Let the diners sprinkle their portions with the desired condiments.

Makes 8 servings. Per serving (without condiments): 443 calories, 31 g protein, 16 g carbohydrate, 29 g fat, 101 mg cholesterol, 179 mg sodium.

Black Bean Chili

Lean chuck and pork shoulder combine in this rib-sticking chili, and the flavor mellows after a day or two. Serve this chili-for-a-crowd with lots of taco chips, both white- and blue-corn.

make ahead

preparation time:
15 minutes

cooking time:
2¼ hours

¼ cup vegetable oil
2½ pounds trimmed lean chuck, cut into 1-inch pieces
2½ pounds trimmed lean boneless pork shoulder or butt, cut into 1-inch pieces
3 large onions, chopped
6 large cloves garlic, minced
1 (28-ounce) can whole tomatoes in purée
1 (6-ounce) can tomato paste
3 cups water
1 cup tequila or beer
1 tablespoon Worcestershire sauce
¼ cup chili powder
1 tablespoon ground cumin
1 tablespoon dried oregano leaves, crumbled
1 teaspoon salt
1 teaspoon freshly ground pepper
3 (1-pound) cans black beans, rinsed

1 • In a large Dutch oven over medium-high heat, heat 2 tablespoons of the vegetable oil. Working in batches, cook the chuck and pork shoulder until the meat is browned on all sides, about 3 minutes per batch, adding more vegetable oil as needed. With a slotted spoon, transfer the browned meat to a large bowl.

2 • Lower the heat to medium. To the drippings remaining in the Dutch oven, add the onions; sauté about 13 to 15 minutes or until the onions are soft and beginning to brown. Add the garlic and sauté for 2 minutes. Add the meat mixture with any juices that have accumulated in the bowl. Add the tomatoes in purée, tomato paste, the 3 cups of water, the tequila or beer, Worcestershire sauce, chili powder, cumin, oregano, salt, and pepper. Stir until the ingredients are well mixed.

3 • Bring the mixture to boiling, stirring. Reduce the heat to low, cover the pan, and simmer the chili, stirring occasionally, about 1 hour and 30 minutes to 2 hours or until the meats are tender. Stir in the black beans for the last 10 minutes of cooking time.

> *Makes 16 servings (16 cups). Per serving: 481 calories, 30 g protein, 24 g carbohydrate, 26 g fat, 89 mg cholesterol, 558 mg sodium.*

Black Bean Chili

El Paso Chili

Like many chili recipes, this dish definitely improves with age. Prepare it a day in advance. Serve with jalapeño cornbread or buttermilk biscuits.

2 tablespoons vegetable oil
2 large red onions, chopped
3 large cloves garlic, crushed
3 pounds ground beef
2 (28-ounce) cans whole tomatoes
2 medium sweet green or red peppers, chopped
1 cup dry red wine
1/4 cup chili powder
2 tablespoons yellow corn meal or masa harina
1 tablespoon sugar
1 1/2 teaspoons ground cumin
1 teaspoon salt
1/2 teaspoon ground hot red pepper
1 (1-pound) can red kidney beans, drained
1 (15-ounce) can whole-kernel corn, drained
Sour cream, shredded Monterey Jack cheese, and chopped green
    onions (optional)

1 • In a large saucepan over medium-high heat, heat the vegetable oil until it is hot. Add the red onions and garlic, and sauté about 5 minutes or until the onions are tender. Add the ground beef and cook until the meat is browned, about 10 minutes. Spoon off and discard any visible fat from the saucepan. Add the tomatoes with their liquid, sweet green or red peppers, red wine, chili powder, corn meal or masa harina, sugar, cumin, salt, and ground hot red pepper. Stir until the ingredients are well mixed. Bring the mixture to boiling. Lower the heat and simmer the mixture, uncovered, for 30 minutes, stirring frequently.

2 • Stir in the red kidney beans and the corn. Simmer the chili for 15 minutes more. If desired, serve the chili with the sour cream, shredded Monterey Jack cheese, and chopped green onions.

Makes 10 servings. Per serving: 462 calories, 30 g protein, 28 g carbohydrate, 25 g fat, 91 mg cholesterol, 802 mg sodium.

Ossobuco

~

Prepare this Italian favorite, tender braised veal shanks, a day ahead and reheat for an easy family meal or a special cold-weather dinner for friends. The Gremolata, a mixture of garlic, lemon and orange zest, and chopped parsley, adds sparkle to the finished dish. Ask your butcher to slice the veal shanks if they're not sold that way.

🌿 🌿 🌿

preparation time:
30 minutes

baking time:
2³/₄ hours

🌿 🌿 🌿

½ cup all-purpose flour
1 teaspoon salt
½ teaspoon freshly ground pepper
8 (2-inch-thick) slices veal shanks (about 5 pounds)
2 tablespoons butter
3 tablespoons olive oil
4 large leeks, green portion trimmed to 3 inches, halved lengthwise, thinly sliced, and rinsed
2 large carrots, pared and finely diced
4 large cloves garlic, finely chopped
8 large sun-dried tomato halves in oil, finely chopped
6 large ripe plum tomatoes, peeled, seeded, and chopped
2 cups chicken broth
1 cup dry white wine
1 teaspoon chopped fresh thyme or ¼ teaspoon dried thyme

GREMOLATA

2 large cloves garlic, finely chopped
Grated zest of 1 lemon (colored part of peel)
Grated zest of 1 orange (colored part of peel)
¼ cup chopped flat-leaf parsley

Hot cooked rice (optional)

1 • In a pie plate, combine the flour, ½ teaspoon of the salt, and the pepper. One at a time, dip the veal shanks in the flour mixture until the meat is completely coated; shake off the excess flour mixture. In a Dutch oven large enough to hold the veal shanks in a single layer, over medium-high heat, melt the butter in the olive oil. Working in batches, cook the veal shanks until they are browned on both sides, about 4 minutes on each side. Transfer the veal shanks to a platter.

2 • Preheat the oven to 300°F. In the drippings remaining in the Dutch oven, over medium-low heat, sauté the leeks and carrots about 10 minutes or until the vegetables are soft. Stir in the 4 cloves of garlic, the sun-dried and plum tomatoes, the chicken broth, white wine, and thyme. Increase the heat to high and bring the mixture to boiling. Return the veal shanks to the pan, arranging the shanks in a single layer under the liquid. Cover the Dutch oven and bake in the 300°F oven about 2 hours and 30 minutes or until the veal is fork-tender; remove the lid for the last 15 minutes of cooking time.

3 • Transfer the veal shanks to a large serving platter. Cover the platter and keep the veal warm. Skim any visible fat from the cooking liquid in the Dutch oven. With a slotted spoon, transfer 1 cup of the solids to a blender or food processor; add the remaining ½ teaspoon of salt. Process until the mixture is puréed. Stir the purée back into the cooking liquid in the pan. Spoon some of the sauce over the veal shanks on the platter.

4 • Prepare the Gremolata: In a small bowl, combine the 2 cloves of garlic, the lemon and orange zests, and the flat-leaf parsley. Sprinkle some of the Gremolata over the veal shanks before serving. Pass the remaining Gremolata along with the remaining sauce. If desired, serve the Ossobuco with the rice for soaking up the sauce.

> *Makes 8 servings. Per serving: 415 calories, 42 g protein, 21 g carbohydrate, 28 g fat, 163 mg cholesterol, 609 mg sodium.*

Cider-Braised Pork Loin

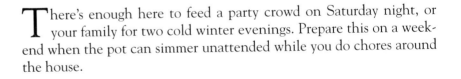

make ahead

preparation time:
20 minutes

baking time:
2½ hours

There's enough here to feed a party crowd on Saturday night, or your family for two cold winter evenings. Prepare this on a weekend when the pot can simmer unattended while you do chores around the house.

> 1 (5½-pound) center-cut loin of pork
> 2 large cloves garlic, slivered
> 1½ teaspoons dried sage leaves, crushed
> 1½ teaspoons dried thyme leaves, crushed
> 1½ teaspoons salt
> 1 teaspoon dried rosemary leaves, crushed
> ½ teaspoon freshly ground pepper
> 2 medium onions, cut into wedges

2 pounds sweet potatoes, pared and cut into 1-inch pieces
3 cups apple cider or juice
1 (12-ounce) package pitted prunes
2 medium Granny Smith apples, cut into wedges
¼ cup all-purpose flour
1 cup light cream or half-and-half

1 • Preheat the oven to 350°F. Using the tip of a paring knife, make tiny slits over the surface of the pork loin. Insert a sliver of the garlic into each slit. In a cup, combine the sage, thyme, salt, rosemary, and pepper. Pat the seasoning mixture over the pork. Scatter the onion wedges over the bottom of a roasting pan. Place the pork loin, fat side up, on top of the onions. Scatter the sweet potatoes on top of the onions around the pork.

2 • Bake the pork loin in the 350°F oven for 1 hour. Pour the apple cider or juice into the roasting pan and scatter the prunes around the pork. Cover the pan with aluminum foil and bake for 1 hour more. Scatter the apples around the pork. Re-cover the pan and bake about 15 minutes or until an instant-read meat thermometer inserted into the center of the pork registers 170°F. Transfer the pork and the potato-fruit mixture to a large serving platter and keep them warm.

3 • Spoon off and discard any visible fat from the surface of the liquid remaining in the roasting pan. Place the pan on the range top. Bring the liquid to boiling; boil until the liquid is reduced to 1½ cups, about 5 minutes. In a cup, combine the flour and the light cream or half-and-half; stir until the mixture is blended. Whisking constantly, pour the flour mixture into the boiling liquid in the roasting pan. Continue to whisk and cook until the gravy boils again and thickens, about 2 minutes.

4 • To serve: Slice the pork loin and pass the gravy separately.

Makes 10 servings and 2¼ cups gravy. Per serving: 760 calories, 64 g protein, 64 g carbohydrate, 28 g fat, 211 mg cholesterol, 488 mg sodium.

Vegetable and Pork Stir-Fry

quick

A selection of colorful vegetables stretches a pound of pork to serve six. Quick and appealing for a weekday family meal, or an easy Saturday-night dinner with friends.

3 large cloves garlic
1 (1½-inch-long) piece gingerroot, pared
3 green onions, cut into 1-inch lengths
¾ cup chicken broth
2 tablespoons soy sauce
3 tablespoons balsamic vinegar
1 teaspoon crushed red-pepper flakes
1 tablespoon brown sugar
1 tablespoon cornstarch
4 tablespoons vegetable oil
1 pound trimmed pork tenderloin, halved lengthwise and cut crosswise
   into ¼-inch-thick strips
6 cups broccoli florets plus thinly sliced, peeled stems (about 1¼
   pounds)
1 large sweet red pepper, cut into ¾-inch cubes
1 large sweet yellow pepper, cut into ¾-inch cubes
Hot cooked rice (optional)

1 • In a food processor, mince the garlic and ginger. Add the green onions and process until they are coarsely chopped. Set aside the garlic mixture.

2 • In a medium bowl, combine the chicken broth, soy sauce, balsamic vinegar, red-pepper flakes, brown sugar, and cornstarch. Stir until the cornstarch is dissolved. Set aside.

3 • In a large skillet over high heat, heat 1 tablespoon of the vegetable oil. Add half of the pork strips. Stir-fry just until the pork strips are cooked through, about 1 minute. With a slotted spoon, transfer the cooked pork to a plate. Repeat with 1 more tablespoon of the vegetable oil and the remaining pork strips. Add 1 more tablespoon of vegetable oil to the skillet. Add the broccoli and sweet red and yellow peppers; stir-fry about 3 to 4 minutes. Transfer the vegetable mixture to the plate with the cooked pork.

4 • Add the last tablespoon of vegetable oil to the skillet. Add the garlic mixture and stir-fry for 30 seconds. Stir the cornstarch mixture to reblend the ingredients; stir the cornstarch mixture into the garlic mixture. Cook, stirring, until the combined mixture has thickened. Return the pork and vegetables to the skillet, and stir until all the ingredients are well mixed. Cook for 1 minute to heat the mixture through. Serve the stir-fry with the rice, if you wish.

Makes 6 servings. Per serving (without rice): 281 calories, 20 g protein, 16 g carbohydrate, 16 g fat, 48 mg cholesterol, 504 mg sodium.

Vegetable and Pork Stir-Fry

Jambalaya

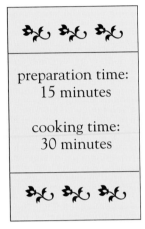

A devilishly spicy stew from the bayou region of Louisiana, our version of this classic is thick with ham and kielbasa. Chunks of crusty bread would be heavenly for dunking into the sauce.

1 tablespoon olive oil
1/2 pound smoked Virginia ham, cut into 3/4-inch chunks
1/2 pound kielbasa, cut into 1-inch chunks
1 large onion, diced
1 sweet green pepper, diced
1 sweet yellow pepper, diced
2 celery stalks, diced
3 large cloves garlic, minced
1 1/2 cups uncooked long-grain rice
1 (14 1/2-ounce) can seasoned diced tomatoes
2 cups chicken broth
1/2 teaspoon freshly ground black pepper
1/2 teaspoon dried thyme, crushed
1/4 teaspoon ground hot red pepper

1 • In a large skillet over medium-high heat, heat the olive oil. Add the ham and kielbasa, and sauté about 6 to 7 minutes or until the meats are browned. With a slotted spoon, transfer the ham and kielbasa to a bowl. Set aside.

2 • Reduce the heat to medium-low. To the hot drippings remaining in the skillet, add the onion, sweet green and yellow peppers, celery, and garlic. Sauté the mixture about 5 minutes or until the vegetables are soft. Stir in the rice, seasoned tomatoes, chicken broth, ground black pepper, thyme, and hot red pepper. Bring the mixture to boiling. Reduce the heat to low, cover the skillet, and simmer the mixture for 15 minutes.

3 • Add the ham and kielbasa to the vegetable mixture in the skillet. Cover the skillet and cook for 3 minutes, stirring once. Remove the skillet from the heat and let the jambalaya stand for 5 minutes before serving.

Makes 6 servings. Per serving: 431 calories, 21 g protein, 51 g carbohydrate, 16 g fat, 45 mg cholesterol, 1,347 mg sodium.

Baked Polenta with Broccoli Rabe and Tomato-Sausage Sauce

P olenta (cornmeal mush) is baked into a soft "cake" that soaks up all the savory sauce. To make the preparation even easier, the polenta mixture can be made up to 2 days ahead; the Broccoli Rabe and sauce can also be prepared ahead. Gently reheat the three mixtures to serve. Spinach may be substituted for the broccoli rabe.

POLENTA

Nonstick cooking spray
2 tablespoons olive oil
1 small onion, chopped
1 clove garlic, minced
2$\frac{1}{2}$ cups chicken broth
$\frac{1}{2}$ cup heavy cream
$\frac{1}{4}$ teaspoon freshly ground black pepper
1 cup cornmeal
4 ounces mozzarella cheese, diced
$\frac{1}{4}$ cup shredded Parmesan cheese
2 tablespoons chopped parsley

BROCCOLI RABE

2 bunches broccoli rabe or 2 pounds fresh spinach, coarse stems removed
2 tablespoons olive oil
2 cloves garlic, minced
$\frac{1}{4}$ teaspoon crushed red-pepper flakes
$\frac{1}{4}$ teaspoon salt

TOMATO-SAUSAGE SAUCE

1 tablespoon olive oil
2 links hot or sweet Italian sausage, casings removed
$\frac{1}{2}$ pound medium mushrooms, sliced
1 teaspoon water
1 (14-ounce) container prepared tomato-basil sauce
1 (8-ounce) can tomato sauce

make ahead

preparation time: 20 minutes

cooking time: 18 minutes

baking time: 18 minutes

Broccoli Rabe

Also known as rapini, this leafy green vegetable is a cousin to both turnips and cabbage. It is long and stalky, with clusters of little buds that look like broccoli. Strongly flavored with a slightly bitter quality, rabe is usually sautéed, steamed, or braised. Look for it at produce stands and better supermarkets during the spring.

Baked Polenta with Broccoli Rabe and Tomato-Sausage Sauce

1 • Prepare the Polenta: Preheat the oven to 350°F. Grease a 9-inch round cake pan with the nonstick cooking spray. In a large saucepan over medium heat, heat the 2 tablespoons of olive oil. Add the onion and the 1 minced clove of garlic; sauté the mixture about 5 to 6 minutes or until the onion is soft. Add the chicken broth, heavy cream, and ground black pepper. Bring the mixture to boiling. Very gradually add the cornmeal, whisking constantly. Reduce the heat and simmer the mixture, stirring, until it is thick and creamy, about 10 minutes. Remove the saucepan from the heat; stir in the mozzarella and Parmesan cheeses and the chopped parsley. Pour the polenta batter into the prepared pan and smooth the top of the batter with a spatula. (The Polenta can be made up to this point, covered, and refrigerated up to 2 days.) Bake the Polenta in the 350°F oven about 18 to 20 minutes.

2 • Meanwhile (or when ready to continue), prepare the Broccoli Rabe: Add 3 inches of water to a large saucepan; add salt to taste, about 1/2 teaspoon or so. Bring the water to boiling and add the broccoli rabe. Cover the saucepan and cook about 1 to 2 minutes or until the broccoli rabe is wilted (if using spinach, cook for 30 seconds). Drain the broccoli rabe well and chop it coarsely. In a large skillet over medium-high heat, heat the 2 tablespoons of olive oil. Add the 2 minced cloves of garlic, red-pepper flakes, and the 1/4 teaspoon of salt. Sauté about 30 seconds or until the mixture is fragrant. Add the broccoli rabe and sauté about 3 minutes or until the broccoli rabe is very tender. Transfer the broccoli rabe mixture to a warm serving dish and keep it warm.

3 • Prepare the Tomato-Sausage Sauce: In the same skillet over medium heat, heat the 1 tablespoon of olive oil. Add the Italian sausage and sauté, breaking up the sausage with a wooden spoon, until the meat is browned. With a slotted spoon, transfer the browned sausage to a plate. Add the mushrooms to the drippings remaining in the skillet. Sauté about 3 to 4 minutes or until the mushrooms are just tender, adding the 1 teaspoon of water to the skillet to prevent the mushrooms from scorching. Stir in the tomato-basil and plain tomato sauces. Return the sausage to the skillet. Stir until the ingredients are well mixed, and cook until the sauce is heated through.

4 • To serve: Cut the Polenta into 6 wedges. Place one wedge on each of 6 dinner plates. Top each serving with some of the Broccoli Rabe and some of the Tomato-Sausage Sauce.

Makes 6 servings. Per serving: 534 calories, 19 g protein, 36 g carbohydrate, 38 g fat, 65 mg cholesterol, 1,432 mg sodium.

Polenta with Pork-Shiitake Sauce

preparation time:
10 minutes

cooking time:
40 minutes

A mound of creamy polenta is crowned with a rich sauce of shiitake mushrooms, tomatoes, and pork.

2 tablespoons olive oil
1 medium onion, chopped
1 large clove garlic, crushed
1/2 pound shiitake mushrooms, stemmed, rinsed, and sliced
1/4 cup dry white wine
1/2 pound cooked pork, julienned (about 1 1/2 cups)
1 (28-ounce) can whole tomatoes, chopped
1/2 teaspoon dried basil leaves, crushed
1/2 teaspoon freshly ground pepper
1/2 teaspoon salt
3 cups chicken broth
1 cup fine yellow cornmeal
1/2 cup grated Parmesan cheese
2 tablespoons chopped parsley
3 tablespoons butter or margarine
Sprigs fresh basil (optional)

1 • In a large skillet over medium-high heat, heat the olive oil. Add the onion and garlic, and sauté about 2 to 3 minutes or until the onion is softened. Add the shiitake mushrooms and sauté for 3 minutes. Add the white wine. Bring the mixture to boiling and cook until the wine has evaporated. Stir in the pork, tomatoes, basil, pepper, and salt. Return the mixture to boiling. Reduce the heat, partially cover the skillet, and simmer for 30 minutes, stirring occasionally.

2 • Meanwhile, in a large saucepan, bring the chicken broth to boiling. Whisking constantly, gradually add the cornmeal to the broth. Lower the heat and simmer, stirring constantly, about 5 minutes or until the mixture thickens. Stir in the Parmesan cheese, parsley, and butter or margarine. Cover the saucepan and remove from the heat. Let the polenta stand for 10 minutes.

3 • To serve, divide the polenta among 4 plates. Spoon some of the pork-shiitake mixture over the polenta and serve immediately. If desired, garnish each serving with sprigs of fresh basil.

Makes 4 servings. Per serving: 555 calories, 30 g protein, 47 g carbohydrate, 27 g fat, 85 mg cholesterol, 1,473 mg sodium.

Pork with Soba Noodles

Garlic and Szechuan chili sauce enliven this simple dish, which is prepared in less than 15 minutes. The soba and saifun noodles and the chili sauce can be found in the Asian foods section in some supermarkets or in food stores specializing in Asian ingredients.

1 pound pork tenderloin, sliced
2 large cloves garlic, crushed
1 1/2 cups sugar snap peas
1/2 medium sweet red pepper, diced
3 tablespoons soy sauce
1/4 pound soba noodles, cooked (see Note)
1/4 pound saifun noodles, cooked (see Note)
1 teaspoon Szechuan chili sauce
1/2 cup coarsely chopped walnuts

1 • In a nonstick skillet over medium-high heat, sauté the pork and garlic for 3 minutes. Add the sugar snap peas and sweet red pepper, and sauté for 3 minutes. Add the soy sauce and sauté for 1 minute. Transfer the pork-vegetable mixture to a serving platter.

2 • To the same skillet, add the soba and saifun noodles, Szechuan chili sauce, and walnuts. Toss to coat the noodles and nuts with the sauce. Transfer the noodle mixture to the platter with the pork mixture and serve immediately.

NOTE: To cook the soba and saifun noodles: In a large saucepan of boiling water, cook the noodles for 3 minutes. Drain well.

Makes 6 servings. Per serving: 297 calories, 26 g protein, 19 g carbohydrate, 3 g fat, 63 mg cholesterol, 591 mg sodium.

low-fat

quick

___

Soba Noodles

These Japanese noodles are made from buckwheat flour and can be found in food shops specializing in Asian ingredients or in the Asian foods section of better supermarkets. In Japan, soba is a symbol of good fortune and longevity.

___

Saifun Noodles

Long and thin, these clear cellophane noodles are made from mung beans. Like other noodles, they can be eaten after being cooked in boiling water until soft, or the dried noodles can be fried until crispy and used as a bed or topping for a stir-fry.

Italian Strata

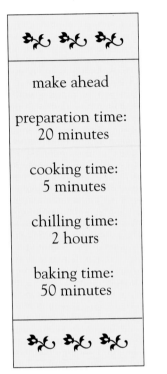

What is a strata? A fabulous concoction made by layering bread, meat, and seasonings, covering it all with a custard sauce, and baking. The whole dish (shown on page 53) can be assembled a day ahead and then baked just before serving.

Nonstick cooking spray
1 (10-ounce) loaf Italian bread
18 thin slices provolone cheese (about $^{3}/_{4}$ pound)
9 thin slices mortadella sausage (about $^{1}/_{2}$ pound)
9 thin slices Genoa salami (about $^{1}/_{4}$ pound)
2 tablespoons butter or margarine
1 large onion, chopped
1 large sweet red or yellow pepper, chopped
1 medium zucchini, halved lengthwise and cut crosswise into thin slices
3 cups milk
6 large eggs, beaten

1 • The day before or at least 2 hours before cooking, grease a shallow 2-quart baking dish with the nonstick cooking spray. Slice the Italian bread diagonally into 18 thin slices. Toast the bread slices on both sides. Cut the provolone cheese, mortadella sausage, and Genoa salami in half. Using 2 slices of toasted bread, 2 slices of cheese, and 1 slice each of the sausage and the salami, make 9 sandwiches. Place the sandwiches in the prepared baking dish, overlapping the sandwiches slightly.

2 • In a large skillet over medium heat, melt the butter or margarine. Add the onion, sweet red or yellow pepper, and zucchini, and sauté about 5 minutes or until the vegetables are tender-crisp. Scatter the vegetable mixture over the sandwiches.

3 • In a large bowl, beat together the milk and the eggs. Pour the egg mixture over the sandwiches in the dish. Cover the dish and refrigerate the strata for at least 2 hours or overnight.

4 • To serve: Preheat the oven to 350°F. Bake the strata about 50 minutes or until a knife inserted in the custard comes out clean. Let the strata stand for 10 minutes before serving.

Makes 8 servings. Per serving: 555 calories, 30 g protein, 31 g carbohydrate, 34 g fat, 236 mg cholesterol, 1,313 mg sodium.

make ahead

preparation time:
20 minutes

cooking time:
5 minutes

chilling time:
2 hours

baking time:
50 minutes

Sausage Ratatouille

Make this a day or two ahead and then gently reheat to serve. You need nothing more than a loaf of bread on the side.

1 medium eggplant, cut into $^1/_2$-inch cubes
$^1/_2$ pound mushrooms, quartered
1 large yellow squash, cut into $^3/_4$-inch dice
1 large zucchini, cut into $^3/_4$-inch dice
1 sweet red pepper, cut into $^3/_4$-inch dice
1 sweet yellow pepper, cut into $^3/_4$-inch dice
1 onion, diced
2 tablespoons olive oil
$^1/_2$ teaspoon salt
$^1/_2$ teaspoon freshly ground black pepper
1 pound hot Italian sausage
1 cup water
$^3/_4$ cup bottled thick-and-chunky spaghetti sauce

make ahead

preparation time:
15 minutes

baking time:
45 minutes

1 • Preheat the oven to 400°F. In a large shallow roasting pan, combine the eggplant, mushrooms, yellow squash, zucchini, sweet red and yellow peppers, and onion. Drizzle with the oil and sprinkle with the salt and black pepper.

2 • Bake in the 400°F oven for 30 minutes, stirring once.

3 • Meanwhile, in a large nonstick skillet, combine the sausage and the water. Heat to boiling. Reduce the heat; cover and simmer for 8 minutes or until the sausage is firm. With tongs, remove the sausage to a plate; cool. Cut the sausage crosswise into $^1/_2$-inch-thick slices. Drain the skillet and place it over medium-high heat. Add the sausage; sauté for 5 minutes or until lightly browned. Stir in the spaghetti sauce. Add the sausage mixture to the vegetables.

4 • Bake the ratatouille in the 400°F oven for 15 minutes or until the vegetables are tender. Serve warm.

Makes 6 servings. Per serving: 282 calories, 13 g protein, 20 g carbohydrate, 18 g fat, 35 mg cholesterol, 757 mg sodium.

Moussaka

Moussaka

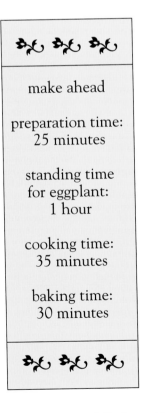

make ahead

preparation time:
25 minutes

standing time
for eggplant:
1 hour

cooking time:
35 minutes

baking time:
30 minutes

The classic Greek dish made with ground lamb, or beef if you prefer, and eggplant. The whole dish can be assembled earlier in the day. Serve with a cucumber and plain yogurt salad.

2 eggplants (about 1³/4 pounds), trimmed and cut crosswise into
¹/4-inch-thick slices
1¹/2 tablespoons coarse (kosher) salt

LAMB FILLING

2 teaspoons olive oil
1 large onion, chopped
2 pounds ground lamb or ground beef
1 cup tomato purée
2 teaspoons dried oregano leaves, crushed
1¹/2 teaspoons ground cinnamon
1 teaspoon salt
¹/2 teaspoon freshly ground pepper

BÉCHAMEL SAUCE

¼ cup unsalted butter
¼ cup all-purpose flour
¾ teaspoon salt
¼ teaspoon freshly ground pepper
1 cup milk, heated
3 large eggs, lightly beaten
1 cup heavy cream, heated

¼ cup olive oil
⅓ cup freshly grated Parmesan cheese
Ground cinnamon for dusting

1 • Sprinkle the eggplant slices with the coarse salt. Arrange the eggplant in layers in a colander placed over a bowl. Place a sheet of waxed paper on top and weight with 2 heavy cans. Let the eggplant drain for 1 hour.

2 • Meanwhile, prepare the Lamb Filling: In a large skillet over medium heat, heat the 2 teaspoons of olive oil. Add the onion and sauté about 5 minutes or until the onion is tender. Add the ground lamb or beef to the skillet, breaking up the meat with a wooden spoon. Sauté just until the meat is no longer pink. Transfer the meat mixture to a sieve set over a bowl. Let the meat mixture stand until all the fat is drained off. Return the meat mixture to the skillet. Stir in the tomato purée, oregano, the 1½ teaspoons of ground cinnamon, the 1 teaspoon of salt, and the ½ teaspoon of pepper. Cook the mixture about 5 minutes or until it is thickened. Set aside.

3 • Prepare the Béchamel Sauce: In a medium saucepan over medium heat, melt the butter. Add the flour, the ¾ teaspoon of salt, and the ¼ teaspoon of pepper, and stir until the mixture is blended. Cook the flour mixture about 1 minute or until it is bubbly. Gradually stir in the warm milk until it is well blended. Remove the saucepan from the heat. Stir in the eggs until they are blended. Return the saucepan to the heat and whisk in the warm heavy cream. Cook, whisking constantly, until the sauce is the thickness of mayonnaise, about 8 minutes; do not boil or the sauce will curdle. Pour into a bowl and set aside.

4 • With paper towels, dry the eggplant slices. In a large nonstick skillet over medium-high heat, heat 1 tablespoon of the olive oil. Add enough eggplant slices to cover the bottom of the skillet in a single layer. Cook about 2 to 3 minutes on each side, until the eggplant slices are lightly browned and cooked through; press the slices with a spatula to squeeze out any liquid. Transfer the eggplant slices to paper towels to drain. Repeat with the remaining eggplant slices, using an additional 1 tablespoon of olive oil per batch.

5 • Preheat the oven to 375°F. Assemble the Moussaka: Arrange 1 layer of eggplant slices over the bottom of a 10 × 9-inch 2-quart casserole dish. Sprinkle some of the Parmesan cheese over the eggplant slices. Repeat the layering, using the remaining eggplant slices and Parmesan cheese until all the eggplant and cheese has been used. Spoon the Lamb Filling over the top layer in the dish, lightly packing the filling down. Pour the Béchamel Sauce over the filling. Dust with the ground cinnamon. Bake in the middle of the 375°F oven about 30 to 35 minutes or until the Moussaka is golden. Cool for 10 minutes before serving.

> *Makes 8 servings. Per serving: 479 calories, 27 g protein, 17 g carbohydrate, 34 g fat, 203 mg cholesterol, 762 mg sodium.*

Lamb Curry

Serve this pungent dish with a variety of condiments, such as shredded coconut, unsalted cashews or peanuts, chopped dried apricots, and raisins.

low-fat

preparation time:
15 minutes

cooking time:
30 minutes

1 tablespoon vegetable oil
1 medium zucchini, cut into 1-inch cubes
1 cup finely chopped onion
2 teaspoons minced garlic
1 teaspoon finely chopped fresh gingerroot
1 tablespoon ground cumin
1 teaspoon ground coriander
1/2 teaspoon turmeric
1/4 teaspoon salt
1/8 teaspoon ground hot red pepper
2 large all-purpose potatoes, pared and cut into 1 1/2-inch pieces
2 carrots, pared, halved lengthwise, and cut into 2-inch pieces
3/4 pound cooked lamb, cut into 1-inch pieces (about 3 cups)
1 (14-ounce) can Italian plum tomatoes, drained and chopped
1 1/2 cups chicken broth
1 cup frozen peas
Plain yogurt
Fresh cilantro sprigs

1 • In a large, deep skillet over medium-high heat, heat the vegetable oil. Add the zucchini and sauté about 2 minutes or until the zucchini is golden brown. With a slotted spoon, transfer the zucchini to a plate. To the skillet, add the onion and sauté about 3 minutes or until the onion is golden. Add the garlic and ginger, and sauté for 30 seconds. Add the cumin, coriander, turmeric, salt, and hot red pepper. Sauté for 15 seconds or until the mixture is fragrant. Add the potatoes and carrots, and sauté for 1 minute more.

2 • Add the lamb, Italian tomatoes, and chicken broth to the skillet, stirring until the ingredients are well mixed. Bring the mixture to boiling. Reduce the heat, cover the skillet, and simmer about 20 minutes or until the vegetables are tender. Return the zucchini to the skillet and stir in the peas. Simmer for 2 minutes more. Garnish each serving with a dollop of yogurt and a sprig of fresh cilantro.

Makes 4 servings. Per serving: 430 calories, 34 g protein, 47 g carbohydrate, 12 g fat, 78 mg cholesterol, 730 mg sodium.

Lamb Curry

Cassoulet

make ahead

preparation time:
15 minutes

cooking time:
10 minutes

baking time:
45 minutes

The recipe for this hearty French country classic makes enough for a Saturday-night party or two weeknight suppers. Serve with a green salad, crusty bread, and fruit for dessert.

3 tablespoons olive oil
1 pound lean boneless leg of lamb, trimmed and cut into $^3/_4$-inch pieces
$^1/_2$ pound kielbasa, cut into $^3/_4$-inch pieces
2 large carrots, pared and chopped
1 large onion, chopped
4 large cloves garlic, finely chopped
1 (28-ounce) can Italian tomatoes in juice
1 teaspoon dried thyme leaves, crushed
$^3/_4$ teaspoon salt
$^1/_2$ teaspoon dried oregano leaves, crushed
$^1/_2$ teaspoon freshly ground pepper
$^1/_2$ teaspoon dried rosemary, crushed
3 (1-pound) cans cannellini beans, rinsed and drained
$^1/_2$ cup fine dry bread crumbs

1 • Preheat the oven to 375°F. In a large skillet over high heat, heat 1 tablespoon of the olive oil. Add the lamb and sauté about 1 to 2 minutes or until the lamb is browned but not cooked through. With a slotted spoon, transfer the lamb to a large bowl. Add the kielbasa to the skillet. Reduce the heat to medium and sauté about 3 minutes or until the kielbasa is browned. Transfer the kielbasa to the bowl with the lamb.

2 • To the drippings remaining in the skillet, add 1 tablespoon of the olive oil. Add the carrots, onion, and garlic. Sauté about 4 to 5 minutes or until the vegetables are tender. Add the tomatoes with their juice, the thyme, salt, oregano, pepper, and rosemary. Stir until the ingredients are well mixed, breaking up the tomatoes with a spoon. Bring the mixture to boiling. Reduce the heat and simmer for 1 minute. Pour the vegetable mixture into the bowl with the lamb-kielbasa mixture; add the cannellini beans. Gently stir until the ingredients are well mixed.

3 • Pour the cassoulet mixture into a 2-quart shallow casserole dish. In a small bowl, stir together the bread crumbs and the remaining tablespoon of olive oil. Sprinkle the bread-crumb mixture over the Cassoulet.

Bake in the 375°F oven about 45 minutes or until the Cassoulet is bubbly and the top is brown. Let the Cassoulet stand for 5 minutes before serving.

> *Makes 8 servings. Per serving: 464 calories, 30 g protein, 51 g carbohydrate, 17 g fat, 50 mg cholesterol, 749 mg sodium.*

Pastitsio

This Greek casserole is similar to moussaka with a layer of pasta added. A no-nonsense one-dish supper for a hungry crowd, this dish can be made earlier in the day and refrigerated, but allow a little extra cooking time if baking it directly from the refrigerator.

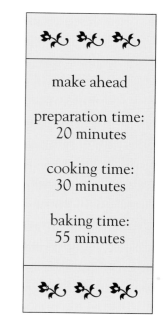

make ahead

preparation time:
20 minutes

cooking time:
30 minutes

baking time:
55 minutes

2 tablespoons olive oil
1 medium yellow onion, finely chopped
3 cloves garlic, chopped
1 1/2 pounds ground lamb shoulder
1/2 cup dry red wine
1 teaspoon salt
3/4 teaspoon freshly ground black pepper
1/2 teaspoon ground cinnamon
1/2 teaspoon dried oregano leaves, crushed
1 (28-ounce) can crushed Italian tomatoes with added purée
1/4 cup finely chopped, pitted oil-cured Greek olives
1/4 cup grated Parmesan cheese
1 pound penne

BÉCHAMEL SAUCE

6 tablespoons butter
6 tablespoons all-purpose flour
3 cups milk
3 large eggs
1/4 cup grated Parmesan cheese
2 tablespoons chopped fresh parsley
3/4 teaspoon salt
1/4 teaspoon freshly ground black pepper
1/8 to 1/4 teaspoon ground hot red pepper

1 • In a large skillet over medium-high heat, heat the olive oil. Add the onion and sauté about 5 minutes or until the onion is soft. Add the garlic and the ground lamb, and sauté about 8 minutes or until the meat is no longer pink. Add the red wine, the 1 teaspoon of salt, the ³/₄ teaspoon of ground black pepper, the cinnamon, and oregano. Cook the mixture about 3 minutes or until the wine is reduced by half. Add the Italian tomatoes. Reduce the heat and simmer the mixture for 30 minutes. Add the Greek olives and 2 tablespoons of the Parmesan cheese. Stir until all the ingredients are well mixed. Set aside.

2 • Meanwhile, cook the penne as the package label directs. Drain the pasta and set aside.

3 • Prepare the Béchamel Sauce: In a medium saucepan over medium heat, melt the butter. Stir in the flour until the ingredients are blended. Cook for 1 minute or until the flour mixture is bubbly. Stir in the milk until it is blended. Remove the saucepan from the heat. Add the eggs, one at a time, whisking well after each addition. Return the saucepan to the heat and cook about 8 minutes, whisking constantly, until the egg mixture has thickened; do not boil or the sauce will curdle. Remove the saucepan from the heat and stir in the ¼ cup of Parmesan cheese, the parsley, the ³/₄ teaspoon of salt, the ¼ teaspoon of black pepper, and the hot red pepper to taste.

4 • Preheat the oven to 350°F. Spread one half of the lamb mixture over the bottom of a shallow 3-quart casserole dish. Place half of the penne over the lamb mixture in the dish. Spread the remaining lamb mixture over the layer of penne and top with the remaining pasta. Spoon the Béchamel Sauce over all. Sprinkle the remaining 2 tablespoons of Parmesan cheese over the top of the casserole. Bake in the 350°F oven about 35 minutes or until the Pastitsio is hot. Let the casserole cool for 10 minutes before serving.

Makes 8 servings. Per serving: 607 calories, 30 g protein, 59 g carbohydrate, 27 g fat, 165 mg cholesterol, 1,039 mg sodium.

Appendix 1: Guide to Wines

Selecting Wine

Contrary to popular belief, there is no hard-and-fast rule about which wine to serve with which food. A wine should complement and highlight the flavor of the food and vice versa, so that your meal is a harmonious blend of flavors, with neither the food nor the drink overwhelming the other.

There is, however, one simple rationale behind the primary guideline of choosing a wine: A delicate food requires a delicate wine; a hearty food requires a robust wine. Chicken or fish, for example, is best paired with a white wine, such as Chablis or Chardonnay, or with a light red wine, such as a Beaujolais; roast beef is best complemented by a full-bodied red wine, such as a Cabernet Sauvignon or Bordeaux.

In addition to red wines and white wines, consider adding specialty wines to your wine cellar: champagne (the traditional choice for a toast), port (a dessert wine), and sherry (an aperitif). Many wines, including specialty wines, are named for their region of origin, where unique grape varieties and growing conditions contribute to the making of the particular type of wine; Chablis, Burgundy, and Bordeaux are examples. Wine that is not named for a particular region or country is usually named for the dominant grape used to make it — for example, Cabernet Sauvignon, chenin blanc, and zinfandel.

Food and Wine Complements

Food: Appetizers; hors d'oeuvres; egg dishes; delicate fish; plain chicken; mild cheese dishes; main-dish salads; Asian food.

Wine: Light to medium-bodied fruity whites, and rosés.
American and imported jug whites
French Sauvignon
Standard Italian whites (Soave, verdicchio, orvieto secco, pinot bianco)
Spanish and Portuguese whites (vinho verde)
California Chablis, chenin blanc, and blush wines
Australian Moselles

Food: Shellfish; oily fish; chicken in sauce; pasta; turkey; creamed dishes; main-dish salads; sandwiches.

Wine: Full-bodied whites, rosés, and light-bodied reds.
Jug red wines from America, France, Italy, Spain, Eastern Europe, Argentina, Chile, and Australia
French, California, and Australian Chardonnays
Alsatian whites
French whites (pouilly-fumé and sancerre) and Beaujolais
Italian whites (frascati, Soave Classico, pinot grigio) and young Chiantis
Spanish white Rioja and red lambrusco
Australian semillons
California Johannisberg Riesling

Food: Pork; ham; sausages; turkey; lamb; pasta.

Wine: Medium-bodied dry reds.
        Italian Valpolicella, bardolino, barbera, Chianti, Chianti Reservas, and
            venegazzu
        Spanish lambrusco
        California light gamays and zinfandels
        French Burgundies and Rhônes
        Spanish red Rioja

Food: Hearty soups; pasta; roast beef; steaks; pot roast; venison; cheese.

Wine: Full-bodied reds.
        California, Washington, and Oregon Cabernets and pinot noirs
        Australian reds
        French Bordeaux, Burgundies, and Rhônes
        Italian barolo, barbaresco, brunello di Montalcino

Buying Wine

- Buy inexpensive wines in a store with a large turnover to avoid overpaying and getting old wines. Be sure corked bottles are stored on their sides to keep the cork moist.

- When trying a new wine, buy only one bottle. Try the wine first and then buy more if you like it.

- If you are undecided, choose wine from a vineyard whose wines you have tried and liked before.

Wine Serving

- Less expensive wines should be consumed shortly after you purchase them.

- White and rosé wines should be refrigerated just until chilled, for 1 to 2 hours.

- Light red wines may be chilled only slightly. Full-bodied red wines are always served at room temperature.

- Cork any leftover wine tightly and refrigerate it. Use up the wine as soon as possible.

Appendix 2: Guide to Herbs and Spices

Herbs and spices should be used as accents to enhance the flavor of food; they should never overpower the flavor. As you gain confidence in your knowledge of herbs and spices, you should try experimenting with them in dishes, but it is best not to try too many varieties at once. Begin by adding $1/4$ teaspoon of a particular herb or spice for every four servings of a dish. Taste the dish and, if desired, add a bit more. Don't overdo the magic: Too much will obscure the flavor of the food.

Is It an Herb or a Spice?

The terms "herb" and "spice" are frequently used interchangeably, but there are differences. As a rule, you can grow herbs or buy them fresh from your greengrocer; spices are generally grown in tropical climates.

Herbs are defined as "the leafy part of a nonwoody plant that grows in a temperate zone." Parsley, sage, rosemary, and thyme are all types of herbs.

Spices, on the other hand, include certain parts (such as dried seeds, stems, buds, fruits, flowers, barks, and roots) of aromatic plants, usually of tropical origin. Allspice, cinnamon, clove, and nutmeg are all examples of spices.

Fresh versus Dried, Whole versus Ground

HERBS

The key to using herbs successfully is to follow the recipe directions. Many recipes calling for herbs are referring to dried herbs. If a recipe specifies a fresh herb, always try to use the fresh variety. If fresh herbs are not available, substitute 1 part dried for 3 parts fresh; for example, use 1 teaspoon dried basil in place of 1 tablespoon fresh basil.

Fresh Herbs: Quick-cooking dishes, such as sautéed fillets of fish and chicken, taste best when seasoned with fresh herbs, such as basil, oregano, tarragon, and parsley. These herbs are not good for prolonged cooking — the extended heat dissipates the flavor — and should be added only in the last few minutes of cooking. However, you can extract the flavor over a long period, such as when using herbs to flavor oils or vinegars.

Dried Herbs: It isn't necessary to use fresh herbs in dishes such as stews and sauces that simmer for an hour or more; dried herbs, especially thyme and bay leaf, are a better choice. The long cooking time allows the dried herbs to absorb moisture and to release their flavor into the food.

If a dish is to be served cold, reconstitute the dried herbs before adding them. Soak the dried herbs for at least 10 minutes in the liquid (wine, stock, milk, lemon juice, oil, or vinegar) that will be added to the dish.

Crushed herbs: Add these to a dish at the end of the cooking time. First measure the herbs, then crush them in the palm of your hand or with a mortar and pestle to break up the leaves and release the aroma and flavor.

SPICES

Whole spices: These are best used in long-simmering foods such as soups and stews. Wrap whole spices in cheesecloth, place them in a tea ball or, if using cloves, stick them in an onion. This makes it easier to remove the whole spices after cooking.

Ground spices: Because they are already broken down, these impart their flavor immediately. Add ground spices to dishes about 15 minutes before the end of the cooking time.

Seeds: To bring out the full flavor, seeds (such as cumin or coriander) should be toasted before being added to foods.

Storage

Fresh Herbs: Store fresh herbs in containers in the refrigerator. Wash, dry, and snip with kitchen shears as needed. Fresh herbs will last in the refrigerator for about a week.

- Stretch the life of fresh herbs by setting bunches upright in jars with their cut stems covered by an inch or two of water. Cover the leaves with plastic wrap and store in the refrigerator.

- If you have purchased or cut too many fresh herbs to use immediately, just rinse them in several changes of water and pat dry with paper towels. Place small amounts of the herbs in freezer-safe plastic bags, foil, or plastic wrap; label, date, and freeze the packets.

Dried herbs and spices: Dried herbs and spices should be fresh tasting and fragrant. To check an herb or spice on your shelf for potency, first pinch or crumble a small amount to see if it has its characteristic aroma. Then taste a pinch. If the flavor and aroma don't come through, the herb or spice certainly can't do much for a dish, so toss it out. Under favorable conditions, dried herbs will last six months to a year; ground spices will remain fresh up to a year. Whole spices will remain fresh indefinitely.

- Don't store herbs and spices over the stove. The hot, steamy environment reduces the flavor, encourages caking, causes color changes, and encourages infestation.

- Use clean, airtight, nonabsorbent containers to store herbs and spices, and keep them in a cool, dark area. In hot climates (or in the summer), it's practical to store capsicum spices (ground red pepper, chili powder, paprika) in the refrigerator to guard against infestation. Be sure to date all spice and dried herb containers with a wax pencil or felt-tip pen.

ALLSPICE (WHOLE AND GROUND)

Has an aroma and a flavor that suggest a blend of cloves, cinnamon, and nutmeg with peppery overtones. Use whole allspice in meat broths, gravies, and pickling liquids. Use ground allspice in fruitcakes, pies, cookies, relishes, and preserves, and with tomatoes and sweet yellow vegetables.

ANISE SEED

Has a distinct licorice taste that resembles the flavor of fennel; it is also reminiscent of tarragon. Use anise seed in cookies, cakes, fruit cups, and compotes. Also an excellent spice for chicken, duck, and veal dishes.

BASIL (FRESH AND DRIED LEAVES)

Flavor can range from licorice to clove. Use dried or fresh basil as a seasoning for pizza, spaghetti sauce, pesto, tomato salad, and tomato sauce. Basil adds a sweet, clovelike flavor to vegetable soups, meat pies, stews, chicken dishes, rice dishes, peas, zucchini, green beans, and cucumbers.

BAY LEAF

Has a unique evergreen fragrance and a sweet flavor. The subtle taste of Turkish bay leaf makes it more prized than bay leaf from California. Delicious with meats, potatoes, stews, soups, sauces, and fish. Be sure to remove the bay leaf from a dish before serving.

CARAWAY SEED

Has a strong peppery taste with a quality similar to anise. Use caraway seed in rye bread and other baked goods, and in cheese dishes. Sprinkle it over pork and sauerkraut dishes, soups, meats, and stews.

CARDAMOM (WHOLE AND GROUND)

A member of the ginger family. Each whole pod contains about 20 very small seeds. Cardamom has a strong flavor and aroma, so use it sparingly. It lends a delightful, spicy-sweet flavor to baked goods, especially apple and pumpkin pies. An important spice in Scandinavian baked goods and authentic Indian stews and curries.

CAYENNE PEPPER

(See Red Pepper)

CELERY SEED (WHOLE OR GROUND)

As the name implies, a flavor reminiscent of celery. Use celery seed with fish and in soups, tomato juice, oyster stews, clam juice, potato salad, salad dressings, egg dishes, and sauerkraut. It is also good in canapé mixtures and spreads.

CHERVIL (FRESH AND DRIED LEAVES)

Has an aroma suggestive of tarragon and a slight anise flavor. Because chervil is an herb that is low in oil (which imparts flavor and fragrance), the fresh form is preferred. It gives a fine aroma to numerous dishes, from appetizers to salads, and is tasty with poultry. Often included in the mixture known as fines herbs.

CHILI POWDER

Consists of a blend of chili pepper (the basic ingredient), ground cumin, ground oregano, powdered garlic, and usually salt. Other seasonings, such as ground cloves, ground allspice, and occasionally powdered onion, are sometimes added. A basic seasoning for Mexican dishes, such as chili con carne, chili powder is also good with scrambled and hard-cooked eggs, in gravies and stews, with shellfish, in ground meat dishes (including hamburgers), and in bean and vegetable combinations.

CHIVE (FRESH, FROZEN, AND FREEZE-DRIED)

Has a delicate onion flavor and aroma. Add chives to cooked green vegetables, green salads, cheese dishes, egg dishes, cream sauces, gravies, dips, vichyssoise, and sour cream–dressed baked potatoes.

CILANTRO

(See Coriander)

CINNAMON (STICK AND GROUND)

Has a robust, spicy flavor. This sweet-smelling spice is delicious in hot chocolate and chocolate desserts. Use ground cinnamon in a wide variety of cakes, buns, breads, cookies, and pies, in savory Middle Eastern meat dishes, especially lamb, and in marinades. Try stick cinnamon in sugar syrups, pickling vinegars, and many hot beverages (cider, mulled wine, etc.). A bit of stick cinnamon gives a delightful fragrance and flavor to beef stew.

CLOVE (WHOLE AND GROUND)

Has a stringent quality and a spicy flavor. Use whole cloves to stud hams and pork, in pickling fruits, spicy sweet syrups, and in cooking stews and meat gravies. Whole cloves are delicious in hot beverages, too. Ground cloves enhance sweet vegetables such as beets, sweet potatoes, and winter squash. Ground cloves are also delightful in baked goods and desserts, especially chocolate mixtures.

CORIANDER (FRESH AND DRIED LEAVES, WHOLE AND GROUND SEEDS)

In fresh leaf form this herb is called cilantro, Chinese parsley, or fresh coriander. The fresh leaves have a distinctive aroma and a pleasant lemony flavor. The whole or ground seeds, known only as coriander, have a delicate fragrance and a lemon-orange flavor. Ground coriander is a wonderful spice for buns, pastries, cookies, and cakes, and in other baked goods containing dried fruits. It is also good in lentil soup, stews, fish dishes, and in vegetable-rice combinations. Try adding it to yogurt dressing for fruit plates.

CUMIN (WHOLE AND GROUND)

Has a slightly bitter, spicy flavor and aroma. Cumin is widely used in Indian, Near Eastern, and Latin American cooking. Add it to pork and sauerkraut for authentic German cooking. Guacamole, bean soup, chili, curry dishes, and vinaigrette salad dressing all benefit from the addition of cumin. Add it to spice cookies, fruit pies, and holiday cakes.

CURRY POWDER

Designed to give the characteristic flavor of Indian curry cooking, curry powder is a blend of 16 to 20 spices. Use this in curry sauces, curried eggs, vegetables, and fish and meat dishes. Add a pinch of curry powder to French dressing, scalloped tomatoes, clam chowder, and split pea soup. To avoid an unpleasant raw flavor, cook curry powder in a little butter or oil before adding it to a recipe.

DILLSEED, DILLWEED (FRESH AND DRIED)

Dillseed has a slightly bitter flavor; it is essential in making dill pickles. Use dillseed in meat and fish entrees, sauces, salads, coleslaw, potato salad, cooked macaroni, and sauerkraut. Dillweed has a slightly sweet and refreshing flavor. Dillweed is particularly suited to salads, sandwich fillings, and uncooked mixtures such as tuna salad, as well as to crayfish and other boiled fish dishes.

FENNEL (FRESH LEAVES AND SEEDS)

Has a delicate licorice flavor and aroma. The seeds add an intriguing flavor to Italian sausage, breads, rolls, and apple pie. Use both fennel leaves and fennel seeds in seafood, pork, and poultry dishes; they are also great in beef stews and bouillabaisse. Fennel is a popular flavoring for rice pudding, cookies, Scandinavian desserts, and holiday pastries.

GARLIC POWDER

Ground from pure garlic that has been dehydrated, garlic powder releases its flavor instantly. It is excellent in all tomato-based sauces, in vegetable soups and creamy Italian dressing, and with roast lamb and roast chicken.

GINGER, GINGERROOT (FRESH, DRIED WHOLE AND GROUND, CRYSTALLIZED)

Chopped fresh ginger and ground ginger give a deliciously spicy, sweet flavor and aroma when rubbed sparingly into meats, fowl, and fish. Add fresh or ground ginger to stir-fries and fried rice; ground ginger is nice in baked goods and on poached winter fruits, too. Use whole or crystallized ginger when making flavored syrups and pickling vinegars. Crystallized ginger is excellent for baking.

MACE (WHOLE AND GROUND)

Has a flavor and aroma like nutmeg, but more intense and not as sweet. Infuse whole blades of mace into milk for white sauces. Use ground mace in pound cake, cherry pie, and fish sauces. Substitute it for nutmeg wherever the lighter color of mace is an asset.

MARJORAM (FRESH OR DRIED LEAVES AND GROUND)

Has a delicate sagelike flavor with mint overtones. Use marjoram with vegetables such as lima beans, peas, and green beans. It also enhances the flavor of lamb and mutton.

MINT (FRESH AND DRIED LEAVES)

Has a fresh, cool, fruity flavor and aroma. Use mint to flavor candies and frozen desserts. Fresh mint teams deliciously with chocolate and many fruits, and is a lively addition to tossed green salad or cooked peas and carrots. Fresh or dried can be used to make mint jelly or mint sauce as an accompaniment for roast lamb.

MUSTARD (WHOLE SEEDS AND POWDERED)

Has a sharp, hot, pungent flavor. Use powdered mustard, popularly known as ground mustard, to enhance meats, fish, fowl, sauces, salad dressings, cheese dishes, and egg dishes. Use the tiny whole seeds of mustard in pickling, with boiled meats and as a garnish on salads. Seeds are also excellent when boiled with cabbage or sauerkraut.

NUTMEG (WHOLE AND GROUND)

Has a spicy, peppery, macelike flavor and aroma, only sweeter and more delicate. Use nutmeg in baked goods, puddings, sauces, vegetables, and beverages. It is also a nice addition to spice blends, in chicken soup, and in butter for corn on the cob. Nutmeg is good with spinach, candied sweet potatoes, and eggnog.

OREGANO (FRESH LEAVES AND GROUND)

Has a spicy, evergreen, sweet flavor with overtones of thyme. Oregano pairs well with meats, fish, cheese dishes, egg dishes, Italian dishes, and vegetables, such as tomatoes, zucchini, and green beans.

PAPRIKA (SPANISH AND HUNGARIAN)

The Spanish variety has a woodsy, slightly sweet flavor. The Hungarian variety has a pungent flavor that can be either hot or mild. Use this garnishing spice liberally to give an appetizing appearance to a wide variety of dishes, including salads and salad dressings, fish, meats and poultry, soups, eggs, and vegetables.

PARSLEY (FRESH AND DRIED LEAVES)

Has a refreshing, slightly sweet, peppery flavor. Use parsley freely in a variety of dishes, such as chicken, fish, salads, soups, meat, and vegetables. Add fresh parsley toward the end of the cooking period. Allow parsley flakes (dried leaves) to soak a few minutes in salad dressings, dips, and sandwich spreads.

PEPPER, BLACK AND WHITE (WHOLE AND GROUND)

Both types of pepper have a spicy, hot flavor, but the white pepper's heat comes through as an aftertaste in the throat, not immediately felt in the mouth. Use white pepper in light-colored foods where dark specks of black pepper might be unattractive. Add black pepper to most dishes, including some desserts, such as spice cookies and cakes, strawberries, and poached pears. Use black pepper as a seasoning corrector just before serving a dish.

POPPY SEED

Has a sweet, nutty flavor. Use whole seeds as a topping for rolls, breads, cakes, cookies, and pastries. Mix seeds with butter and use over noodles, rice, broiled fish, and vegetables such as green beans, boiled onions, and new potatoes. Crush and mix seeds with sweetening to use as a filling for a variety of pastries.

RED PEPPER (GROUND AND CRUSHED)

This very hot spice should be used with discretion. Ground red pepper, also known as cayenne pepper, is indispensable for flavoring meats and sauces. Use small amounts of red pepper to add zest to eggs, fish, and vegetables. Use crushed red pepper in spaghetti sauces, pizza, and other Italian dishes, and in Mexican dishes.

ROSEMARY (FRESH AND DRIED LEAVES)

Has a piney aroma and a refreshing flavor. Use this potent herb with restraint for the best effect. An excellent spice for lamb, chicken, shrimp, and spoon bread, and for vegetables such as eggplant, turnips, cauliflower, green beans, beets, fried potatoes, and summer squash. Rosemary enhances the flavor of fruits, especially citrus fruits.

SAFFRON (THREADS AND POWDER)

Has a strong, bittersweet, spicy flavor and aroma, and adds a distinctive yellow color to food. The spice is actually the stigma from the purple crocus. Use saffron sparingly — a little goes a long way. Add saffron powder (or threads steeped in hot water) to fancy rolls and biscuits to impart a rich golden color as well as an exotic aroma. Essential to bouilla-baisse, risotto, paella, and arroz con pollo (a great Spanish chicken dish), saffron — the world's most expensive spice — is particularly good in rice dishes. (Steep or dissolve a pinch of saffron powder in boiling water before adding the mixture to the rice.)

SAGE (FRESH AND DRIED LEAVES, GROUND AND RUBBED)

Has a pungent aroma and a woodsy flavor. Use chopped sage leaves and rubbed and ground sage sparingly. Whole leaves can be used to season short-cooking broths for gravies, stews, and soups; remove the leaves before serving. Try ground sage with pork, poultry, and baked fish, and in poultry stuffings, salad dressings, and chowders. Rubbed sage has a fluffy consistency compared with the fine powder of ground sage.

SAVORY (FRESH AND DRIED LEAVES AND GROUND)

Has a delicate sagelike flavor; winter savory has a stronger flavor than summer savory. Add savory to beans, meats, meat dressings, chicken, soups, salads, and sauces. Try a pinch of savory in scrambled eggs and omelets.

SESAME SEED

Has a rich nutlike flavor when toasted. Bake in or on rolls, breads, and buns. Toast sesame seeds before using if they will not be exposed to the direct heat of the oven. Use sesame seeds as you would finely chopped almonds.

TARRAGON (FRESH AND DRIED LEAVES)

Has a slightly bitter, mild licorice flavor. A distinctive herb that is a delightful seasoning for poultry, seafood, sauces, tartar sauce, seafood salad, and egg salad. Best known as the flavoring in tarragon vinegar and tarragon salad dressing.

THYME (FRESH AND DRIED LEAVES AND GROUND)

Has a bright, spicy, clovelike flavor; the lemon variety has a delicate, spicy lemon flavor. Add thyme to New England clam chowder, Creole seafood dishes, and poultry stuffings. Thyme also teams well with cottage cheese, creamed chicken, and roasted meats. Mix thyme with butter and use over creamed white onions, braised celery, asparagus, green beans, eggplant, and tomatoes.

TURMERIC

An ancient spice related to ginger with a woodsy aroma, exotic bitter flavor, and bright yellow color. Use turmeric with poultry, in seafood and egg dishes, curries, chowchow, and corn relish, or with rice, creamed potatoes, and macaroni. Add a little to mayonnaise for seafood salads or to melted butter for corn on the cob. Like curry powder, turmeric is best used after it has been cooked in butter or oil (or in a pickling mixture) to avoid an unpleasant raw flavor.

Index

[handwritten:] — 5 - 278 very good